M000215123

GOOD
DATA

GOOD DATA

An Optimist's Guide to Our Digital Future

Sam Gilbert

WELBECK

Published by Welbeck
An imprint of Welbeck Non-Fiction Limited,
part of Welbeck Publishing Group.
20 Mortimer Street,
London W1T 3JW

First published by Welbeck in 2021

Copyright © Sam Gilbert, 2021

Sam Gilbert has asserted his right under the Copyright, Designs
and Patents Act, 1988, to be identified as Author of this work.

All rights reserved. No part of this publication may be
reproduced, stored in a retrieval system, or transmitted
in any form or by any means, electronically, mechanical,
photocopying, recording or otherwise, without the prior
permission of the copyright owners and the publishers.

A CIP catalogue record for this book is
available from the British Library

ISBN
Paperback - 9781787396333
eBook - 9781787396357

Typeset by seagulls.net
Printed and bound in the UK

10 9 8 7 6 5 4 3 2 1

www.welbeckpublishing.com

For Jennie, who sees what else is possible.

Contents

Introduction   1

Part I: Paranoia

1. The New Oil?   15
2. Mind Games   39

Part II: Prosperity

3. Collective Consciousness   71
4. Data Abundance   97
5. It's Not All About 'Us'   139

Part III: Power

6. Taking Over the Panopticon   163
7. Tech CEO Hubris   193

Part IV: Proposals

8. Digital Legitimacy   221
9. Data Ethics for Big Tech   245

Conclusion   269
Acknowledgements   275
Notes   277
Index   307

INTRODUCTION

In 2018, at the age of thirty-nine, I went back to university. Ray, who I had found online, helped me load a suitcase and a few boxes of books into the back of his van, and drove me from London to Cambridge. September is a busy time in the student removals business, and on the journey we chatted about other moves he was doing that week – to Southampton, to Manchester, to Cambridge again. I noticed from his key ring that he liked German shepherds, so I asked him about them. He had two, Lola and Charlie. Both were rescue dogs: Lola was five, and just as affectionate as when she was a puppy; Charlie was older and more wary, especially around strangers. We talked about the huge difference that dogs can make to people's physical and emotional wellbeing. When Ray asked me what I was going to study in Cambridge, I told him I was going to do politics. He thought for a moment before responding – I imagine about Brexit, Donald Trump, or both. 'You certainly picked an interesting time to do that,' he said.

Not everyone was as phlegmatic about my decision as Ray. For the previous six years, I had been chief marketing officer at Bought By Many, one of the fastest-growing tech companies in the UK. After handing my notice in, I posted my news on LinkedIn, and an old colleague got in touch to ask if I fancied a coffee. I said yes, assuming he was interested in hearing about my academic research, and we agreed to meet in a hipsterish café in Clerkenwell. 'Well,' he said, after our flat whites had arrived, 'you've gone from the sublime to the ridiculous.' He assumed I was having a midlife crisis. Alone in Cambridge, wiping down the drawers in the basement kitchen of my student flat, I could see where he was coming from.

Why had I taken this apparently baffling career path? The roots of my decision are in a *Guardian* live event on the evening of 17 April 2018. Everything was going well in my life at that time, but the outside world seemed to be falling apart. Things had recently gone from bad to worse for liberal democracy, with right-wing populists winning votes and parliamentary seats in France, the Netherlands, Germany and Austria. But something had also changed. The world had finally found someone, or something, to blame for Brexit, Trump and everything else: Facebook. The crisis of liberal democracy was Mark Zuckerberg's fault.

The *Guardian* event was a conversation between the Cambridge Analytica whistleblower Christopher Wylie and Carole Cadwalladr, the *Observer* reporter who had broken the scandal. I was there with my friend Jim, who I had known since he had hired me to work at the data company Experian in

2008. We had worked together on a strategy to develop Experian's software and data products for digital marketers, which included the acquisition of Techlightenment, a start-up with a platform for running large-scale Facebook ad campaigns. Jim had since gone on to run the marketing business of VisualDNA, a company that used personality quizzes to tailor online ads, while I had signed up hundreds of thousands of new customers for Bought By Many, mainly by targeting people with Facebook ads based on the breeds of dogs and cats the data suggested they liked. As I sat in the dark auditorium, listening to Wylie describe how Cambridge Analytica had exploited Facebook data to wage psychological warfare on ordinary people on behalf of its political clients, something began to dawn on me. I glanced at Jim and could tell he was forming the same troubling thought. Was it also our fault? Were we the bad guys? I had a horrible sinking feeling.

But then I realised that I was losing touch with reality. There was no doubt that Wylie was engaging, charismatic and witty. In his ripped jeans and big glasses, with his nose piercing and hot pink hair, he fitted the archetypal image of the data geek. It was easy to see why Cadwalladr, a feature writer, had found him such a compelling source – and why he was able to command the audience's attention. He was an excellent storyteller, with a gift for articulating the complex technicalities of data analytics in terms they could understand. But I knew from my own professional experience that much of what he was saying about Facebook and the capabilities of targeted digital advertising was misleading. Worse, some of it was plain wrong.

As we were leaving the event, we bumped into a friend who used to run a healthcare think tank, there with her husband. They were distressed and angry about what they had heard. Though they are active members of the Green Party, this wasn't about party politics; it was about the integrity of democratic institutions. Facebook was undermining the basic foundations of democracy, and something had to be done. I share their concerns about contemporary politics, but I did not agree that bringing down Facebook was the answer. I wanted to explain what was wrong about the story Wylie had told, and why it was dangerous that so many intelligent and thoughtful people were being taken in by it. After all, I'd worked in data analytics and digital marketing for eighteen years and had nearly been taken in by it myself.

Despite wanting to, I didn't say anything – I realised that I didn't have the right vocabulary. At that time I spoke the arcane, technocratic language of the data-driven marketer. I could have talked about segmentation, prospecting, cookies and lookalike audiences, but that wouldn't have helped. I needed a new way of communicating about data, so I quit my job and went back to university to learn it.

*　*　*

In a relatively short time, a highly influential theory has been developed to explain the apparent connection between technology companies like Facebook and the political and social convulsions of the last few years. It focuses on the role of data, and it's called 'surveillance capitalism'. The term was coined by the Harvard Business School professor Shoshana Zuboff in 2015, but it was the recent publication of her 700-page book *The Age of Surveillance Capitalism* that propelled it into the mainstream. Many other high-profile scholars with critical perspectives on technology, including Zeynep Tufekci, Siva Vaidhyanathan and John Naughton, also subscribe to it. This is the case it makes against Facebook.

When you sign up for Facebook, Instagram or WhatsApp, you give Facebook some of your personal data, in order that you can construct a profile and find other users. This might include your phone number, your date of birth, what school you went to, your favourite music and so on. As you continue to use Facebook, this is supplemented with other data, such as the friends you connect with, the groups you join and the organisations and public figures you follow. We'll call this kind of data *profile data*. Facebook also collects data about your activity – for example, which news stories you like or share, which videos you unmute and which of your friends you interact with most frequently. Because it is integrated with other websites through features like 'Login with Facebook', it's also able to collect data about your browsing elsewhere on the web. We'll call this second kind of data *behavioural data*.

Your profile data and your behavioural data are then combined by Facebook in a way that means you can be put into a near-infinite number of possible audiences, which advertisers can then pay to target using Facebook's tools. For instance, a mattress company might want to promote its new product to women aged between twenty-nine and forty-five who like yoga.

Data on Facebook enables that to happen. If you fit that profile, an ad with, say, a woman floating above a mattress in the lotus position will appear in your feed. If you don't, it won't. If the mattress company was advertising in traditional media, it would have to make do with placing its ads in magazines aimed at health-conscious women, or on billboards in the train stations of major cities. With these approximations, most of the people who saw the advert wouldn't be the target audience.

Collecting and compiling data in this way helps make Facebook's advertising space more valuable than most advertising space in magazines and billboards. It's an important part of how Facebook makes money. The theory of surveillance capitalism calls this business model 'fundamentally illegitimate'. That's a pretty strong claim. If something is illegitimate, we must not stand for it – it means it is not only unjust, but actually intolerable. A classic example of illegitimacy might be an armed group seizing control of a democratic state through a coup. There are three reasons why surveillance capitalism theory says Facebook's use of data is just as grave.

Firstly, you didn't give Facebook your permission to use your profile data in this way. You didn't consent to it. Facebook's terms of service or its data use policy might talk about it, but these documents are long and impenetrable. It isn't fair to expect that people actually read them, so any consent implied by your acceptance of them can't be regarded as *informed* consent.

Secondly, the collection of behavioural data is both intrusive and essentially covert – in other words, it amounts to surveillance. As such, it's a violation of privacy rights that is equivalent to someone secretly filming you in your house or wiretapping your phone. Again, whatever it says in Facebook's terms and conditions is irrelevant, because understanding the technical processes they describe is beyond the capability of most Facebook users. Furthermore, it is practically impossible to opt out of your profile and behavioural data being used without losing access to the services Facebook provides.

Thirdly, the social relations created by Facebook's business model are expropriative and extractive. Profile data should be seen as your digital property, and behavioural data as the surplus from your digital labour. Facebook takes these from you, making you the modern-day digital equivalent of a serf toiling to enrich a cruel feudal lord. So the power that Facebook derives from data is 'illegitimate' because it has been gained by means that no reasonable person would agree to if they understood them.

The graphic on the website promoting the conversation between Christopher Wylie and Carole Cadwalladr is straight out of a sci-fi dystopia: two giant hands bear down on a row of people sitting at computer screens. They are literally being manipulated: the tip of each finger fuses with the head of each figure, making data pour out of their devices, as if they are having the lifeblood drained out of them. The caption reads, 'The internet has been corrupted into a propaganda tool for the powerful,' but it could just as well have been entitled 'Surveillance capitalism in action.'

But that's not all. Surveillance capitalism theory alleges that Facebook's pursuit of growth is motivated by a desire to accumulate more of this data and that its rapid expansion into almost

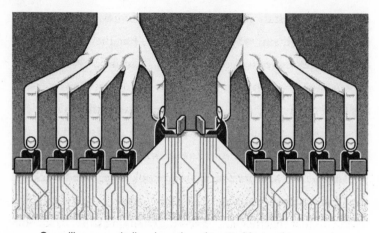

Surveillance capitalism in action: the graphic used to promote
the *Guardian* event with Christopher Wylie and
Carole Cadwalladr on 17 April 2018.

every country in the world is explained by its voracious quest for
profit. The use of its apps to disseminate political propaganda,
extremist content and fake news serves its objectives; prurience
and outrage lead to more clicks and shares, and therefore to the
generation of more behavioural data. The ethnic cleansing of
Rohingya Muslims in Myanmar, the rise of alt-right conspiracy
theories, the anti-vaxxer movement and the election of populists, from Donald Trump to Rodrigo Duterte in the Philippines
and Matteo Salvini in Italy, are among the catastrophic consequences of Facebook's business model.

At the same time, surveillance capitalism theory claims that
Facebook diminishes human freedom. The design of its user
interfaces, informed by vast quantities of behavioural data, is
intended to encourage you to spend more time using its apps,
which has a detrimental effect on your wellbeing. The more

extreme manifestations are increases in anxiety, self-harm and suicidal thoughts among young people, but they also include more generalised feelings of distraction, dissatisfaction, boredom and malaise. Facebook is using the data it has illegitimately acquired from you, along with the talents of the data scientists, software engineers and designers it employs, to create an epidemic of digital addiction. As the former Facebook employee Antonio García Martínez puts it, Facebook is 'legalised crack on an internet scale'.

Put all that together, and this is the terrifying story. Facebook steals personal data from you and uses it to manipulate you into becoming addicted to its apps, so you produce even more data, which it also steals. Facebook then sells the data it has stolen from you to advertisers, so they can manipulate you into buying their products or voting for their side in a referendum or election. Facebook doesn't care why its advertisers want your data, how they use it or what the consequences for society are, because all it cares about is profit – as long as your likes, shares and comments keep producing data it can sell, it's all the same to them. Cambridge Analytica helped the Vote Leave campaign and the Trump campaign use your data as a weapon against you, and Facebook couldn't care less.

Convinced? If you are, I completely understand why. We are at a moment of extreme pessimism about data. Every day seems to bring news stories implicating social media and mobile phones in cyberespionage, organised crime or authoritarian repression. The risks of speaking your mind online have never felt more acute, so it's hardly surprising that encrypted private messages on platforms like WhatsApp and Snapchat are fast becoming our preferred way of communicating. Meanwhile, tech companies seem to grow ever more powerful. A decade ago, just one of the world's largest ten corporations was a technology company; today, seven out of ten are. The market capitalisation of tech giants like Facebook, Google, Amazon, Microsoft and Apple is now bigger than the GDP of most countries – an ascendency that has made their founders and executives spectacularly wealthy. By restricting how data can be used, policymakers promise to repair the damage to world order, civility and equality that tech companies seem to have inflicted.

However, there is another, more optimistic side to the story – the story of good data. In telling it, I begin from a different position to most people writing about data and big tech. Many of the academics, cultural commentators and journalists who shape public opinion on these issues are deeply knowledgeable, but they also tend to be outside observers, who haven't run ad campaigns on Facebook or analysed Google data to grow a business. By offering the inside perspective of someone with real-life experience of digital marketing and data science, I hope to provide new insights and ways of thinking about these important issues.

It's a story that might seem contrarian at first. After all, it highlights the reasons *not* to be worried about how big tech companies are using our data. It shows that targeted digital advertising isn't as personal, sinister or persuasive as you might think, and that most of the data we produce isn't a precious commodity that we're being cheated out of. It explains why the power of big tech companies, despite their scale, is *not* like the power of states, and it reveals how they can be reformed to better serve the public interest without banning them. But most importantly, it's the story of the huge societal benefits that we can unlock by putting more, rather than less, data into the public domain. Governments' data. Tech companies' data. And our data.

* * *

Digital technology is so pervasive that almost every aspect of our daily lives generates or consumes data. It will only continue to proliferate. Whether or not this data is harnessed as a force for good depends on choices we make together about social norms, and choices about laws and regulations that politicians make on our behalf. At the moment, surveillance capitalism theory is framing those choices. But from my perspective, the risks associated with tech companies' use of data have been dramatically exaggerated, while the benefits of data openness, both to individuals and society, are being undervalued or even forgotten. It's time to rediscover the possibilities for data to make life better for all of us. It's time to talk about good data.

PART I

PARANOIA

Chapter One
THE NEW OIL?

In April 2018, Mark Zuckerberg was summoned to Washington, DC to appear before the US Congress and answer questions about the Cambridge Analytica scandal. At home in London, I sat up late into the night on two consecutive evenings and watched the livestream of the hearings. It was sober viewing, though there was one enjoyable moment of comedy when Orrin Hatch, an octogenarian senator from Utah, asked Zuckerberg, 'How do you sustain a business model in which users don't pay for your service?' The Facebook founder, wearing a dark suit and blue tie, had answered questions respectfully, even when they were motivated by party political point-scoring or displayed a weak understanding of technology, but this level of disconnection from the modern world was too much for him. After a pause in which he struggled to suppress his amusement, Zuckerberg drily replied, 'Senator, we run ads.'

Advertising-based business models have been around for hundreds of years and form the commercial basis of many newspapers, magazines, radio stations and TV channels. They are an accepted part of life and are not generally regarded as controversial. News, opinion and entertainment are provided for free, financed by the sale of advertising space to companies that wish to promote their products to readers, listeners and viewers. The value of this advertising space depends on how many potential customers it is expected to reach, and how inclined those customers are to spend money on the advertisers' products. The business model of Facebook – and of other owners of digital advertising space, such as Google and Twitter – is basically the same: spaces in the user interfaces of websites and apps are reserved for ads and auctioned to advertisers, which generates revenue; services like social networking, messaging, email and search can therefore be provided to users for free. Where this business model differs from that of traditional media companies is in its use of data that enables advertisers to target specific audiences. The claim of surveillance capitalism theory that the business model of companies like Facebook and Google is 'illegitimate' therefore rests on claims regarding their use of data.

At the beginning of this book's introduction, I mentioned Ray's German shepherds. He hadn't told me about them, but I'd noticed his 'I heart GSDs' key ring. If he'd been wearing a claret and sky blue scarf, I might have asked him about West Ham United instead. Until I asked, I didn't know for certain that he had German shepherds. There could have been other plausible explanations for the key ring – it might have come into his possession by chance, or he might have borrowed the van from a friend. But I made an educated guess that turned out to be correct, and we had a warm, meaningful conversation about his dogs as a result.

Statisticians call this a *probabilistic inference*. Ray made one about me too when, without consciously thinking about it, he put together the time of year, my destination in central Cambridge and the high proportion of books in the small load, and calculated that I was probably a student. Probabilistic inferences like these are what is happening when you are targeted with Facebook ads; advertisers define which audience they would like to see their ad (for example, women who like yoga, German shepherd enthusiasts or West Ham fans), and Facebook uses data to make educated guesses about who those people might be.

Neither Facebook nor its advertisers really know these things about you, and they don't need to. If a sports retailer shows you an ad for West Ham merchandise and you're not a West Ham fan, it doesn't really matter – you scroll past the ad in half a second and then it's gone. When Facebook guesses correctly it can seem uncanny, which is why some people are convinced that Facebook must be listening to them through the microphone on their laptop or mobile phone. We might say, 'I said to my friend this morning that I was thinking about getting the new West Ham shirt, and now there's an advert for it on my Instagram feed!' A more likely explanation would be that the conversation and the ad have the same underlying cause: West Ham releasing their kit for the coming season. Retailers will want to sell the kit, and fans – many of whom will have liked the team's Facebook page – will be talking about it. Most of the time, though, you barely notice that ad targeting is happening.

One of the key claims of surveillance capitalism theory is that this kind of targeting is intolerable because it's an invasion of privacy. But privacy is subjective – what we consider private varies from society to society and from person to person. Did I infringe Ray's privacy by asking him about German shepherds after spotting his key ring? I don't think I did, and I don't think Ray thought I did, either. The keys were in the ignition, so the key ring was in plain view of me or any other client in the passenger seat of Ray's van. It was in the public domain. Perhaps this might have been different if we'd been in a country where people have different expectations about interactions with strangers – in Sweden, for example. My Swedish alter ego might have noticed the vallhund key ring but decided it would be impolite to comment on it. It might also have been different if Ray preferred to keep his work separate from his private life. If that had been the case, he probably would have chosen a neutral key ring and kept Charlie's muzzle out of sight, instead of hanging it from the rear-view mirror.

Ray's choice of key ring is an analogue version of what we are calling *profile data* – the kind of data that's expressed by your Facebook profile. Similar examples of actual profile data would be liking the page of the German Shepherd Dog Community on Facebook (which has nearly 2.5 million followers), or joining the German Shepherd Owners group (which has over 100,000 members). Pages you like and groups you join appear on your profile and are visible to other Facebook users – including advertisers. They are in the public domain unless you choose to hide them, and probabilistic inferences about your interests can be made from them.

Is it an invasion of your privacy for Facebook to show you an ad based on inferences from your profile data? I want to suggest that this is a matter of personal preference and not – as surveillance capitalism theory argues – a matter of ethics. To bring this to life, let me tell you a story about the early days of Bought By Many, the tech company where I worked between 2012 and 2018.

Why Facebook Ads?

In the initial start-up phase, before they know what their product is or who their customers are, entrepreneurs will generally do whatever they can to save money. One obvious way to do this is to economise on office space. My two co-founders and I agreed on a mutually convenient location for our first office – Farringdon in central London – and started viewing the cheapest places we could find online. Eventually we settled on a single whitewashed room in a serviced office building. The compromise was square footage: it was officially a two-person room, but we decided that with small desks we could all fit in. There was just about enough space for Bought By Many's only physical assets: a basic printer and a coffee machine. When we had a visitor, we would borrow a chair from another office and install them behind the closed door. The first person to visit us was our seed investor, John. He had put £300,000 into Bought By Many, so obviously we wanted to be hospitable and make a good impression. We made him a latte and placed the borrowed chair behind the door. My co-founder Steven launched into an update about what we'd achieved in our first couple of weeks as John sat down. As he put his weight on the chair, the back right chair leg went straight through the floorboard and into the void below. John was tipped suddenly and violently backward. Luckily, he managed to keep hold of his coffee cup: we were mortified enough as it was, without having to administer first aid and arrange dry cleaning. When we made our first hires and moved into a five-person room a few months later, our tiny office with the hole in the floor was turned into a stationery cupboard.

Another way we conserved funds was by paying ourselves as little as possible. Steven retained a part-time interim CEO job, which meant he only needed a minimal salary from Bought By Many but also that he couldn't be in the office all the time. Guy and I managed on 50 per cent of what we were used to by reducing our living costs. Some of the time, rather than paying the train fare to come into London from Maidenhead, Guy would work from the shed at the bottom of his garden, which meant there were often days when I'd be in the office on my own. I prefer being in physical proximity with people I'm working with, so those days were quite tough. The office had a high ceiling and a big Crittall steel window: these gave it character, but also meant it was very cold in the winter. Much as I would do six years later in draughty corners of Cambridge libraries, left by myself I would sink into melancholy doubts about the choices I had made. It was during those times that I learned what makes Facebook so valuable.

At that time, Bought By Many had a hypothesis that if we got people who shared the same need for insurance together in an online group, we could use the group's collective buying power to negotiate a better deal with insurers. While Guy wrote code for the website and Steven negotiated agreements with insurers, my focus was on coming up with ideas for groups and then testing them out with real people. The first idea was to create an insurance policy that would pay out a million pounds if a young person suffered a life-altering injury while playing amateur rugby. In search of people who might be interested, I started following school rugby results obsessively so I could work out who the top teams were. On Monday mornings I would individually email the coaches at ten or fifteen schools to congratulate them on Saturday's result or commiserate with them. Then I would tell them about Bought By Many's insurance. My efforts were met with indifference. Eventually one of the coaches kindly explained that there were two major problems with our proposition. Firstly, the schools were reluctant to draw parents' attention to specialist insurance products, as it would imply that rugby wasn't safe and that their existing insurance arrangements were inadequate. Secondly, there was an expectation that the players' union, the RFU and the wider 'rugby family' would take care of anyone who was seriously hurt playing the game. That was what had happened when the England under-21 prop Matt Hampson was paralysed after a scrum collapse. I went to interview him at his home in the Rutland countryside and he spoke movingly about the financial, practical and emotional support he had been given after his accident. We had managed to pick a problem that people were hesitant to talk about openly and where there were already solutions that – while not immediately obvious to outsiders – were more than good enough.

Our second idea was equally flawed. A home insurer wanted to acquire new customers in Yeovil in Somerset and agreed to offer a group discount if we signed up one hundred customers. I tried various tactics to get the town's residents excited about clubbing together with their neighbours to get cheaper home insurance. I ran a disastrous Google Ads campaign, in which I paid £26 for a single click to our website. Then I persuaded Steven and Guy that we should decamp to Yeovil for two days, with the vague idea that we'd be able to meet 'community influencers'. We wandered the streets talking to people at random, but it was hopeless – nobody was interested. The only useful thing we learned was that a lot of people found our messages about Bought By Many's 'new', 'different' and 'innovative' way of getting insurance alienating, and that they valued the established ways of doing things that they understood and could trust.

It was while I was smarting from these lessons one November afternoon in the little office, that I turned to Facebook. At a networking event for start-ups, Chris, an entrepreneur who had founded a social network for PAs, had told me how he had acquired his first 500 users. He had logged on to LinkedIn, joined every group he could find that was aimed at PAs and started answering people's questions. Which hotel in Kowloon had the best gym? And was it feasible to have a meeting with a supplier on a Eurostar train? After a couple of weeks, he felt he had enough credibility to start posting links to articles on his website that were relevant to the discussion. Other members of the group followed them and found them useful enough that they were willing to sign up for Chris's network. I wondered if I could do something similar with my new idea for Bought By Many: travel insurance for people with diabetes.

There aren't many diabetes-related groups on LinkedIn, but there are a lot on Facebook. With some help from two data scientists called Steve Johnston and Liam McGee, Guy and I had built a huge database of anonymous internet searches for insurance, which also showed how many pages of content there were on the internet about each search topic. Analysing this data revealed that thousands of people were searching for travel insurance that covered the complications of diabetes, but almost no insurance companies included information about these conditions on their websites.

I felt like I had a valuable insight into where the insurance industry was failing to serve the needs of people with diabetes. Could I join the Facebook groups for people with diabetes, get involved in the conversations and pick my moment to mention Bought By Many's travel insurance, in order to repeat Chris's success? Having browsed the groups, I decided that I couldn't. Firstly, unlike Chris, I didn't have anything useful to contribute apart from one highly specific insight. Secondly, most of the groups didn't allow participation by commercial organisations; even where this wasn't explicitly prohibited, it was clear that it wouldn't be appropriate for me to join in. These were conversations between people whose lives were directly affected by their condition: advice about glucose monitors was being shared, stories about awkward insulin injections told and consolations about pain offered. There is a lot of scepticism in academia about using the language of 'community' to describe online groups, but that was exactly what I was observing. I suppose I could have pretended, but it would have been disrespectful – a violation, even. I needed to think again.

This was what brought me to Facebook ads. I had some understanding of them, shaped by working on the integration of Techlightenment into Experian, the data company I was working for at the time. Techlightenment's software made it easy for retailers to generate thousands of ad variations for their large product catalogues. As that wasn't relevant for Bought By Many, I'd deprioritised testing Facebook ads. But now, having seen how lively the conversation about diabetes on Facebook was, they seemed to be the obvious answer. I loaded up Audience Insights, Facebook's tool that shows you roughly how many people you can reach based on the criteria you set for your marketing campaign. I set the geographic filter to the UK, typed 'diabetes' into the 'interests' filter and hit the return key. 1.5 million people. Wow! I typed 'diabetic retinopathy' and hit return again. 216,000 people. 'Diabetic foot' gave me 66,000 people. It was incredible – analysing the anonymous internet search data had given me an important insight about an unmet insurance need, and now I had found a way of telling the people who would benefit from knowing about it without violating the norms of their online community. Clearly this was better than emailing school rugby coaches and wandering around Yeovil. Within an hour I had set up some simple Facebook ad campaigns for our Travel Insurance for People with Diabetes group. Within a week, Steven had identified an insurance broker who could cover diabetic complications and negotiated a 12.5 per cent discount for Bought By Many members. Within a fortnight, we had over a thousand members – we were in business.

The Rights and Wrongs of Micro-targeting

The kind of targeting I was doing when I set up those initial Bought By Many campaigns is known as *micro-targeting*, which simply means defining an audience with a high degree of specificity – for example, people aged over eighteen in the UK who appear to have an interest in diabetic retinopathy, based on their Facebook data. Since the Cambridge Analytica scandal, micro-targeting has become a byword for everything that's regarded as being wrong with data-driven advertising. So you might expect that the people who saw my micro-targeted ads for diabetes travel insurance would have been appalled. But in fact, in the vast majority of cases, they really liked them. Why was that? I think partly because they recognised a challenge people face as a result of having complications of diabetes – access to affordable travel insurance – and offered practical help with it. Even more than that, people valued the creation of a space for the discussion of that specific challenge. The comment threads on the ads became a place where the pros and cons of travel insurance were debated, and experiences of different insurers and different countries' healthcare systems shared. Just as Ray wasn't offended by me asking him about German shepherds, most people who responded to the ads didn't mind Bought By

Many speaking to them about diabetes; in fact, they actually welcomed it. In both cases, something new and of mutual value was created as a result of starting a conversation based on an inference from data.

We can break the minority of people who didn't like the ads into two groups. The first, less than 1 per cent of everyone who saw the ads, consisted of people who loathe all advertising so much that they are willing to devote time and energy to making their displeasure known. This involved using the comment thread to post insulting messages and gifs. For these people, it seemed like privacy was not the issue; they were affronted by advertising per se, and regarded targeted ads using their profile data and undifferentiated spam as the same thing. The second group, larger than the ad rejectors but many times smaller than the group that valued the ads, consisted of people who had concerns about being targeted. They expressed this in private messages to the company Facebook page, or by posting comments like 'How does Facebook know I've got diabetes?' To understand why targeting can be an emotive issue, it's worth considering their perspective in some detail.

Bought By Many now employs over two hundred people, including teams dedicated to replying to questions by Facebook Messenger, email and phone. Back then, however, it was just me – I was a one-man marketing, product, operations and customer services organisation. There were significant downsides to this: for two years until we could afford to hire Heidi, our first social media manager, my weekends were spent communicating with strangers in the comment threads of Bought By Many Facebook ads. I would answer questions while eating breakfast on Saturday mornings, and from the sofa during *Antiques Roadshow* on Sunday evenings. If I went out for the day, I would answer questions from bus stops, restaurants, shops and museums. It wasn't great for my quality of life, but there was a huge upside: I came to understand how the people I was advertising to thought and felt. I gained so much insight from it that for the next three years I made everyone in the company take turns answering questions on our Facebook comment threads when Heidi was on holiday. A lot of these insights were about insurance, but I also learned a lot about people's attitudes to and understanding of data.

I had some very interesting exchanges with the minority of people who objected to being targeted. They typically didn't dislike targeting that was based on things discernible from their profile – it was targeting based on *behavioural data* that they thought was inappropriate. You'll recall that Ray's German shepherd key ring was an analogue version of his profile data. By contrast, the things that enabled Ray to conclude that I was probably a student were analogue versions of my behavioural data – the kind of data that is generated as you live your digital life on Facebook apps and across the wider web. Examples of my actual behavioural data might be liking multiple posts by students at Jesus College, Cambridge or spending hours on the University of Cambridge admissions website at the time of year when applications for graduate programmes are made. It is one thing to be shown a Facebook ad for diabetes travel insurance when you're openly following the Facebook pages of the major diabetes charities; it's quite another if you're targeted with it having avoided putting anything about diabetes on your profile. Similarly, I didn't feel Ray had infringed my privacy when he asked what I was going to study, but I might have felt differently if he'd been driving me to an address near Addenbrooke's Hospital and asked what I was going in for.

What I'm suggesting here is that data-driven advertising isn't *inherently* privacy-infringing, as surveillance capitalism theory argues – people sometimes like targeted ads and get genuine value from the conversations that can develop around them in social media. Even when they're indifferent to ads, most people aren't troubled by those that speak to interests they've publicly disclosed in their social media profiles; where ads do feel invasive, it's typically because something that you regard as private has been inferred from your behavioural data and directly addressed. There are two ways to mitigate the risk of that happening. One is through law – we'll discuss that a bit later. The other is by taking control of how your data is used. And contrary to what you might have heard from proponents of surveillance capitalism theory, it's not at all hard to do.

You Are *Not* the Product

'If you're not paying, you are the product' is a hugely popular claim among Facebook's critics. It's one of John Naughton's *95 Theses about Technology*, Niall Ferguson made the claim in *The Square and the Tower*, his book about the power of networks, and Zeynep Tufekci made it in a TED Talk. It's an idea that seems to resonate because it draws attention to the fact that Facebook's paying customers are advertisers rather than its users, as well as highlighting the role that users' data plays in creating value for advertisers. It's become a commonplace in academic scholarship and political debate, as well as in tech journalism, but unfortunately it's unfounded.

As a statement to be taken literally, 'you are the product' doesn't accurately describe what is sold by Facebook and bought by advertisers; Facebook's 'product' is the advertising space in its apps. Understood metaphorically as a claim about the relationship between the company and its users, it suggests that Facebook treats you *as if you were its product* – in a disempowering way that doesn't respect your rights or your wellbeing. A typical example is the assertion by the UK Department of Digital, Culture, Media and Sport Select Committee in their inquiry into fake news that Facebook 'make it extremely difficult, in practice, for users to protect their data' through user interface design and 'complicated and lengthy terms and conditions'. If this were true, there would be a case for saying that Facebook mistreats you, but it's all wrong. In contrast to the vast majority of legal terms, Facebook's data use policy is designed for readability. Its 'Ad Preferences Center' gives a user transparency and control over if, when and how their data may be used to target advertising. Users can opt out of profile data about their relationship status, job title, employer, education and interests being used. They can opt out of their behavioural data being shared across different Facebook-owned apps and third-party websites. They can opt out of lists of customers that companies who already have their contact details – like their bank or mobile phone provider – have uploaded to Facebook. These opt-outs are accessible from the main Facebook settings page and via the 'Why am I seeing this?' link that appears in the menu of every ad. They are simple to use, and activating them won't degrade the social networking features available. If users want a more detailed explanation, Facebook even provides visual guides to explain how its ad targeting and privacy controls work. Short of getting rid of ads altogether, an idea we'll examine in Chapters Five and Eight, it's hard to think what more they could do.

What's more, if these controls are news to you, it seems that you're in the minority. A Reuters survey in April 2018 found that 69 per cent of Facebook users knew how to change their privacy settings and that 39 per cent of users had recently done so. If you know about the privacy settings and haven't done anything to change them, it's worth pausing to reflect on why that is. If the truthful answer is that you can't be bothered, how egregious can the use of your data in ad targeting really be?

Navigating from an ad to Facebook's Ad Preferences Center.

If, on the other hand, you have changed your settings, you might have noticed that the quality of your Facebook and Instagram feeds has suffered. Behind the above image of how to navigate to the Ad Preferences Center is an ad for the 'all-new Chilli Beef Loaded Fries Box', apparently available at my local BP petrol station. It is taken from my own Facebook feed, but since I don't eat meat or own a car, it's hardly an appealing prospect.

Facebook's explanation for why I was shown this ad indicated that BP wanted to reach people aged over eighteen in Cambridge. That's a good example of 'broad targeting'. Where micro-targeted ads are specific, broad-targeted ads are generic. As they need to appeal to a wide audience, they tend towards the lowest common denominator. It's unlikely that meaningful conversation will develop around them in the way that it did on our ads at Bought By Many that talked about the challenges diabetic retinopathy presents for getting travel insurance. When my friend Jim, who I mentioned in this book's introduction, opted out of data in his Gmail account being used for targeting advertising, he began to see more ads for payday loans and hookup apps. Jim and I might have had more privacy by opting out of data-driven targeting, but it negatively affected our experience of the internet.

The alternative way to mitigate the privacy risks associated with the use of data in advertising is through law. Recent legislation like the European Union General Data Protection Regulations (GDPR) requires companies to obtain consent before collecting behavioural data from consumers. Most behavioural data relies on cookie technology, and GDPR's requirement that you consent to cookies is why you now see so many pop-ups asking you to click a button or check a box when you visit a new website. The main drawback with this approach is that it interferes with everyone's experience of browsing the internet – regardless of your personal preferences about data privacy, if you're in the EU you must either accept or decline cookies at every website you visit. Ironically, this can be just as irritating as the ubiquitous pop-ups that characterised online ads in the bad old days, when advertisers relied on cheap tricks instead of targeting to try and catch your attention. The point is that when laws like GDPR are implemented, we are no longer able to choose which trade-offs to make between privacy and convenience.

Data is the New Manure

Perhaps I've persuaded you that what surveillance capitalism theory has to say about the privacy implications of targeting may be too simplistic. But what about the argument that Facebook has stolen your data and sold it to advertisers for a vast profit? Surely that's unjust, even if targeted advertising isn't so bad? Let's explore it with the help of another proponent of surveillance capitalism theory, the musician and entrepreneur will.i.am, who has captured the logic of this argument rather well:

> The ability for people to own and control their data should be considered a central human value. The data itself should be treated like property and people should be fairly compensated for it. As a musician, I benefit from the

copyright system that attaches ownership rights to my lyrics and instrumental tracks. Why should the data that I generate be handled any differently? It makes no sense that the information is used as the raw material to produce billions of dollars of income for massive 'data monarchs' yet is of no financial value to me [...] all one gets is a 'free' account bursting with advertising, faux news and lame 'sponsored content'.

For will.i.am, data is the fruit of your labour, in the same way that 'lyrics and instrumental tracks' are the fruit of a musician's creative endeavours. Data is therefore your property, and it follows that when it is used as a 'raw material' by 'data monarchs' like Facebook or Google, you are being exploited – the services these companies provide in return aren't fair compensation. In other words, your property is being stolen.

There's a fundamental assumption underpinning will.i.am's argument: that your data is economically valuable. That is what people are getting at when they call data 'the new oil'. *The Economist*, the magazine in which will.i.am's op-ed appeared, famously depicted the big tech companies as offshore oil rigs on its cover in 2017, calling data 'the world's most valuable resource'.

But here's the thing: data is nothing like oil. Metaphors matter a lot for how we think about intangible concepts, so it's worth unpacking a few of the reasons why this particular metaphor misses the mark. Firstly, oil is scarce, plus it's difficult and expensive to extract. By contrast, data is superabundant, and it's produced effortlessly and in unimaginably large quantities.

The cover of *The Economist* in May 2017.

Secondly, oil is gone once it has been burned, while data can be used again and again. Thirdly, and most importantly, oil is a commodity. It's homogenous: one barrel of crude oil is worth the same as any other. Data is the opposite. Most of it, including things that might matter deeply to you, like your gender identity or religion – is economically worthless, as it expresses little about your preferences as a consumer. Some of it – including things that are entirely banal, like the fact that you left four pairs of jeans in your Amazon basket without checking out – can be very valuable indeed, though only to a small number of organisations at a specific moment in time. Oil is traded in a marketplace operating on the basis of supply and demand, but you won't hear the BBC economics editor reporting that the price of data has dropped below $100 a byte, or Mark Zuckerberg announcing that Facebook is going to limit their production of data. That's because selling data simply isn't the business Facebook is in. That may seem like a surprising claim if you've watched *The Great Hack*, the Netflix documentary about the Cambridge Analytica scandal, but let's dig into Facebook's business model to see how it really works.

As we've touched on already, Facebook sells advertising space to advertisers – not your data. Data is just one of many components in its advertising-based business model. The other components include the post format, the virtual canvas on which ads are displayed and commented on in the newsfeed. They include 'Ads Manager', the sophisticated software that enables marketers to create and manage Facebook ads and campaigns. And most importantly, they include Facebook's reach – 2.5 billion people, who look at Facebook-owned apps for an average of almost an hour a day.

It is all these components working together, rather than data by itself, that makes Facebook ads so valuable. What excited me on that quiet afternoon looking at Facebook's ads system was not the ability to reach people with diabetic retinopathy – if Bought By Many only had something to say to that one community, I could have contacted Diabetes.co.uk about sponsoring a thread on the retinopathy forum, and it probably would have worked just as well as a Facebook ad. But Bought By Many also had things to say about travel insurance to people with other medical conditions, like Crohn's disease, angina or fibromyalgia. And we had things to say about pet insurance, too, not just to German shepherd owners like Ray, but to owners of pugs, cockapoos and giant schnauzers. What excited me most was the ability to speak to all these different communities instantly, through a single piece of software and in the familiar environment of a news-feed. I didn't need to research the most popular internet forums for each medical condition or dog breed, haggle with different webmasters or cobble together imagery in multiple formats to fit the requirements of different websites. From my desk in the tiny Bought By Many office, it felt like I could reach more or less anyone in minutes.

So the data gets its value from this context. It's sometimes suggested that you can calculate what Facebook 'owes' you for your data by dividing its ad revenue by its number of users. Based on Facebook's financial results for 2018, that calculation comes out at just under $25 per person per year. But that massively overstates what the average Facebook user's data is worth, as it doesn't recognise the importance to Facebook's revenue of having developed the software and apps that have become part of daily life for billions of people.

Rather than oil, a better metaphor for data might be manure. Like most data, manure is a mundane by-product of life, and there are businesses that have built the logistics to collect it on a large scale and process it into something useful: fertiliser for their crops.

Let's imagine a business that specialises in growing black-eyed peas. It spreads the manure-based fertiliser on the fields, and the plants grow tall. Eventually the pods are harvested, and the peas are picked, sorted, canned and shipped. You happen to live near the farm, so your household must have contributed a small amount of the manure. You see the peas on the shelves of your local supermarket and think of a recipe you'd like to try, so you buy a couple of tins. Now, let's say will.i.am shows up while you are sitting down to enjoy your black-eyed pea salsa with some tortilla chips and a cold beer. He tells you that your effort to produce the manure that went into the pea fertiliser was work, that the manure was your property and that you should receive a share of the agribusiness's revenue as compensation for it. I suspect he would have a hard time persuading you. It would be obvious that manure was only a part of the overall picture, and that its economic value was contingent on everything else the agribusiness did. And besides: you'd have your salsa to enjoy and other things you'd rather talk to will.i.am about.

Chapter Two
MIND GAMES

My first visit to Facebook's international headquarters in Dublin got off to a terrible start. It was February 2016 and we had been building Bought By Many for about three-and-a-half years. We had grown to sixteen employees in total, and there were seven in my marketing team. I'd persuaded Helen, who I knew from Experian, to leave her job at JustGiving and lead customer acquisition at Bought By Many. She in turn had hired Gordon, an expert in Google advertising, and Lyes, a bright graduate to train in Facebook ads. For about eighteen months, Helen and Lyes had tried in vain to persuade Facebook to assign us an account manager, so we could talk to a specific person about issues with our campaigns and ideas to improve their performance. Suddenly, out of the blue, I received a phone call from what looked like an Irish number. 'Sam,' it began in an East Coast drawl, 'my name is Sean Maloney, and I'm your dedicated Facebook account manager.' Sean was calling to invite us to a workshop in Dublin with a group of other start-ups and various members of Facebook's team. When he followed up by email, he told me we'd been transferred to a different account manager called Joe. I wondered why, but was too excited by the prospect of finally being able to engage with people at Facebook to dwell on it for long.

I also had the immediate task of convincing Steven that the whole acquisition team should go to Dublin. By this time, over one hundred thousand people had become members of Bought By Many groups and the revenue from introducing them to insurance companies was growing quickly. However, we were still a long way from turning a profit, and the time when raising another round of investment would become urgent was approaching. In other words, money was tight. Steven thought one of us should just go for the day and report back on what they'd learned, but I was thinking more broadly: here was an opportunity for us to start building a real relationship with Facebook, get answers to the questions we had about the mercurial ways of their algorithm and bond as a team in the process. I worked out that if we caught an early morning Ryanair flight and stayed one night in a cheap hotel, all four of us could do the trip for less than £500. I pointed out to Steven that it would only need a tiny improvement in the click-through rate of our Facebook campaigns to return this small investment, and he gave in.

Things started going wrong at Gatwick. Bleary-eyed, we met for breakfast in the terminal at 6 a.m. to find that our flight had been delayed by three hours, meaning we had no chance of being at Facebook's offices in time for the 11 a.m. start. To make matters worse, we couldn't reach Joe; for reasons I didn't yet understand, we hadn't been given his mobile number, and he hadn't replied to the email Lyes had sent him. I had visions of us being turned away at the door of Facebook's office and booted out of their account management programme. When we finally made it to Dublin, we sprinted through arrivals and piled into a taxi, only for the driver to warn us that it would be a slow journey: a funeral was taking place for a prominent gang member, and there were traffic restrictions and heightened security on the roads.

Finally the taxi dropped us off among the generic office buildings of Dublin's docklands. Having heard about the grandiosity of Apple Park in Cupertino, California, seen the playfulness of the Googleplex in the film *The Internship* and read about the 'village' feel of Facebook's campus in the San Francisco Bay Area, I was a little underwhelmed. Still, we had got there, even if we were an hour and a half late. We walked up the concrete steps and through a revolving door into an atrium. While the receptionist tried to get hold of Joe, I looked around at banquette seating, security pass-operated barriers guarding access to the lifts and a contraption dispensing covers for wet umbrellas. One or two people wearing lanyards were standing around chatting. There were a few slogans on posters at the mezzanine level – 'DONE IS BETTER THAN PERFECT', 'PROCEED AND BE BOLD', 'WHAT WOULD YOU DO IF YOU WEREN'T AFRAID?' and the now-infamous 'MOVE FAST AND BREAK THINGS' – but little else to let you know you were at the international HQ of one of the world's most innovative companies. Posters aside, we could have been visiting one of Bought By Many's insurance clients.

Eventually, a rosy-cheeked young man in a hoody wandered over and asked, 'Are you Brought By Many?' This was Joe. I introduced him to the team, explaining our roles and what each of us was hoping to get from the workshop, while emphasising the word '*Bought*' as many times as possible. I apologised for our lateness and said that I hoped we'd be able to catch up on what we'd missed. 'Oh,' he said, 'actually, we didn't start the meeting yet. Some other people got delayed too, so we thought we could have a tour first and do the presentations after lunch. So tell me, what does Brought By Many do?'

As we joined the rest of the tour group, I asked Joe how long he had worked at Facebook and what he'd done beforehand. He explained that he'd moved to Ireland after graduating to work for a small digital advertising agency. A year later he'd got a job at a larger agency in Dublin, and then Facebook had approached him. This was his first account management role and he was only a few months into it. 'So how many clients do you look after?', I asked him. 'Hmmm,' he replied, 'perhaps seventy-five or eighty? To be honest with you, I lose count!'

At Experian, like most B2B companies, we'd employed a lot of account managers. As an Experian client, if you spent in the tens of thousands of pounds on our products each year, you'd have an account manager. They would probably be relatively early in their careers, but they'd have a good understanding of Experian's product range, and they'd ask enough questions about your business to show that Experian was interested in your success. If you'd been invoiced incorrectly or couldn't log in to an Experian system, they would immediately sort it out for you. If you spent in the hundreds of thousands of pounds each year, a more senior account manager would look after you. They would take you out for lunch, invite you to drinks receptions and make sure you had priority access to new product features. They might even proactively conduct analysis to identify business opportunities for you. If you spent in the millions of pounds each year, you were assigned a 'strategic account director', who would bring the regional CEO or other luminaries to meetings with you, while knocking heads together to make sure you got whatever you needed. You'd be under no illusions about how much your business was valued.

Facebook, however, does none of this. At the time of our Dublin visit, Bought By Many was spending close to half a million pounds a year on Facebook ads, but that got us barely 1 per cent of Joe's time. A few weeks later, we were late paying an invoice when our finance manager was off sick and our access to Facebook's ad platform was instantly suspended. We couldn't contact Joe by phone, as Facebook account managers aren't allowed to give out their mobile numbers. When Joe eventually replied to an email from Lyes, he told him the process for accounts in arrears couldn't be overruled, no matter how much we had spent in the past or how many times we had paid promptly before. Our sales ground to a halt, as we waited eleven days for Facebook's accounts payable department to acknowledge our belated payment.

What explains this disregard for normal account management practice? I think it's because, for Facebook's sales and account management organisation, revenue accumulation is effortless. They have been able to surf a wave created by extraordinary user growth and the resulting shift of advertising budgets away from other channels. At the same time, they have benefited from the unprecedented user-friendliness and accessibility of the self-service advertiser tools that Facebook's product managers and developers have created. Their job is so easy that *not* hitting their targets might be a greater achievement. Unfortunately, that doesn't create the conditions for appropriately resourcing an account management function, or for a culture of providing good service to clients.

I wasn't enjoying the tour. We were shown a cavernous cafeteria with napkin dispensers, tubs of ketchup sachets and a passive-aggressive sign indicating which direction to queue in. We went up one floor to an open-plan office area that was depressingly familiar, with banks of rectangular desks on grey carpet tiles, under strip lights and ducting. There were coats on the backs of wheeled office chairs and rucksacks on top of wheeled pedestals. There were bottles of hand sanitiser and discarded takeaway coffee cups. There were laptop docking stations with electrical safety testing stickers and trailing ethernet cables. A4 printer paper was stacked in corners next to neglected houseplants. Old leaflets and brochures spilled out of cardboard boxes. Whiteboards stood vacantly in front of windows or next to concrete pillars. The roller blinds were down, keeping the daylight off generic monitor screens. Quirky conference room names like 'Ted and Dougal' and 'Quantum of Salads' only served to underline how utterly ordinary the epicentre of Facebook's international operations was.

My mood did not improve when the workshop finally started. A couple of Facebook account managers who were even younger and less experienced than Joe went through a presentation that explained the absolute basics of measuring online ad effectiveness. I finally let go of my hope that we were going to get the inside track on the newsfeed algorithm. A guy from Facebook's creative team Skyped in from London and encouraged us to spend more on awareness-building video ads, until he got kicked out of the booth he was using and abruptly left the meeting. It was clear by this point that there would be no great revelations. Nobody at Facebook could teach us anything, and there was nothing worth knowing about Facebook ads that Helen and Lyes weren't already doing. Like the characters in *The Wizard of Oz*, we'd gone behind the curtain and found that there was no magic. I wondered how I was going to explain this to Steven when we got back to London.

Then something unexpected happened. A young man in black jeans and a crisp white Oxford shirt took to the stage. Joe introduced him as Kristian Larsen, the co-founder of a specialist Facebook ads agency called PL & Partners, and said that he would be presenting a client case study. With a modesty and dry humour that I recognised as typically Danish, Kristian described the approach he'd taken to helping a T-shirt store develop its online business using Facebook ads. Budget was tight, so he'd started with a 'retargeting' campaign – he showed Facebook ads to people who had already visited the T-shirt website but left without buying anything. Using the Facebook ads feature called Custom Audiences, he'd shown different images to people, depending on which T-shirts they'd looked at. At the same time, through a process marketers call *optimisation,* he'd made sure the performance of the campaign kept improving by iteratively testing variations of the ads' other ingredients – the headline, the message, the positioning of the company logo and whether the wording on the button should be 'Læs mere' or 'Køb nu' ('Read more' or 'Shop now'). Once he was sure he was getting the most from the store's existing audience, Kristian had turned his attention to attracting new customers. He'd created a list of the email addresses of the customers who had spent the most on T-shirts in the past and uploaded it to Facebook. With Facebook's Lookalike Audiences feature, he was able to target a much larger group, whose profile and behavioural data suggested they were similar to the store's most valuable existing customers.

The results were impressive: in just four months, the store's website traffic had nearly doubled, its sales had grown 57 per cent and the return on investment in the Facebook ads was 10x. Even more impressive to me was the structured, data-driven and repeatable approach Kristian had described; I'd never heard Facebook articulate how to use its tools with such clarity. After the workshop had ended, I made a point of seeking him out and introducing myself to him and his co-founder, Mads. We agreed to meet up at their offices the next time I was in Denmark.

Buoyed by this conversation, Helen, Gordon, Lyes and I made our way over the River Liffey and checked into our hotel. We had some friendly banter with the receptionist as he noticed that we had three rooms between four and speculated about who would be sharing with who. Having dropped off our bags, we headed out for a bite to eat and a pint of Guinness, unaware that at that very moment he was using the details from my company card to order £1,500 worth of garden furniture from the Argos website.

Psychological Manipulation?

In relaying Kristian's presentation, I touched on the most important techniques and technologies that Facebook marketers have at their disposal: optimisation, Custom Audiences and Lookalike Audiences. Surveillance capitalism theory argues that these techniques amount to psychological manipulation, another strong claim. Manipulation is different from legitimate forms of influence, such as inducement, encouragement or persuasion, because it conflicts with the interests of the person on the receiving end of it. If Facebook ads are manipulative, it means they are so powerful that they make people do things they would not otherwise do. I think surveillance capitalism theory gets this badly wrong, and believe that media reporting of the Cambridge Analytica scandal is partly to blame.

The whistleblower Christopher Wylie, who worked as a part-time contractor at Cambridge Analytica for nine months in 2014, revealed that the company had promoted personality quizzes to a sample of Facebook users. People's answers to the quiz questions enabled Cambridge Analytica to build a 'psychographic' model intended to predict any Facebook user's personality based on their profile data. In this context, 'personality' is defined in terms of the so-called OCEAN segmentation, which classifies individuals according to openness, conscientiousness, extraversion, agreeableness and neuroticism. By subsequently obtaining profile data from tens of millions of Facebook users, Cambridge Analytica was able to apply its model's predictions to a much larger population. It then targeted different political ads to these people, depending on their personality type: for example, American Facebook users with high neuroticism saw ads that stressed the risks posed to national security by immigration, while users with high openness saw ads that emphasised its benefits to the economy. Secret filming by Channel 4 News of Cambridge Analytica's senior staff, including its CEO Alexander Nix and managing director Mark Turnbull, appeared to substantiate Wylie's claims that Cambridge Analytica had used Facebook as a 'psychological warfare tool' on behalf of its political clients.

Most proponents of surveillance capitalism theory take these claims at face value, but there are two good reasons to be sceptical of them. The first is to do with the incentives created by the structure of the digital advertising market. Owners of digital advertising space like Facebook are on the supply side of the market, and have incentives to talk up the value of their product (advertising space) to their clients. Their objective is often to persuade advertisers that they should pay a premium for space that will be seen by a high proportion of their target audience. The advertising market, meanwhile, is full of intermediaries, including agencies like PL & Partners and so-called 'adtech' firms – businesses that use software and data to improve the returns of media owners or advertisers. Acting for the sellers of advertising space, media sales agencies and supply-side adtech companies are incentivised to exaggerate its value. Acting for the advertisers, media buying agencies and demand-side adtech companies are incentivised to give a rosy account of the benefits of purchasing premium advertising space in order to justify the commission or software licence fees their clients are paying them.

All claims about the power of Facebook data, the precision of its targeting and the effectiveness of campaigns on its platform need to be understood in this context. Offering political advertisers a mixture of Facebook media buying and technology, Cambridge Analytica, like other demand-side intermediaries, had strong incentives to talk up both the value of Facebook's advertising space and their ability to exploit it. Put simply, the sales messages articulated by Wylie, Nix and Turnbull are not reliable evidence of Cambridge Analytica's capabilities, let alone of the effectiveness of those capabilities. The data scientist Aleksandr Kogan, who created the psychographic model, claims that it correctly predicted OCEAN personality traits in only 1 per cent of cases. However, Cambridge Analytica didn't care that it was 'useless', because their client – the Ted Cruz presidential campaign in 2016 – was willing to continue paying for it. Even if the model had been good at predicting personality traits, there is no evidence that tailoring Facebook ads using psychographics is any more effective than conventional forms of targeting. As with subliminal TV advertising in the 1950s, the fact that marketing techniques seem creepy doesn't mean they work. And from my own perspective as a marketer, psychographic targeting seems unnecessarily complicated compared to approaches like the one Kristian used to help his client sell more T-shirts.

The second reason to be sceptical about the Cambridge Analytica claims is that they muddle distinct techniques and technologies. You might have heard that Facebook and other tech companies continually modify the user interfaces of their apps to 'nudge' you towards particular actions. This is true: just as Kristian tested small variations of T-shirt ads to maximise the number of clicks, Facebook continually tests new ideas to see which designs encourage the greatest number of people to tap on a Messenger notification or include more hashtags on an Instagram post. You'll recall that marketers refer to this technique as 'optimisation'. It's highly data-driven, but contrary to what surveillance capitalism theory suggests, the data involved isn't individual profile data – it's aggregated behavioural data. If people's psychological profiles were being used to nudge them there would be every reason to take offence, but that isn't how optimisation works; instead, it's conducted on a mass scale and without differentiation between users. It doesn't make sense to talk about optimisation manipulating people based on their individual psychological vulnerabilities, as it's not remotely personal.

There are some well-known examples of optimisation playing a role in politics. Dominic Cummings wrote that during the UK EU referendum, Vote Leave 'ran many different versions of ads, tested them, dropped the less effective and reinforced the most effective in a constant iterative process'. For some proponents of surveillance capitalism theory, being advocated by Cummings is reason enough for optimisation to be regarded as illegitimate.

However, the approach he describes is methodologically identical to those used by the 2012 Obama presidential campaign, who found that an image of the president with his wife and children combined with a button marked 'Learn More' generated 40 per cent more donor registrations than an image of Obama by himself with a button marked 'Sign Up'. When I interviewed Kristian for my academic research on Facebook three years after meeting him in Dublin, I asked him about Cummings's account of Vote Leave's Facebook ads strategy and he called it 'Digital Marketing 101'. There is no wizard behind this curtain, either.

I think surveillance capitalism theory is also in a muddle over Custom Audiences – the Facebook feature that enables advertisers to target their existing customers with ads. To use it, the advertiser uploads a list of its customers' emails, addresses, mobile phone numbers or Facebook IDs. Facebook then compares this list to its database and shows ads only to the people who appear on both lists. Proponents of surveillance capitalism theory seem to think this means that with the right data, people can be targeted with individually customised messages. But this simply isn't the case: the minimum size for a Custom Audience is one hundred people, and you can't show a specific ad to a group smaller than that.

Part of the confusion stems from language. Encouraged by software companies whose products make it easier to run optimisations and measure results robustly, marketers now commonly refer to their tests as 'experiments'. This has the added benefit of reminding one's colleagues that marketing is no longer about mood boards and boozy lunches: it's a rational, quantitative discipline. Unfortunately, however, it has also led proponents of surveillance capitalism theory to conclude that Facebook users are continually being 'experimented on' without their knowledge or consent. This conflates an ethically dubious 'experiment' run by Facebook in 2012 to see whether the words people were exposed to on social media affected their emotional state with everyday common-or-garden optimisation 'experiments' of the type outlined in Kristian's presentation. Another example is the renaissance of the term 'dark post'. In the early days of Facebook ads, when the system was more rudimentary, the easiest way of advertising was paying to 'boost' something you'd already posted on your company's Facebook page. 'Dark post' referred to a new post created for promotional purposes that you didn't want to appear on your page in perpetuity. In other words, it was a synonym for 'advert'. As Facebook Ads Manager became more sophisticated and the types of ads you could run multiplied, the term lost its meaning and declined in use. However, it's now been revived by Facebook's critics, seemingly because it implies that covert tactics and nefarious intent are inherent in Facebook ads.

It should not be assumed that Facebook ads are as persuasive as the sellers of them claim, and nor are the optimisation techniques used by marketers to increase their effectiveness as sinister as surveillance capitalism theory suggests. The dystopian narrative that has emerged from the Cambridge Analytica scandal is simply not supported by the often mundane reality of digital advertising operations.

Lookalike Audiences at the Experian Museum

If there is magic in Facebook ads, Lookalike Audiences is it. Explaining what it does is fairly straightforward: it enables advertisers to target prospective customers with similar characteristics to their existing customers. As with Custom Audiences, the advertiser uploads a list of its existing customers to Facebook, but this time Facebook shows ads to a new audience that it deems similar on the basis of their profile and behavioural data. When an advertiser uses Lookalike Audiences, they don't make decisions about targeting criteria themselves, as I did with my diabetes travel insurance campaign; instead, the targeting decisions are made by Facebook's machine learning algorithm. Explaining how the Lookalike Audiences algorithm works and why it is so powerful is more complicated.

I may have given the impression that meeting Kristian and Mads was the only good thing about visiting Facebook in Dublin, but that's not quite true. On the top floor of their offices was a sort of company museum. It had installations about Facebook's most technologically ambitious projects like the Oculus Rift virtual reality headset and the Aquila drone, a prototype for beaming Wi-Fi into remote parts of the developing world. It also showcased products from successful Facebook advertisers, including scooter helmets, collapsible water bottles with charcoal filters, luxury vegan chocolates, slippers with detachable soles, subscription boxes of scented candles, custom-painted cake stands and much more besides. The exhibits in the museum highlighted the fact that Facebook ads make possible a huge range of online businesses that wouldn't have existed before. By enabling makers and inventors to market their products directly to the public, they level the playing field between small business owners and massive retail groups, increasing consumer choice and encouraging innovation. A venture capitalist I spoke to for my academic research went further: she believed that the explosion of UK start-ups centred around London's 'Silicon Roundabout' couldn't have happened without entrepreneurs having access to Facebook ads. Lookalike Audiences plays a key role: if you want to grow your cake stand business, you no longer need to run expensive focus groups or surveys to understand what sort of people are buying your cake stands, and then devise a marketing campaign around the TV programmes they watch or the newspapers they read. Instead, you can upload your existing customers' email addresses to Facebook and let the Lookalike Audiences algorithm magically show your cake stands to the right people.

The methodology of Lookalike Audiences isn't new. In fact, it was invented in the 1980s at data companies like Experian, where I used to work. If Experian had a company museum, a humble and largely forgotten object would have pride of place: the Kays mail order catalogue. You could turn its pages and browse Casio digital watches, coffee makers with integrated clock radios, He-Man action figures, Clairol foot spas and countless other retro items. Tucked into it would be an order form on which you could fill in the alphanumeric codes for the things you liked, and an envelope with a freepost address to send it off in.

The Kays catalogue was over a thousand pages long. Printed in colour, it was expensive to produce and to post. As a result, mail order companies needed to be selective about who they sent catalogues to in order to remain profitable. There was one obvious group to include in a catalogue mailing: people who had bought items from a previous edition. However, if you wanted to grow your mail order business, you couldn't rely solely on existing customers – you needed to find new ones. But how on earth were you supposed to know which prospective customers to send your catalogues to? The answer was a technique called *geodemographics*.

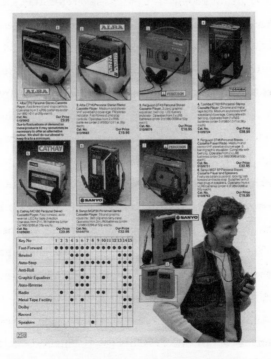

Alternatives to the Sony Walkman in a 1980s mail order catalogue.

The principle of geodemographics is the old saying that 'birds of a feather flock together'. In other words, your postcode can predict the sort of person you are – or at least, the sort of things you buy. For example, if you live in a detached house in a suburb where there is no public transport, you are far more likely to be interested in child car seats than someone who lives in a city-centre Edwardian terrace that's been converted into studio flats.

To help visitors understand geodemographics in practice, my imaginary Experian museum has a virtual reality installation. You put the headset on and find you've travelled back in time to 1989 and are looking at the world through the eyes of the database marketing manager for the Kays catalogue. You catch sight of your own reflection: you're wearing a stonewashed denim jacket and have massive hair. There's a sickly-sweet taste in your mouth: it's the Hubba-Bubba gum you're chewing. You're wondering how to meet a target your boss has set you for orders of electronics from new customers. You've already looked at the customer database to see which postcodes have the highest concentrations of past orders for hi-fi systems, VHS video recorders and radio cassette players. You know that by comparing the existing customer database with data from the electoral roll, you'll be able to send a catalogue to the addresses in those postcodes that haven't received one in the last two years; that should get you off to a good start, but it probably won't be enough by itself. You go over to a boxy Amstrad computer terminal and monitor. At the top of the screen it says 'MOSAIC'; below it is the instruction, 'ENTER POSTCODE', and a command line with a blinking cursor. You choose a postcode with a high share of past electronics orders and hit return. After a moment, the computer gives you a result 'FIVE MOST SIMILAR POSTCODES TO MK45 1SN: SO40 3QN, BH16 5HQ, WA5 2NB, NG10 3JB, NR33 7BT.' Now you know which addresses elsewhere in the country are most likely to order a colour TV or a microwave oven if you send them a catalogue. And what's more, you don't need to waste money sending catalogues anywhere else.

'Mosaic' is the name of Experian's geodemographic classification system. Other data companies have similar systems, and they all work in a similar way: starting with a table of millions of names and addresses from the electoral roll, they add data points to as many rows as possible, building up a detailed picture of the type of people who live in each postcode. The data can come from publicly available sources like the census, from large-scale consumer surveys or it can be purchased from third-party companies (provided they've obtained consent from the people who shared it with them in the first place). The data includes a wide range of things, from the age and income of household members to whether they have pets and prefer caravans to hotel accommodation. It's important to note that it isn't necessary to have data for every row in the table; what matters is having enough data points for each postcode to paint an accurate picture. Once that's done, they can be grouped with others sharing similar data characteristics. To make its groups more intuitive and easier to remember, Experian Mosaic gives them names: when I moved across London in 2013, from leafy Dulwich to edgy Hackney, I went from 'Uptown Elite' to

'Flexible Workforce' – from an area that was in a group with Morningside in Edinburgh ('High status households owning elegant homes in accessible inner suburbs where they enjoy city life in comfort') to one similar to Chorlton in Manchester ('Successful young renters ready to move to follow worthwhile incomes from service sector jobs'). Meanwhile, the postcodes that offer the best prospects for selling 1980s electronics are in the group 'Suburban Stability' ('Mature suburban owners living settled lives in mid-range housing').

In the next room of the Experian museum would be interpretive boards explaining that since the 1980s, the real-world applications of geodemographic classification have extended far beyond mail order catalogues. By adding driving time data, Mosaic was able to show Experian clients like Greene King and Vue where they should open new pubs and cinemas. And it was geodemographic analysis using Mosaic that identified 'Motorway Men' – sales professionals living on the M1 and M6 corridors – as the key swing voters in the 2010 UK general election.

You might have noticed that my description of Experian Mosaic is similar to Facebook's Audience Insights tool with which I identified people with an interest in complications of diabetes. Just as geodemographic targeting works by making inferences from postcode data, Facebook's targeting works by making inferences from profile and behavioural data. Like the geodemographic targeting of people who are more likely to buy child car seats, the examples of Facebook targeting we've discussed so far have common-sense explanations: you like the Facebook page of a diabetes charity and you see an ad for diabetes travel insurance in your Facebook feed; you put a black V-neck T-shirt in your shopping basket and it follows you onto Instagram. Lookalike Audiences goes further: it upgrades geodemographics for the era of big data. Machine learning finds patterns in millions of points of profile data, behavioural data and metadata – the data about the data – that a human analyst would never be able to uncover. With these, it can create a classification system that is much more granular than Mosaic or anything else that has gone before.

It's up to you whether you want to call Lookalike Audiences 'magic' or just 'data science', but is it fair to call it *dark* magic? Surveillance capitalism theory certainly thinks so. It points to the ways in which Lookalike Audiences has been used in elections – most famously in efforts by Donald Trump's election campaign in 2016 to depress voter turnout among groups favouring Hillary Clinton. Through Facebook ads targeted using Lookalike Audiences, the attention of younger women was drawn to allegations of sexual harassment levelled at Clinton's husband, while audiences likely to contain a high proportion of African-American men were reminded of comments she had made about 'super predators' twenty years previously.

Does responsibility for this cynical and unsavoury use of Lookalike Audiences rest with the Facebook technologists who created the tool? And do digital marketers in political parties share some of the blame, for finding ways of using Lookalike Audiences that Facebook didn't think of? I'm not so sure. For better or for worse, we accept smear tactics as part of electoral

campaigning: in this example, Lookalike Audiences is a transmission mechanism rather than a cause.

However, there is a darkness in the use of Facebook ads in
political campaigning that the company needs to do more to
address. Just as they are an incredibly efficient way of finding
new customers for a T-shirt store, Lookalike Audiences are
an incredibly efficient way for marginal political parties to
recruit new supporters. Take Germany's right-wing populist
Alternative für Deutschland (AfD), which promotes nation-
alism and military conscription while opposing immigration,
feminism, investment in renewable energy and equal rights
for gay couples. It used Lookalike Audiences in its campaign
for the 2017 federal election, and won ninety-one seats in the
German parliament just four years after its founding. Lookalike Audiences has enabled the AfD to amass a following on
Facebook that is more than twice the size of the followings of
Germany's main parties, the Christian Democratic Union and
the Social Democratic Party. Furthermore, during the 2019
European elections, the AfD's Facebook ads were systemati-
cally amplified by a network of Facebook groups and pages
managed by a private individual who was sympathetic to the
party's policies.

It is beyond my pay grade to make claims about whether
political parties like the AfD are legitimate, but I do think it's
a problem that Lookalike Audiences makes it so easy for new
entrants in the political arena – including those whose views and
policies are outside the mainstream – to find supporters. Facebook places hardly any controls on access to its advertiser tools,

including Lookalike Audiences. Anyone can attempt to exert influence in an election, regardless of their agenda; you don't need to be a member of the campaign team for a candidate or a political party – all you need is a Facebook Page and a credit card. The AfD's European election ads were amplified by one of its supporters, but if a civil rights activist wanted to run Facebook ads criticising the AfD's position on 'traditional gender roles', there would be nothing to stop them. In fairness to Facebook, the roll-out of its 'ad authorization' process means that in an increasing number of countries, it's no longer possible to run Facebook ads about elections, social issues or politics without proving that you live there. That at least mitigates the risk of interference in domestic politics from overseas, but the fact that the barriers to entry in political Facebook advertising are so low is a real problem.

Another area in which Facebook disowns responsibility concerns the truthfulness of claims made in Facebook ads. Mark Zuckerberg's rationale for this, which we'll explore in Chapter Seven, arises from his commitment to upholding free speech. That might be a reasonable justification for Facebook not acting to remove ordinary posts or comments about politics unless they break the law, but for a long time I thought extending this logic to advertising was nonsensical. After all, freedom of speech is a human right, but freedom to advertise is not. In the UK, advertising on TV, in newspapers and in direct mail is kept honest through a combination of rules set by regulators like the Advertising Standards Authority and norms fostered by bodies like the Direct Marketing Association. The idea that ITV would allow an advertiser to make an unsubstantiated claim and invoke freedom of speech as a justification seems absurd. Similarly, it's unthinkable that a mailing house could justify delivering tens of thousands of leaflets which made claims that were provably false. So why is this allowed on Facebook?

In 2010, the US Supreme Court ruled that laws restricting political advertising by independent organisations were unconstitutional, based on the free speech protections in the First Amendment. And as Facebook is an American company, it sees political advertising in these terms. Its default setting is to allow anyone to say whatever they like in political Facebook ads – even in Germany, the UK and other countries where the US Constitution doesn't apply.

Meanwhile, ads that Facebook doesn't regard as being about social issues, elections or politics are a total free-for-all. Multiple state-run Chinese news organisations have been able to amass larger Facebook followings than the BBC, the *New York Times* and CNN by promoting their content using Facebook ads. Throughout 2019, the China Global Television Network (CGTN) ran campaigns featuring iconic images of China, from baby pandas to high-speed trains, with a simple request to like their Facebook page. *China Daily* used the same tactics, but with a clickbait approach; nothing says 'soft power' like a video of a cockatoo eating shrimp. Both campaigns were seen by hundreds of millions of Facebook users all over the world.

Though overseas broadcasting by state media can be perfectly legitimate, Facebook is banned in China which creates an asymmetry: these advertisers benefit from Facebook's reach but can't

be reached with ads themselves. This may reflect Mark Zuckerberg's longstanding aspiration to enter the Chinese market, but
it seems to run counter to the idea of Facebook as a community in which members have reciprocal responsibilities, not to
mention America's strategic interests.

Just as it does nothing to check the truthfulness of claims
made in ads or the integrity of advertisers, Facebook does almost
nothing to verify that advertisers using Lookalike Audiences
have permission to use the data they are uploading – advertisers simply check a box confirming that their use of data is
compliant with the applicable laws and regulations. In practice,
unscrupulous advertisers use whatever data they can get. Of the
eighty-eight advertisers who uploaded my data to Facebook in
the seven days to 21 May 2019, sixty-nine of them didn't have
my permission, and the majority of them were car dealerships in

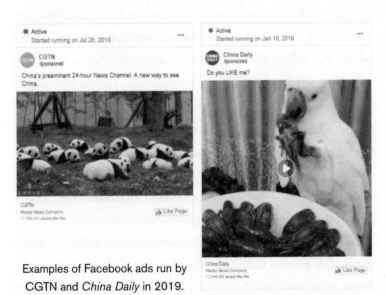

Examples of Facebook ads run by
CGTN and *China Daily* in 2019.

the United States, where I have never lived. The consequences of this specific example are hardly grave: at worst, I might see ads that are irrelevant to my life. The point is to demonstrate the weakness of Facebook's controls on Lookalike Audiences.

The Graph API

There is a final aspect of the Cambridge Analytica scandal that we haven't yet touched on: how the data used to build a psychographic model was obtained in the first place. Many media reports called it a 'data breach', but that's misleading. A breach is when data ends up in the hands of someone who doesn't have permission to access it. That can happen deliberately when a hacker attacks a company's computer systems, or accidentally if an employee leaves their laptop in a pub. By contrast, Aleksandr Kogan – the data scientist who built Cambridge Analytica's notorious model – had Facebook's permission to access Facebook users' data through its Graph API, a pipe built into their system for third-party developers. At the time, Facebook was actively encouraging developers outside the company to collect huge quantities of users' data in this way. It wasn't a mistake that allowed Cambridge Analytica to harvest data: it was company policy.

Why would Facebook want to do that? Ironically, this goes back to Mark Zuckerberg's personal dislike of advertising. Like a lot of software engineers, he doesn't care for ads. In a parallel universe where he stayed at Harvard instead of dropping out to build Facebook, Zuckerberg might easily have been one of the ad rejectors I mentioned in Chapter One, posting rude gifs in the comment threads of travel insurance ads. He never wanted to build an ads business; he wanted to build a *platform*.

Rather than earning money by selling advertising space, platform businesses earn money by receiving small commissions on enormous volumes of third-party transactions that they play a part in facilitating – Airbnb and Paypal are two examples. The Graph API was designed to enable a platform business model; one example of the way Facebook intended it to be used involved the business directory Yelp. Pulling data from the Graph API enabled Yelp to improve restaurant recommendations for its users by taking into account the restaurants that they and their friends had liked on Facebook. Ironically, another early adopter was the *Guardian*, who worked with Experian to develop an app that allowed users to see which news stories their Facebook friends were reading. Ultimately, Facebook hoped to become ad-free and generate revenue from third-party developers whose apps benefited from Graph API data.

Note that both these examples from Yelp and the *Guardian* require not just Facebook users' own data, but their *friends'* Facebook data. That's what I think was the only truly shocking aspect of the Cambridge Analytica scandal: the profile data of tens of millions of Facebook users was given away when their friends completed a personality quiz, entered a competition or installed a Facebook app. These users had no way of knowing that was happening, let alone of opting out. As a result, the $5 billion fine Facebook received from the Federal Trade Commission is hard to argue with.

But here's where subscribers to surveillance capitalism theory get into a muddle again. Expressing his view that the fine was insufficient, Federal Trade Commissioner Rohit Chopra remarked, 'The settlement imposes no meaningful changes to the company's structure or financial incentives, which led to these violations. Nor does it include any restrictions on the company's mass surveillance or advertising tactics.' Did you see what he did there? Chopra made a causal connection between Facebook's current advertising-based business model and its historic bad practice with the Graph API, even though the Graph API was created so that Facebook could develop a business model that didn't involve targeted advertising!

One outcome of this confusion among regulators has been challenges to the legitimacy of the data analytics and targeting techniques I've described in this chapter. When I was bogged down in this during my research, I realised I needed to talk to someone who had thought deeply about the ethics of marketing over many years: Nigel Wilson, who was managing director of Experian Mosaic between 2007 and 2015, has been incredibly influential on the practice of targeted marketing. I caught the train to Nottingham to see him, and over lunch I asked him what he thought about a recent report from the Information Commissioner's Office that had questioned whether the use of data analytics in political campaigning should be allowed. Nigel folded his arms and gave this bracing reply.

'I disagree with the ICO. They're missing the point. It's not about the use of data for messaging and targeting – it's about understanding the wider context and purpose of the people who are doing it. For decades, consumers have been receiving highly targeted messages that appeal to their wants, desires, hot buttons – that's just the way commerce works. If you're a political party, why wouldn't you build segments that help you understand your audience better and tailor a message accordingly? Why shouldn't you be able to tell young families about your plans to reform education, or tell commuters you'll invest in transport infrastructure? The context for Cambridge Analytica is surely that people's data was used without the necessary permission being granted. On top of that, Facebook didn't apply the right controls. They didn't check whether the targeting was being done by a wealthy citizen, an interest group, a foreign power. They didn't check whether messages were appropriate or whether claims were accurate. Back in the 1990s, you couldn't have used direct mail to target people with disabilities, say, with unsubstantiated claims about a miracle cure – the controls were in place to stop that happening. Frankly, it pains me that geodemographic targeting is identified as the issue.'

Rereading Nigel's words, I feel like I've stepped out of a stuffy room into the sea air. It isn't targeted marketing or Facebook's advertiser tools that cause political problems: it's the lack of controls on who can use them and on what they can say.

PART II

PROSPERITY

Chapter Three
COLLECTIVE CONSCIOUSNESS

Every day, people make around 5.6 billion Google searches. What's more, they tell Google things that they wouldn't share with their friends and family – perhaps not even their partner or their doctor. If you have your phone or laptop to hand, go to Google, type 'I've just h' into the search and you'll see what I mean. As I'm writing this, here are some of the searches Google anticipates, based on what people have searched for before:

- 'I've just had enough'
- 'I've just had a car accident'
- 'I've just had a panic attack'
- 'I've just had the craziest week'
- 'I've just had a baby, what am I entitled to?'
- 'I've just had a period but feel pregnant'
- 'I've just had a poo and there was blood'

What this set of searches highlights is that people turn to Google not just for practical information, but for advice at life's most significant moments. Because we are unfiltered when we use Google, the data created by our internet searches is hugely powerful. The data scientist Seth Stephens-Davidowitz has called it 'the most important data set ever collected on the human psyche', and I don't think he's exaggerating. You can think of search data as a vast reservoir of human needs and desires, which grows deeper every minute. It's a profound expression of our collective consciousness.

I started learning about search data when I was head of strategy and development at Experian, and quickly became obsessed. One of the company's marketing businesses, Hitwise, had a software tool called Search Intelligence. Through partnerships with internet service providers and web browser companies, it worked by anonymously compiling the internet searches made by millions of internet users in Australia, America and the UK. Logging in to the software allowed you to mine the data, using keywords you were interested in. You could also look at which searches were driving traffic to a specific website, or which websites were gaining traffic for a specific search.

As I talked to Hitwise's account management team, I realised that most of our clients were using the tool in rather mundane ways: someone from the customer insight department at a bank might take a screenshot of the twenty most popular searches for mortgages and paste them into a monthly PowerPoint report; someone from marketing might use data on a competitor's website as evidence that they needed more budget to spend on

Google ads. It was while I was mulling over other possibilities for the data that I was introduced to Steve Johnston and Liam McGee, the data scientists I mentioned in Chapter One. Their company Kaiasm had partnered with Hitwise to offer a service they called 'demand taxonomy' to Experian's clients in the retail sector. It involved comparing which searches were driving traffic to the client's e-commerce website with all the searches happening on Google for products that the client stocked. The idea was simple – to find gaps between demand and supply that the client could capitalise on – but it took a lot of data and analytical smarts to execute it.

Steve gave me a real-life example of a demand taxonomy he had built for the DIY brand Screwfix. By analysing internet search data from Hitwise and comparing it to product listings on Screwfix's website, Steve could see all kinds of commercial opportunities that Screwfix had been oblivious to. What would you call a tool that uses compressed air or gas to drive nails into wood? Screwfix called it a 'nailer' and listed it as such on their website. However, search data indicated that literally ten times as many people called the tool a 'nail gun'. How about a lamp mounted on an exterior wall of a building, that illuminates when an infrared sensor is triggered by the approach of a person or animal? Screwfix categorised it as an 'outdoor light', but a large majority of people call it a 'security light'. Lastly, if you were renovating your kitchen and had installed a new induction hob, granite worktop and double-door fridge freezer, what would you search for if you wanted to replace the strip light bulb on the ceiling? Search data suggests that most people would google 'kitchen lighting', yet Screwfix, thinking, not unreasonably, that downlights, spotlights and recessed LEDs can feature in lots of different places around the home, hadn't listed them by room at all. By changing how they described and classified their existing products to align with what people were searching for, Screwfix was able to win much more traffic from Google and increase sales as a result.

I was inspired by this story, and as I got the train to play squash one Friday, my head was spinning with ideas. My opponent that evening was a friend who ran the digital marketing department at the Open University. It seemed obvious that education was an ideal sector to try big search data analysis. I lost the match, but in the pub afterwards I sold a six-month taxonomy project on further and higher education demand.

Little did I know that at the same time, venture capitalists were cooking up an even more ambitious scheme to use search data. One day, an account manager at Hitwise received a call from someone at Forward Internet Group, casually enquiring how much it would cost to license Hitwise's search data for the past ten years; because the storage costs of making such a large data set available online would be very high, Hitwise only allowed users of Search Intelligence to access two years of search data. In putting together a quote for Forward Internet Group, the account manager eventually managed to find out from them what they were planning to do with the data. Their idea was to get their data scientists to mine it for the single best untapped opportunity for a new online retail business. The methodology would be similar to the one Steve and Liam's team had used to show Screwfix and the Open University how to describe and classify their products and courses to gain more traffic. However, the important difference was that Forward Internet Group weren't trying to drive more sales for a business they had already established; they wanted to start a business from scratch, which meant there was a far greater volume of search data to analyse.

The monumental scale and complexity of this challenge meant Forward Internet Group's data scientists disappeared into a metaphorical bunker for months. Fuelled by coffee and Haribo, they would work long into the night. Colleagues started to notice their increasingly unkempt appearance and a wild look in their eyes: they were becoming obsessed. Eventually, the executive team lost patience and summoned the data scientists to the boardroom. At the head of the table sat Neil Hutchinson, the company's founder and CEO, flanked by his most trusted advisers. 'Let's hear it,' he began. 'What have you found?' There was an uncomfortable silence as the data scientists, incongruous in their hoodies and trainers, looked at each other. 'Come on,' said Hutchinson, 'We asked you to mine the data to find the best opportunity for a new business – what is it?' Finally, one of them found the courage to pipe up: 'It's parrot cages.' 'Parrot cages?' Hutchinson repeated. 'Are you winding me up?'

They weren't. The search data had revealed that the biggest gap between demand and supply in the online retail market was for parrot cages. To his great credit, Hutchinson put aside his scepticism and committed himself to entering the parrot cages business. As a first step, Forward Internet Group set up a simple

one-page website called Just Cages and spent a small amount
advertising it in Google listings. It wasn't possible to actually
buy a cage from Just Cages at this point, but two weeks of clicks
to the website showed that the data scientists were right – there
really *was* unmet demand for parrot cages on the internet. Next,
they found a so-called 'dropshipper' in India – a wholesaler who
would send the parrot cages directly to the customer, meaning
that Just Cages didn't have the financial risk and practical incon-
venience of holding stock. The final piece of the jigsaw was to
build e-commerce functionality – the capability to list products,
take payments and process orders online. To keep Just Cages
as simple as possible, Forward Internet Group used Shopify, an
off-the-shelf product for online stores.

The results were remarkable: within a year, Just Cages had
turned over £3.2 million, and set up ten further e-commerce
websites to sell kennels, hutches, aquariums and vivariums
(environmentally controlled enclosures for pet reptiles). What's
more, the opportunities for new online stores turned out not to
be limited to accommodation for pets. Just as Forward Internet Group's data scientists were falling down their search data
rabbit hole, the entrepreneurs Richard Tucker and Joe Murray
were crafting a vision to change the world of home and garden
retail, using the gaps between demand and supply that their
analysis had uncovered. The company they founded, World-
Stores, consisted of a multitude of niche websites with names
like MattressesWorld, ShedsWorld and even TrampolineWorld
– all designed to meet the consumer demand for unusual home
and garden products that was being expressed through Google

searches. By continually monitoring search data for emerging trends, WorldStores stayed one step ahead of its traditionally minded competitors. 'One year there was a thing about trundle beds,' recalls Tucker. 'None of us had a clue what they were, but people were typing it into search. So we got them in stock and they sold like hell!' (It's a low wheeled bed that is stored under another bed, by the way.)

While Just Cages was a clever experiment that exceeded expectations, WorldStores was a serious business based entirely on analysing search data. By the time of its sale to the Dunelm Group in 2016, it listed over half a million home and garden products across its network of online stores, had annual sales of more than £100 million and employed 650 people. It's a powerful example of the way that big data can enable consumer choice, economic growth, job creation and prosperity.

I remember sitting at my desk in the Experian office in spring 2012, reading news coverage of a recent venture capital investment in WorldStores, when my phone rang. It was my friend and marketing mentor, Ruth. 'I won't beat about the bush,' she said. 'I've called to ask you a favour.' Ruth told me that one of her old colleagues from the strategy consultancy McKinsey was planning to set up a new business offering unusual types of insurance online. Immediately my ears pricked up. 'Steven's very smart commercially and he's got a technical co-founder,' Ruth continued, 'but he needs digital marketing expertise. Would you meet him to see if there's someone you could recommend?'

Although I was intrigued by the idea of applying internet search data analysis to the insurance market, I wasn't looking for a new job. My work at Experian was varied, intellectually stimulating and came with perks including business trips to Paris and New York. Why would I swap that for the chaos and uncertainty of life at an early-stage start-up? I told Ruth I'd be happy to meet Steven for a coffee and offer some advice, but that was as far as I expected it to go.

However, as I began analysing the search data I'd downloaded from Hitwise in preparation for the meeting with Steven, my intrigue turned into excitement. To outsiders, big data analysis sounds dull and laborious, but it can be profoundly rewarding. It is the sort of activity you can completely immerse yourself in: distractions melt into the background and time seems to stand still, as all your mental resources become absorbed by it. Talk of being in a 'flow state' is more often associated with yoga, painting, or rock climbing, but it is there in data analysis, too. I sometimes liken it to swimming silently through a deep blue ocean, looking for pockets of phosphorescence. In the insurance search data I'd downloaded from Hitwise – this great outpouring from millions of minds – lights were glowing in every direction. There were so many opportunities that I couldn't decide which ones to swim towards and examine more closely, so I decided to take a sort of underwater picture instead.

Because I was interested in the consumer demand that the current competitors in the market were missing – just like Forward Internet Group and WorldStores – I started by getting rid of the searches that were more than 80 per cent likely to result in a click; a lower percentage of clicks on a search would indicate that people couldn't immediately see what they were looking for on the search results page. I then made a long list of 'stop words' – words and phrases that wouldn't tell me about consumer demand for products. This included brand names of insurance companies like Direct Line and Aviva, synonyms for insurance like 'policy' and 'cover' and generic words about the process of buying and using insurance like 'quote' and 'claim'. Once I had filtered these out, I dragged and dropped the data into an online visualisation tool called TagCrowd, and asked it to show me the words that appeared most frequently. This was the result:

abroad (6) accident (12) bike (8) black (6) box (6) building (17) business (12) campervan (6) car (369) caravan (10) cat (8) classic (7) conditions (11) contents (9) credit (7) critical (6) dental (7) dog (9) drivers (24) driving (17) employed (6) employers (7) gap (11) green (6) health (28) hire (10) holiday (18) home (74) horse (9) house (5) illness (9) indemnity (14) landlord (8) learner (6) legal (10) liability (24) market (10) medical (21) mobile (12) mortgage (8) motor (15) motorcycle (5) motorhome (7) multi (5) mutual (5) ni (7) office (12) party (8) personal (8) pet (42) platinum (6) premier (5) premium (5) private (15) professional (5) property (5) protection (13) provident (5) public (18) rental (5) self (11) taxi (6) third (7) top (7) trade (6) traders (5) travel (136) van (14) vehicle (8) warehouse (6) white (6) work (8) year (7) young (6)

'Photographing' big data: a word cloud visualisation of consumer demand for insurance, as expressed by internet searches.

Parts of this picture were reassuringly obvious: there was clearly plenty of demand for car insurance, travel insurance, home insurance and so on. More interesting, though, were clusters of lower-volume searches. Together, searches for words like 'business', 'liability', 'professional', 'indemnity', 'market', 'traders', 'van' and 'taxi' suggested a great opportunity to respond to insurance demand from small business owners, and perhaps explained why the specialist direct broker Simply Business seemed to be growing so quickly. Searches for words like 'campervan', 'caravan' and 'motorhome' on the one hand, and 'young', 'drivers', 'black', 'box' and 'learner' on the other implied that the opportunity in motor insurance might lie outside mainstream vehicles and motorists. And, of course, the early signs of the future success of Bought By Many were already apparent in words like 'medical', 'conditions', 'pet', 'cat', 'dog' and 'horse'.

Rush hour had begun as I crossed London Bridge on my way to meet Steven, and masses of City workers were marching in the opposite direction towards the station. I held the line I was walking and noticed how easily the crowd parted in front of me. I realised that it was possible to go against the flow, and thought I might enjoy doing it.

I got to Pret, bought a coffee and texted Steven to tell him I'd arrived. I added that he might not recognise me, as I had grown a beard since the photo on my LinkedIn profile had been taken. I recognised him, though – tie-less in a grey suit, he looked serious, lean, energetic and restless. Ruth had told me he could be very direct, and in that first meeting he certainly was, at one point asking, 'So why are you here?' I replied that I wasn't looking for a job, but that I had a lot of respect for Ruth and liked meeting interesting new people. I'd brought a printout of the search data analysis with me, and Steven was clearly impressed. He told me it was the first time someone had come to a meeting with him having properly thought about what Bought By Many could be rather than turning up expecting to be sold to, before spouting the conventional wisdom that millions of pounds would need to be spent on TV and above-the-line advertising to drive brand awareness if Bought By Many was going to be successful. He showed me a PowerPoint deck he had been using with potential investors and insurance partners, which asserted that the insurance market was ready for disruption and that Bought By Many was the company to do it. Insurance companies' profit margins were under pressure from price comparison websites, and new regulations meant that insurers would be forced to hold more capital unless they diversified into new product lines and geographic areas. At the same time, group buying was gaining acceptance among consumers, thanks to Groupon and collective energy switching clubs. Steven told me a story about leaving Close Brothers, where he had worked after McKinsey. He had phoned AXA PPP, who provided the company health insurance scheme that he'd been covered by as an employee, and asked for a quote to continue the same cover as an individual. He knew Close Brothers had been paying just over £1,000 a year on his behalf, but now AXA wanted over four times that amount. Nothing about his or his family's health had changed – it was simply an example of financial services companies giving preferential treatment to large corporations, and taking advantage of ordinary people to subsidise it. His vision for Bought By Many was to use the collective buying power of like-minded individuals to redress such power imbalances.

The following week I met Guy; in contrast to Steven, he was very laid-back and at first they seemed like unlikely business partners. Guy told me his side of the Bought By Many foundation story: after building some software to make it easier for his group of friends to split the expenses of their annual ski trip, he had started thinking about what else online groups might be capable of doing. He had been working at a bank where Steven was running the wealth management arm, and their ideas had collided. Guy had built tech businesses before, in San Francisco during the dotcom bubble and then in Europe, but they had always been structured as consultancies, which had made it hard to create equity value. There was not much of a start-up scene in London at that time, but he was convinced that the opening of the Google Campus in Shoreditch, along with new tax incentives for early-stage investors, meant that it was about to explode into life.

Here was a chance to push the boundaries of search data analysis and transform financial services, with people I'd instantly gelled with. My mind was made up. I accepted Steven's offer to join Bought By Many as chief marketing officer, and agreed to resign from Experian as soon as the seed money from our investor was in the bank.

In Chapter One, I mentioned what we spent money on in the early days of Bought By Many: a printer, a coffee machine and rent for our miniscule office. Once we had sorted out these basics, my top priority was to build a 'demand taxonomy' for the insurance market. I haggled with Hitwise for a discounted licence, and hired Kaiasm to help crunch the data. My initial word cloud analysis had been based on 10,000 rows of search data from one twelve-week period in 2011. That might seem like a lot, but it was unlikely to be representative because of seasonality: people need different types of insurance at different times of year, the summer peak in demand for travel insurance for family holidays being one obvious example. It was also only a small sliver of all the data that was available, and like Forward Internet Group and WorldStores, I wanted the motherlode. I downloaded every search that had been made for insurance in the previous two years and sent it to Steve and Liam to compile and deduplicate. It turned out that in the UK during that period there had been 105 million searches for insurance, distributed across almost 850,000 distinct search expressions. Kaiasm's team of data scientists used software they had built to count the number of web pages that contained each search expression in their title – that would be our measure of how well existing websites were meeting the demand people were articulating through their Google searches. Finally, Guy built an online tool to make it easier for us to query the database, and Liam created a visualisation of all the best opportunities, which we mounted on the office wall.

How did we use this magnum opus? At first, we tested the ideas we already had, including the schools rugby insurance and diabetes travel insurance examples I described in Chapter One. Next, we tested ideas from the insurance companies that Steven had started commercial discussions with, but they were all terrible. The insurers wanted to sell things like insurance for wine collections, kidnap-and-ransom insurance and indemnity insur-

The insurance demand taxonomy visualisation.

ance for planning consultants. The data showed that there was an abundance of supply for these products, but almost zero demand – the ideas all involved types of insurance that would be unlikely to result in many claims, and would therefore be highly profitable. Instead of responding to what potential customers actually wanted, the insurers preferred to develop products that met their own needs and then hope they could convince people to buy them.

Having rejected the insurers' ideas, we decided to start groups on the Bought By Many website for types of insurance where there was clear demand that insurance companies weren't meeting. I would see if I could recruit fifty or a hundred people to a group, and then Steven would go and present insurers with this tangible evidence of consumer demand. Like the proverbial kid in the candy shop, I picked the quirkiest opportunities first: quad bike insurance, canal boat insurance, even stage hypnotist insurance. Sure enough, people quickly began to join, and from them I learned that:

- Insurers over-charge for quad bikes that are used for track racing but aren't road-registered.
- There is only one dominant provider of insurance for narrowboats, and owners think more competition would 'keep them honest'.
- It's surprisingly hard for stage hypnotists to get the public liability insurance that's mandatory for performing in many venues.

The trouble with these opportunities from a commercial perspective was that they weren't very scalable. To meet these three niche demands would have required signing deals with three separate insurance companies, and Steven was discovering that closing deals could be a protracted process. I realised I needed to find clusters of related opportunities in the data – or, returning to my diving metaphor, to swim towards a bigger, brighter patch of phosphorescence.

That was how I discovered the golden opportunity that would shape Bought By Many's corporate strategy for years to come. Imagine me, crazy-haired, looking up from my laptop for the first time in days, and announcing to Steven, Guy, Helen and our newest recruit David, 'I've found something that's going to change the face of financial services forever: *Pug insurance*.' With that, I strode out of the room and went to make a celebratory cup of tea.

Pug Insurance

Why was I so excited about it? Firstly, because a lot of people seemed to be searching for pet insurance that was specifically for pugs, yet there wasn't a single page on the web with 'pug insurance' in the title. Secondly, and just as importantly, it was clear that there were tangible reasons why pug owners weren't satisfied with generic dog insurance. It's worth going into them in some detail.

At the time, pugs were on-trend: statistics from the Kennel Club showed that they were close to becoming the UK's most popular puppy. As a result, prices for pug puppies were skyrocketing, which in turn seemed to be leading to a spike in thefts. By quickly analysing data from DogLost.co.uk, a free service that owners can use to post notices about missing pooches, I could see that pugs had been the most-stolen breed in the previous twelve months, their small stature and friendly nature presumably also contributing to their 'thieveability'. If you had a mainstream pet insurance policy at that time and your pug went missing, £1,000 was the maximum payout you would receive, but buying another pug puppy would cost you as much as £5,000. The theft cover offered by insurers was totally inadequate.

What's more, many pet insurance policies also contained a blanket exclusion for so-called 'breed-specific conditions' –

medical problems that particular breeds are known to be prone to. For the growing population of pug owners, this meant that vet treatment for encephalitis (an inflammation of the brain) or hip dysplasia (a problem with the hip socket that can result in dislocation) would not be covered. Facebook comment threads and discussions on online forums showed that pug owners took a dim view of this: what was the point of having insurance, if it wasn't going to pay for the problems that would be most costly to treat? When it came to pugs, pet insurance products were behind the times – and Bought By Many had a great opportunity to bring them up to date.

Thirdly, I was excited because almost every other dog breed I checked showed the same pattern as pugs: there was an abundance of demand that insurance companies had failed to address. French bulldog insurance, Neapolitan mastiff insurance, Siberian husky insurance and, of course, German shepherd insurance – I had a list of more than seventy groups for Bought By Many to start, before it occurred to me that I could be looking at cats as well.

Once I'd explained my findings, the rest of the team quickly rallied behind them. While Helen and I got to work writing content and setting up multiple Facebook ad campaigns, Steven and David pitched the list of breed groups to the major players in pet insurance. There was a bidding war for pug insurance that was eventually won by Petplan, who agreed to increase the theft and loss cover on their product for members of our group. More Than agreed to offer a 20 per cent discount on dozens of breeds they liked the risk of or wanted to diversify into, while a smaller broker offered £25 cashback on a further ten breeds. While discounts and cashback offers didn't tackle the shortcomings of the products, it at least left Bought By Many members with more money to deal with problems that insurance wouldn't help with.

This was the platform from which we built the company as it is today. In 2017, three years later, we were fed up of waiting for our insurance partners to improve their pet insurance products so we designed our own, transforming Bought By Many from a distributor of third-party products into an online broker with the authority to take binding decisions on insurers' behalf. Quantitative insights from analysing the demand taxonomy and qualitative insights from tens of thousands of interactions with pet owners on Facebook and Twitter told us what our products should look like. We set the maximum claim limit for theft and loss at £6,000. We did away with breed-specific exclusions and the age-old insurance industry practice of charging higher renewal prices to existing customers than to new customers. Recognising that for most people pets are part of the family, we included cover for travel, complementary therapies and the costs associated with the death of a pet as standard. The data told us that some people feel unhappy about paying for insurance they don't claim on, so we invented a product that offers cashback for every year that no claim is made. The data told us that other people worry about the cost of pet insurance increasing over time, so we invented a product for puppies and kittens where the price is guaranteed for the pet's lifetime. Some people hate paying the excess – the amount an insurer asks you to contribute to the cost of any claim

– so we gave them the option to set it at zero. With annual sales of £141 million, Bought By Many now employs 220 people and protects more than 325,000 pets. No insurance company has higher customer satisfaction scores. It is the UK's most trusted pet insurance brand, Europe's fastest-growing insurance company and the world's number one insurance provider for pet businesses and unusual pets.

It was search data – an effortless by-product of online life – that made this possible. The availability of large quantities of aggregated and anonymised internet searches was a necessary condition for Bought By Many to succeed – exactly as it was for Just Cages and WorldStores. If you played along with the experiment at the start of this chapter and still have a Google window with 'I've just h' in the search box, go back to it and hit return. Now look at the address bar in your browser; you'll see a long string containing various parameters, like the search query you've just made ('q=i%27ve+just+h'), where it originated ('source=hp', short for the Google 'homepage') and when exactly it happened ('ei=', followed by an encoded version of the time in microseconds). This data now exists somewhere on servers belonging to Google and your internet service provider. If you're using a browser that isn't Google Chrome or have browser extensions installed, it might also exist on servers belonging to the developers of those pieces of software. If you click on one of the search results, Google will send your query, 'i%27ve+just+h', to the destination website.

There are two possible futures for this data: it can be deleted or it can be used. If you'd prefer that it was deleted, you can use a privacy-preserving search engine like DuckDuckGo instead of Google, or a privacy-preserving browser like Brave – they will see to it that your search data vanishes almost as soon as it's created. But I hope to persuade you that it's better if search data is used to make something. With apologies to my old colleagues at Hitwise, they are like the manure collection and processing functions of the agribusiness we imagined in Chapter One. They compile search data from internet services providers and browser software and refine it into something useful: Search Intelligence. Just Cages, WorldStores and Bought By Many are like farmers, whose products depend on Search Intelligence for nourishment.

While human life sometimes improves in great leaps, most of the time it advances in tiny increments, like having more parrot cages to choose from and being able to find unusual types of pet insurance. Even infinitesimally small improvements can make a big difference to some people. Take Micah Carr-Hill, a food scientist from south London who insures his yellow Labrador, Chief, with Bought By Many. Chief is a trained autism service dog, who helps Micah's son stay safe and increases his independence. Autism service dogs are expensive, and Chief cost £6,000. Losing him would have a serious impact on Micah's family, which is why it was such a relief to find pet insurance that would cover the full cost of buying another dog.

Small improvements can have a ripple effect. In 2014, a researcher at Boston Consulting Group was working on a report about innovation in the insurance industry for Ping An, China's largest insurer. She'd read an article about Bought By Many in *Wired* magazine, and contacted Steven for an interview. A few months later, one of her colleagues got in touch to say that the chairman of Ping An's general insurance division was bringing his leadership team to London and wanted to meet Bought By Many. Steven found the thought hilarious: Ping An had 1.5 million employees, over 400 million customers and annual sales of more than $100 billion. At 115 storeys and 562 metres, its soon-to-be-completed HQ in Shenzhen would be the fourth tallest building in the world. Meanwhile, Bought By Many had eight employees shoehorned into a six-person room on a Clerkenwell backstreet.

We welcomed the chairman, Mr Sun, and his team to the largest of the shared meeting spaces in our serviced office building, a low-ceilinged basement room with a hot pink carpet. We had been asked to set up a video link so more Ping An colleagues could join the meeting remotely, but as there were no video conference facilities in the room, Guy had Blu-Tacked a webcam to the whiteboard. I sensed we were all feeling slightly hysterical by this point, aware that we were winging it and that the meeting would end in either triumph or disaster. After much hand-shaking and an elaborate exchange of business cards, Steven began his introduction. After a few minutes, Mr Sun noticed that neither Steven, Guy nor I were wearing ties, and respectfully removed his own. Noticing that Mr Sun was now tie-less, the other male members of the Ping An team did the same. I was next to present, with an overview of Bought By Many's data-driven approach to product development and marketing. During a brief pause when I was a few slides in, Mr Sun got up and strolled to the hospitality trolley at the back of the room. He picked up the hot water flask, and I watched in horror as he poured it into a glass tumbler which he must have assumed was heatproof. The awful memory of our investor John plunging through the floor, latte in hand, flashed before my eyes. Incredibly, Mr Sun's glass remained intact. However, no sooner had he sat down, than several of his colleagues began getting up to help themselves to their own glasses of hot water. I couldn't look.

Somehow, we got to the end of our presentations without any breakages or scaldings. There had been a lot of questions from the Ping An team, and now Mr Sun was ready to tell us what he thought. He said that he agreed with Boston Consulting Group that Bought By Many had an innovative approach to insurance, and that Ping An was committed to partnering with smaller companies at the cutting edge of financial services technology – would we work with them to design and launch a new portfolio of travel insurance products for Chinese consumers?

We weren't sure how to respond. It was a hugely flattering offer, but our agenda was at that time about scaling up customer acquisition for our partners in the UK. Conventional start-up wisdom tells you not to get distracted by speculative opportunities; you should have a laser-like focus on your goals. We turned to our investors for advice, who were sceptical; they warned us that Ping An could copy our intellectual property, and that something as simple as getting an invoice paid was fraught with difficulty when doing business in China. The more we thought about it, the more reasons there were to say no. We would have to find Mandarin-speaking staff with expertise in insurance and digital marketing. There were Chinese equivalents of Google and Facebook – Baidu and WeChat – that we would have to over an opportunity, but Ping An took a decision immediately. Within two weeks, they had launched seven new travel insurance products based on our insight.

The ripple effect quickly spread beyond China, and coverage of our work with Ping An brought us a slew of enquiries. Insurers wanted to know if search data analysis could help them with product development in Switzerland, Poland, Korea and Australia. Still in a single-room office, we created Bought By Many International and took on projects involving mobile phone insurance in Mexico, life insurance in Canada and car insurance in Italy. It didn't seem to matter what combination of insurance and country we tried; our approach just worked. Using search data to address the problems of UK pug owners has made insurance better for people all over the world.

Chapter Four

DATA ABUNDANCE

It may not surprise you to learn that I've developed a reputation among my colleagues in Cambridge for being obsessed with search data. They would probably tell you that it's my answer to everything. From predicting the outcomes of elections and evaluating the popularity of alternatives to representative democracy and measuring mental wellbeing, there isn't a research question in the social sciences that I can't bend search data to.

In a series of workshops I ran recently in Cambridge, simple search data queries provided a range of fresh insights. Matthew, a sustainability expert, identified a turning point in UK public attitudes to climate change in February 2019, when climate-related Google searches suddenly increased. Saite, who is researching the impact of the 2008 economic crisis on household finances, found that Google searches in the US were a leading indicator of demand for mortgages. A simple model based on search data could therefore enable him to estimate demand for mortgages in countries and periods where official statistics were unavailable or unreliable.

Our colleague, the renowned economist Diane Coyle, has a long-term interest in improving the accuracy and usefulness of economic measurement. As Diane discusses in her book *GDP: A Brief but Affectionate History*, the most famous economic metric of all has a number of shortcomings that can lead to poor decision-making by governments and those of us who elect them. One of these shortcomings is that GDP doesn't account for the benefit people receive from the free goods and services that the digital revolution has made possible. For billions of us, free email, video and social networking software are a crucial part of our daily lives – we rely on them for work, entertainment and to keep in touch with friends and family. And yet its value is completely missing from GDP, for the simple reason that no money changes hands.

The challenge for economists is to find a way of calculating what free software is really worth, and this is where search data could come in. In the workshop, Diane tested a small example: free statistics software. Comparing Google searches for the paid statistics software product MATLAB with searches for a free alternative, R, gave her a proxy for the number of people using each product. By multiplying the number of R users by the annual cost of a MATLAB licence, she could estimate how much R was contributing to the global economy. Google search data also indicated changes in user preferences over time, with searches for MATLAB gradually declining while searches for R book *Everybody Lies*. Google searches for pornography would suggest that 2.9 million gay men are still in the closet. The best predictor of support for Donald Trump in the 2016 Republican primary was racist searches – that is, people googling the N-word. The biggest concern parents have about their children is their intellectual potential, but only if they have boys – fewer than half as many people search 'Is my daughter gifted?' as 'Is my son gifted?', while twice as many search 'Is my daughter overweight?' as 'Is my son overweight?'

At the time of writing, some 265 articles using search data have been published in peer-reviewed academic journals. The Italian epidemiologist Nicola Bragazzi is the most prolific exponent of search data in academia. He has co-authored more than twenty journal articles, using search data to shed light on a wide range of public health issues – a technique known as 'infodemiology'.

Many of these papers focus on the public's reaction to infectious diseases. Bragazzi and his collaborators have looked at Google searches for Ebola during the 2014 epidemic in West Africa, for the Zika virus during the 2016 outbreak in Brazil and for West Nile fever over an eleven-year period in Italy. They demonstrate that monitoring aggregated search data can help track the spread of diseases in countries where most people have access to the internet. Even in countries where only a small proportion of people

h data can give health agencies vital clues about ion needs. There is often a gap between expert sease and what ordinary people believe and do; ta can highlight this gap, enabling health agen- e effective communication strategies.

In the case of Zika, search data suggested that the public was disproportionately focused on microcephaly – babies being born with abnormally small heads. In reality, being infected with Zika during the first trimester of pregnancy only leads to a 1 per cent to 13 per cent risk of microcephaly, with fever, skin rash and conjunctivitis being much more common symptoms of infection. Furthermore, there was little evidence of people searching for information about actions that could be taken to reduce the risk of catching the virus, such as using mosquito nets and insect repellents, and avoiding standing water. These insights are potentially life-saving.

Having established the power of Google search data in researching infectious diseases, Bragazzi has extended it to other public health questions. Researchers seeking to understand trends in self-harm among young people typically work with statistics that are months or even years old, but Bragazzi showed that aggregated, anonymised search data was a robust alternative that was available in real time. In the field of occupational health, a team led by Bragazzi analysed patterns in worldwide searches for silicosis, a lung disease affecting people who work in trades like stonemasonry, quarrying and construction, where inhaling dust is unavoidable. This underlined the potential for search data to inform clinicians about patients' concerns, and for its use in evaluating the effectiveness of preventative practices in workplaces and of health and safety legislation.

Finally, Bragazzi has demonstrated that search data can objectively quantify the public health impact of advocacy initiatives. In 2015, the actor and humanitarian Angelina Jolie announced that she had undergone a double mastectomy because her genes put her at high risk of developing breast cancer. In the US, this led to an increase in public discussion of hereditary breast cancer and referrals to clinics offering genetic screening – often referred to as the 'Angelina Jolie effect'. Bragazzi and his team wanted to measure the effect in Europe. Analysing Google data showed that searches for breast cancer had increased by 18 per cent following Jolie's revelation, reversing a long-term decline, while searches for mammography had increased by 71 per cent. While there was no shortage of opinion about the importance of Jolie's intervention, Bragazzi's team used search data to provide hard evidence.

The applications of search data in academic research do not stop there. The digital marketer Eeva Koutaniemi teamed up with the sociology researcher Elina Einiö to look at the seasonality of domestic abuse in Finland. By correlating police data with Google searches for helplines, shelters and information about intimate partner violence, they demonstrated that search data could anticipate seasonal peaks in domestic abuse in countries where official statistics aren't collected. Elsewhere, academics have shown that search data can predict large-scale movements of people – whether in response to natural disasters or to pursue economic opportunity. I could go on, but you get the idea: there is almost no limit to the important truths that data can reveal. In deep sea diving terms, the ocean is vast and full of phosphorescence.

If you know how cash-strapped most universities are, you might be wondering how researchers are able to afford all this data. The answer is simple: they aren't using paid sources of search data, but instead rely on a free tool, Google Trends. Designed to allow ordinary Google users to explore search data, it has a straightforward online interface. You enter a search term or a topic you're interested in, and Google Trends returns the relative volume of searches over time, going back to 2004. If you look back at the image illustrating Diane's experiment with searches for statistics software products, you'll get a sense of Google Trends' other key features. First, you can compare search volume for up to five terms or topics, over different time periods. Second, you can see national variations in searches, and regional variations within countries. Third, you can toggle between different types of searches, such as image search and YouTube search. Fourth, you can download the data into a spreadsheet and conduct your own analysis of it. Finally, you can look at the top twenty-five related search queries: for example, some of the most popular queries Matthew saw when investigating climate change search data were 'greta thunberg', 'trump on climate change' and 'extinction rebellion'.

Google Trends is a fantastic tool, but this last feature highlights its major limitation: it only gives you twenty-five search term variations. Remember how many search term variations were in the demand taxonomy of the insurance market that Steve Johnston and I built for Bought By Many? 850,000. While smart start-ups find commercial opportunities by plumbing the depths of search data, researchers' reliance on Google Trends means they are confined to the shallows. If they could dive deeper with tools like Hitwise, who knows what world-changing discoveries they might make.

The Strange Death of Jumpshot

On 30 January 2020, big search data analysis was dealt a terrible blow. Following reporting by *PCMag* and *Vice* magazine on alleged privacy infringements, the anti-virus software provider Avast announced that it was closing down its subsidiary Jumpshot, which provided behavioural data and analytics to the tech and retail sectors. This news won't have meant much to anyone except digital marketing specialists, but it has had seismic repercussions for the issues we've already discussed.

Jumpshot supplied the data that enabled Hitwise – and numerous other analytics tools like Moz and SEMrush – to provide search intelligence capabilities. In the previous chapter, I explained what sort of companies are able to collect search data: you might remember that anti-virus software providers were one of the examples. It turned out that in recent years Hitwise had become increasingly reliant on data collected by Avast anti-virus software. Jumpshot's role was to anonymise this data and then pipe it to Hitwise. Without this data feed, Hitwise's products (including Search Intelligence) simply stopped working.

Jumpshot's demise also matters because it signals that data companies have begun to doubt the viability of digital analytics as a business model. Jumpshot did not break the law or fail to comply with regulations like GDPR. It did not share any personally identifiable information with its clients; its data was aggregated and anonymised. No privacy experts went on record to say that there was any material risk of harm to individuals from Jumpshot's operations. Avast explained to users of its anti-virus software how and why data was shared, and made it easy for them to opt out. Nevertheless, under the influence of surveillance capitalism theory, perceptions around data analytics have shifted sufficiently for Jumpshot to be driven out of business. As a result, it seems highly unlikely that an alternative supplier will choose to fill the void they've left.

The social costs of this are significant. Hundreds of people at Jumpshot and Hitwise lost their jobs, including many of my old colleagues. Other analytical tools that helped smaller e-commerce retailers to compete with Amazon were hobbled. The US Congress had been using Jumpshot data to investigate monopolistic practices by Google in the search market, but has been unable to continue. And as you will recall, without Hitwise there would have been no trundle beds and no pug insurance. Bought By Many and WorldStores (now part of the Dunelm Group) are established businesses, so are generally unaffected, but it will be harder for entrepreneurs to build new socially useful 'long tail' businesses in the same mould. This type of cost is known as 'deadweight loss' by economists, but I prefer the more emotive phrasing of the tech writers Ben Thompson and James Allworth: it is 'the silent screams of all the companies that never get started'.

What's more, many untapped opportunities for search data in academic research and policy-making have been foreclosed. I'd worked out how Hitwise data could inform policies for LGBTQ inclusion, and how it could amplify the effectiveness of campaigning organisations in areas like asylum, electoral reform and privacy rights. Sadly, those projects died on the vine.

I am not saying that anyone should be forced into pooling their anonymised search data against their will, or that companies should be allowed to collect it in an opaque manner. But I am concerned that norms are being reshaped without sufficient attention being paid to the trade-offs involved. As we've seen, big tech companies offer a surprising amount of control over how our data is used, while privacy-preserving browsers and search engines, VPNs, adblockers and encrypted messaging services are widely available. It's already fairly straightforward for us to prevent our data being collected, but there is increasing support for the view that we shouldn't have to – in other words, that the default settings should be changed to opt us out.

To illustrate the trouble with this, we might consider organ donation. I think most people would agree that greater availability of donor organs is a good thing, but the approach taken to individual consent for donation varies from place to place. Countries like Spain, which opt people in to donor programmes by default, typically experience higher rates of organ donation than countries like Germany, where the default is to opt people out; in 2017, there were more than five times as many organ donations per capita in Spain as in Germany. I don't want to overstate the causal link with opt-out as opposed to opt-in consent, but I do think it's helpful to consider consent for the reuse of search data and other forms of behavioural data in this context. By allowing your search data to be anonymously collected and aggregated with the data of billions of other people around the world, you are donating something for the greater good – just as organ donors are. The more search data is available, the better –

just as the more donor organs are available, the better. I would therefore argue that it is in the public interest for search engine users to be opted in to the pooling of their search data by default – just as citizens are opted into organ donation by default in Spain, France, Italy and (as of spring 2020) the UK.

In the week that Jumpshot closed, it became clear that more than 40,000 people around the world had been infected with coronavirus. Hundreds had already lost their lives and the outbreak was on the verge of being declared a pandemic. The mortality rate among those infected appeared to be as high as 2 per cent. Google Trends shows the day when global interest in coronavirus began to surge: 20 January. It also shows where in the world people were most concerned about it: China, Singapore, Australia, Canada and New Zealand. But not much can be learned from Google Trends' shallow data on the top twenty-five related queries, which were mostly generic searches for things like 'coronavirus update', 'coronavirus symptoms' and 'coronavirus cure'.

In the last few days before it closed its doors, I turned to Hitwise and downloaded UK search term variation data on coronavirus for the four weeks to 25 January. There were 3,664 distinct search queries. Just as Nicola Bragazzi and his team had found when analysing searches for Zika, I could see both information needs and gaps between the advice experts were giving and what people believed. No fewer than fifty-three of the search queries were variations on 'coronavirus face mask' – despite the World Health Organization at that time advising that masks would only help if people who had already been infected wore them.

The forty-fourth most popular search was 'coronavirus japan' and there were many other searches formulated as 'coronavirus <country>', with France, Thailand and Malaysia featuring prominently. I suspected these searches were being made by people who had planned holidays and business trips and wanted to assess the risks of travelling. The searches 'packages from china coronavirus' and 'chinese restaurants coronavirus' were in 137th and 178th place respectively, hinting at safety concerns I had not heard discussed in media reporting and at the damage the outbreak would do to businesses in China and among the Chinese diaspora. Twenty-nine search queries featured cats, with people wanting to know not just about the symptoms of feline coronavirus, but if transmission between cats and humans was possible. These questions didn't feature in any of the advice from health agencies or news coverage I had read.

Other searches highlighted the pervasiveness of misinformation. There were four variations on 'coronavirus bat soup' in the top 200 searches – a reference to a video circulating on social media that falsely claimed to show a restaurant in the Wuhan market where the virus originated but was actually filmed in Micronesia in 2016. Conspiracy theories also seemed to be rife, with 'coronavirus cover-up', 'coronavirus china not telling' and 'coronavirus man-made' also in the top 200. Overall, the picture was one of anxiety, paranoia and even panic.

Within a couple of hours of downloading the Search Intelligence data from Hitwise, I had a clear understanding of how the UK population was thinking about coronavirus, based on a sample of millions of internet users. I knew what existing messages public health officials needed to reinforce, what emerging concerns they needed to address and what misinformation they needed to counteract. Imagine how powerful these insights could be in the hands of the people tasked with controlling the spread of the disease. With access to deep search data, they could run this kind of analysis every day, getting real-time information about the effectiveness of their communications and what to prioritise next. Search data might have become integral to the response to all future public health emergencies, but without Jumpshot, that isn't going to happen.

To sum up the argument I've made so far in this part of the book: allowing your search data to be collected, anonymised, aggregated with other people's data and put into the public domain is a benefit to society. It's an act of good digital citizenship that enables scientific progress and better health outcomes, as well as new consumer products and economic development. There is no financial benefit to you in hoarding your search data; it's true that companies like Hitwise and Jumpshot made money from it, but only because they processed it in very large quantities and refined it into something useful.

But I am also making the case for a bigger concept: *data openness*. It isn't just the data of individuals that can benefit society: companies' and governments' data can, too. And there are movements afoot to make available data that has traditionally been hoarded by organisations, where entrepreneurs, innovators and researchers can use it.

Open Banking

One of these movements is open banking. Following recent regulation designed to encourage competition in the financial sector, banks in Europe, Mexico, Singapore, Hong Kong and Malaysia are now obliged to enable their customers to share their online banking data with third parties. Though that might sound dull, it creates some exciting possibilities.

Most people's financial accounts are spread across many different providers: you might have a current account with HSBC, a credit card with American Express, a mortgage with a local building society, a savings account with an online bank and so on. That fragmentation makes getting an overall picture of your finances tricky. You might copy and paste the figures from your statements into a spreadsheet from time to time, but the information will quickly go out of date. It also makes it difficult to spot money-saving opportunities; better rates of interest on your mortgage or your savings balance might be available, but how do you know when to look for them?

This problem was well known when I started my career in financial services in 2001, and there was a lot of enthusiasm for the solution: a single view of all your financial accounts in one place, with automated recommendations of better deals. Sometimes this solution was referred to as 'account aggregation'; at other times as 'personal financial management'. Over the following two decades, many companies have tried to bring this vision to life – most famously Mint.com. However, they all faced an insuperable barrier: in order for the companies to be able to collate data from multiple accounts, customers had to hand over all their online banking login details. Not only did this increase the risk that customers' accounts would be compromised by hackers, it also breached the terms and conditions of most online banking services, meaning that they would not be protected in the event that they suffered any kind of financial loss. As a result, most account aggregation companies were unable to recruit enough customers for them to become viable businesses.

Open banking changes all that. There is now a set of technical standards that allow online banking data to be securely shared, and the race is on to create the personal financial management apps that will do for financial services what Airbnb has done for holiday rentals and Uber has done for the taxi business. Some of these apps focus on visualising day-to-day spending in a more helpful way, some automatically sweep surplus funds into a savings account at the end of each month and others use feeds of information about loan rates to alert you to cheaper deals. In their different ways, they all give you a clearer view of your personal finances.

But something else is even more helpful than having a clearer view of your personal finances: being able to benchmark yourself, anonymously, against other people. How does your credit card debt compare to other people of the same age, doing similar jobs and living in similar areas? What about your energy consumption – are you using more or less gas than other people in terraced houses in market towns? What's more important to prioritise – getting new double glazing or paying off your credit card?

My first job at Experian was to set up a comparison website business called Lower My Bills. We put a lot of work into sophisticated algorithms that matched people to the appropriate loans and mortgages based on their Experian credit score, but our users' favourite feature was a simple tool called Compare My Bills. In exchange for entering guesstimates of their credit card bill, energy bills, phone bill and so on, users got to see how they compared to other users. Technologically speaking, Compare My Bills was quite crude – we had no way of knowing whether the data people were providing was correct, and it didn't do anything to tailor the comparison: as long as they shared a postcode, a wealthy retiree in a sprawling bungalow and a young warehouse worker in a cramped flatshare would see the same comparative information. Nevertheless, people loved it. An insatiable appetite for benchmarking ourselves against others seems to be part of human nature.

Some of the most exciting opportunities for open banking are in this area. Instead of the hassle of finding your last four quarterly energy bills, or the vagueness of trying to calculate your average credit card repayment from memory, so that you can fill in a Compare My Bills-style questionnaire, agreeing to share anonymous data with an open banking app could enable you to see how you compare with others automatically. Our instincts at this moment of fear and pessimism about data may be to share as little as possible, but imagine the benefit of knowing where we stand financially. It might motivate us to increase our pension contributions, galvanise us to deal with a debt we've been ignoring or allow us to stop worrying about how we're doing. Embracing data openness is the key to it.

Furthermore, the possibilities of open banking data are not limited to personal finance apps. In the same coffee shop where I had first met Steven eight years previously, I met Zoe, the data strategy director at a major high street bank. She told me that analysis of card transaction data from the bank's customers could identify gambling addiction and mania among people with bipolar disorder, as both behaviours manifest themselves in distinctive spending patterns. What's more, it was possible to predict these scenarios up to three years in advance: early warning signs are hidden in the data. Nobody wants to be a gambling addict, and it's a reasonable assumption that at least some people with bipolar disorder would welcome more support in managing their condition. If the bank could use data analytics to help, surely it had a moral responsibility to do something about it?

However, the issues Zoe would face if she was to take action were manifold. There were straightforward commercial considerations: to make money, banks have to manage their customers' access to credit and are constantly reviewing their overdraft and credit card limits, as well as the probability that future mortgage or loan repayments won't be made. It seemed inevitable that using the analytics would lead to people losing access to credit – something that is rarely welcomed, at least in the short-term.

Zoe would also have to figure out how the bank could communicate its insight to the people affected. As we saw with targeted Facebook adverts in Chapter One, using probabilistic inferences means that some of the customers identified would be so-called 'false positives'. Imagine logging into your mobile banking app and a pop-up screen saying something like, 'We think you have bipolar disorder and are about to have a manic episode, so you might want to get help.' That would likely be received as an awful invasion of privacy by people who did have the condition, and as offensive by people who didn't. Zoe wondered if it would be better to be less overt and quietly add links to a page on the bank's website explaining how to set limits on cash withdrawals in advance, or block card translations with particular retailers. This seemed like a better option, but it lacked transparency.

Thirdly, the regulatory and reputational risks for the bank were significant. Regardless of Zoe's good intentions, the Financial Conduct Authority might think she was trying to exploit vulnerable customers. Journalists could stoke outrage about big companies using our most intimate secrets against us. It was for this reason that Zoe suspected she wouldn't be able to do anything with her insights into problem gambling and bipolar disorder. Current norms mean that it's safer for companies with data-driven businesses to sit on their hands.

Luckily, open banking can help. Rather than intruding on people as they browse their statements or standing orders with awkward nudges about wellbeing, third-party organisations could use the bank's API – the pipe into the card transaction data – to build specialised apps. A mental health charity like Mind could build one for people with bipolar; GamCare could do something similar for people at risk of problem gambling. Once again, though, the effectiveness of these ideas depends on a willingness to pool our data anonymously for the greater good, as well as on banks to go beyond the minimum requirements imposed on them by open banking regulations.

Although I hadn't met Zoe before, she's a type of person I know well: energetic, optimistic and keen to push the boundaries. Such people are often found in the strategy, innovation and new product development departments of large corporations. Her counterparts in public and third sector organisations are no less savvy, but they tend to have a quite different outlook.

Take Phil, for example. He co-founded the tech company entitledto, one of the UK's main providers of the software tools that enable people to figure out their eligibility for benefits and rent affordability on government, housing association, charity and money-saving websites. It's a hugely valuable service that is used by millions of people every year and generates a lot of data – about household composition, disabilities, caregiving, special educational needs, childcare arrangements, English language skills, employment, income, housing and homelessness, rental and mortgage payments, savings, pensions, debt and arrears, internet usage, drug and alcohol addiction, domestic violence, asylum and much more besides. Think of all the valuable insights this data might contain, and the correlations that might be revealed if data scientists could analyse it. What could it uncover about the relationship between homelessness and service in the armed forces? Or between caring responsibilities and levels of indebtedness? What about the pay gap for people with disabilities? The data could also be a source of revenue; generating leads for, say, shared ownership properties, credit unions or selected gas and electricity providers could fund new software developments, as well as providing a helpful service to users of entitledto's existing tools.

Phil has had all these ideas, but acting on them is dangerous. GDPR threatens fines of up to 20 million Euros for non-compliance, and the reputational damage of being seen to undermine users' privacy would be just as bad. Even though entitledto doesn't capture personally identifiable information, like the names or email addresses of the people who use its service, the risks of doing something useful with the data are just too great. Advice from an in-house legal and compliance team with an understanding of privacy legislation and a relationship with regulators might give Phil the assurances he would need to start unlocking the potential of the data. But like many smaller organisations, entitledto can't afford an in-house legal and compliance team. So instead of being open and contributing to making the world a better place, the data sits on a server, unused.

Open Data

My hope is that the growth of another movement, *open data*, will help change that. Despite sounding rather broad, open data usually refers to data that has been made available in a reusable format by governments and other public sector organisations. No restrictions are imposed on who can use it, or what they can do with it. Before publishing the data, organisations might have an inkling about how third-party uses of it might benefit them, but that isn't their main motivation. Rather, open data has the same philosophical basis as open-source computing and open-access research: the idea is that treating information as a common good is the best way to enable human progress. It should be open by default and available for everyone to draw on, provided they reciprocate by contributing themselves. Unsurprisingly, open data has been challenging for public sector organisations, as it demands a complete reversal of their normal practice – the hoarding of data as a means of maintaining influence, or (as in Phil's case) minimising risk.

So what are the benefits of open data in the real world? The most obvious is that it creates greater transparency for citizens over political decision-making, public spending and institutional performance. Many countries are dealing with a legacy of kleptocracy and corruption; in these contexts, open data initiatives can help rebuild public trust and hold officials to account. For instance, Open Development Cambodia is an online portal that provides economic indicators on labour and industry, along with data on demography, land use, infrastructure, the judiciary and development aid. It's accessible to Cambodian citizens and has been used by journalists and NGOs to highlight issues such as the mass displacement of small farmers by large-scale sugar plantations. Elsewhere, open data projects enable citizens to make more informed choices about education and health, empowering them with the evidence they need to demand improvements from their political representatives. In Mexico, Mejora tu Escuela, a website that compares the performance of different schools, is visited by more than 40,000 people every day. In Uruguay's mixed public-private healthcare system, an open data-driven service called A tu Servicio allows citizens to compare the performance of different providers. In all these cases, open data stops knowledge being concentrated inside governments and public sector institutions, instead distributing it among citizens. And as the saying goes, knowledge is power.

A less obvious benefit of open data comes from new kinds of private enterprise. You might be aware of Citymapper, the ingenious app that integrates data on every form of transport, making it easy to get around cities – even ones that are unfamiliar and confusing. Not only will Citymapper tell you the best way to get from A to B, it will also keep you posted on when your stop is approaching, when the next bus will arrive and the location of the nearest pay-and-ride bike or scooter. What you might not know is that Citymapper only exists because of open data: according to the company's former president Omid Ashtari, it's 'the essential backbone' of the service. It's because transport authorities make reliable feeds of public transport data openly accessible that commercially motivated developers have been able to design and build travel planning apps. Previously, when the data was hoarded, apps could only be developed by the transport authorities themselves – and they often lacked the skills and resources to do that effectively.

Citymapper is an example of a private company using open data to improve a type of service that already existed. But open data also paves the way for brand new services that public sector organisations never would have had the capacity to build, or even think of. The online real estate portal Properati uses open data to help people to find their next home in unexpected ways. Hayfever sufferers in Buenos Aires can use a Properati app that uses data from the local government's woodland census to avoid areas with the most pollen-producing trees. In five cities

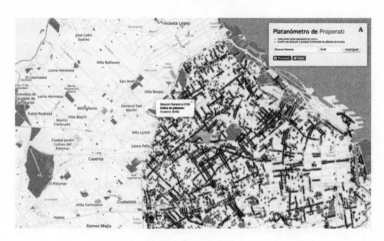

Properati's hayfever map of Buenos Aires.

including Berlin and San Francisco, Place I Live does the same thing with sports facilities: with a single tap you can find the nearest ping pong table, martial arts club or driving range to any home. These open data-enabled services enrich our experience of the environments we move through every day.

A third way in which open data creates real-world benefit is through academic research and the public policy innovations that flow from it. A striking example is the Opportunity Insights group at Harvard, led by the economist Raj Chetty. Using the anonymised census returns and tax records of millions of citizens, Chetty and his team have proved that the American Dream of social mobility is fading. Children born in 1980 had a 50 per cent chance of earning more than their parents at the age of thirty-five – a dramatic fall from the 92 per cent chance enjoyed by those born in 1940. At the same time, Ivy League universities are admitting more students from the richest 1 per cent of families than from the poorest 60 per cent. What's more, there are stark racial and geographic inequalities. Boys born into affluent black families are more than twice as likely to end up poor as boys born into affluent white families. Children born into the poorest 20 per cent of households in Charlotte, North Carolina have barely a 5 per cent chance of being in the richest 20 per cent of households as adults, while the odds for poor children in Salt Lake City are more than twice as good. Even the street you live on as a child can make a huge difference to your prospects: in Oakland, California, men who grow up in the neighbourhood of Fruitvale Station have a 70 per cent chance of going to prison; a few miles away in San Leandro, that likelihood is below 5 per cent. Life chances in America are largely determined by the accidents of birth, throwing the country's meritocratic ideals into sharp relief.

Opportunity Insights is not just interested in highlighting America's problems with inequality; it is also committed to gener-ating solutions. It is clear that moving to a better neighbourhood during childhood makes a huge difference to one's future income; this suggests that inequality would be reduced by making housing vouchers for poorer families conditional on them moving to properties in higher-opportunity neighbourhoods, an approach Opportunity Insights is piloting with local authorities in Seattle.

Another finding is that there are currently two necessary conditions for becoming an inventor and filing patents: innate ability, as measured by excellent scores on third grade maths tests; and being born to rich parents. Chetty estimates that educa-tion policy targeted at realising the neglected potential of poorer, high-ability children could quadruple America's innovation rate. Importantly, Opportunity Insights also seeks to empower other researchers and policymakers. True to the principles of open data, its outputs and data sets are available for download and reuse on its website, and the lectures from the introductory economics course Chetty designed for Harvard students can be viewed for free on YouTube.

Many other fascinating stories have emerged from Opportunity Insights' research, and I encourage you to go and play with their interactive online visualisation tool, the Opportunity Atlas. But the point I want to emphasise is that Opportunity Insights depends on the availability of anonymised tax record data. If Chetty and his fellow researchers hadn't been allowed to access it because of privacy concerns that individuals and families might be reidentified, their insights into economic inequality wouldn't have been possible. In that alternate reality, while Amazon and Netflix used big data analytics to perfect home entertainment recommendations, policymaking to improve social mobility would be stuck in the analogue era.

We have a choice to make about the kind of world we want to live in. We can choose the world we are currently accelerating towards, in which privacy is treated as the supreme human good. In such a world, we would celebrate the demise of Jumpshot and feel satisfied that internet search data was deleted at the moment of its creation. We'd want bank employees like Zoe to think only about the financial realm, and we'd want their public and third sector counterparts like Phil to fear the punitive consequences of using data about individuals to enable innovation.

We'd block researchers' access to tax record data as a matter of principle: after all, it's among the most sensitive information that exists about us.

Alternatively, we can choose the world of data openness that I've sketched in this chapter. It brings with it some privacy trade-offs, like opting all of us in to pooling our anonymised data by default. It also brings some risk of harm, as figuring out an individual's identity from their behavioural data is possible in some circumstances. But there is an abundance of good that we can get in return.

Search Data against Coronavirus

As the coronavirus pandemic unfolded in March 2020, I considered how I could contribute to the response. 'If you work in tech and are wondering what you can do to help with coronavirus,' one wag had posted on Twitter, 'wash your hands for twenty seconds, use a tissue for coughs and avoid touching your face.' I found that amusing, but didn't agree with the suggestion that we should leave the immunologists and epidemiologists to fight the virus alone.

My friend Ed had created an open, crowdsourced library of information, tools and resources called the *Coronavirus Tech Handbook* – a sort of Wikipedia about coronavirus. I thought the least I could do was publish the data I had downloaded from Hitwise in it, in case other researchers could make use of it.

Then it occurred to me that I could contact Sophie Coley at AnswerThePublic and ask if they would consider including their search term variation data about coronavirus and Covid-19, too. Almost immediately, Sophie replied with a link to a Google Sheet, where she had collected daily data for multiple countries for several months. AnswerThePublic compiles Google autocomplete suggestions, which reflect Google's expectation of what you are likely to be looking for, based on the first things you type into the search box. The data isn't as deep as Hitwise Search Intelligence, but it's way better than Google Trends at highlighting the specifics of what's on people's minds.

Better still, Sophie had also been doing her own coronavirus analysis. By tracking searches beginning 'Should I...', she had highlighted how the UK public's concerns were evolving as the weeks passed, from 'Should I travel to Italy?' and 'Should I close my business?' to 'Should I delete Houseparty?' and 'Should I shave my head?' Building on her idea, I looked at the top questions beginning 'Can coronavirus...' in AnswerThePublic's data and saw:

1. Can coronavirus live on food?
2. Can coronavirus live on paper?
3. Can coronavirus live on cardboard?

These immediately resonated with me: I had been washing fresh fruit and vegetables in soap and water, and where possible leaving deliveries in a 'decontamination zone' under the stairs for seventy-two hours before opening them. I knew it might be out of proportion to the risks, but in the absence of explicit public health advice it felt like a sensible precaution. My father was going a step further by heating his Sunday newspaper in the oven at a low temperature before reading it.

I was struck by the continuity from the questions about transmission through packaging and food that had appeared in the Hitwise data back in January, two months earlier. The data showed that this had been a major public concern for months, and yet the government and NHS websites had barely any information about it. Instead, the top results on Google were from news sources like the *Guardian*, and even the website of the radio station Heart FM. There was an obvious explanation for this: journalism is fiercely competitive, so digital marketers in the sector are used to updating website content on a minute-by-minute basis, using insights from search data to gain traffic. That's not something that public sector websites would ordinarily need to do, so they can hardly be blamed for losing out. But the outcome was that the most authoritative sources in the UK were silent on the public health information questions that were of the widest concern.

Sometimes, such information voids are filled by rumour and conspiracy theories. To their great credit, Microsoft started publishing data about coronavirus searches from Bing in a format that made it easy for researchers to run their own analysis. I downloaded their data set and looked for searches about public health information, so I could build on the insights Sophie and I had drawn from the AnswerThePublic data. But I was quickly distracted by something I wasn't expecting: searches about 5G. In the UK, there had been a spate of arson attacks on mobile phone masts, seemingly motivated by the unfounded idea that 5G radiation was the cause of Covid-19. The Bing data showed that the UK was in the top five countries in the world when it came to searches for the 5G coronavirus conspiracy theory, along with Ghana, Nigeria, South Africa and Zimbabwe. It also revealed specific stories that were capturing people's imagination: several were about celebrity endorsements for 5G conspiracy theories, while another was about a viral video uploaded by a former Vodafone employee who claimed that Bill Gates was planning to use coronavirus vaccines to implant humans with tracking chips. There was plenty of talk in the news about the dangers of a coronavirus 'infodemic', but it was clear that Bing's data set could be used to highlight which bits of misinformation most needed to be contested.

Even in the absence of new Hitwise data, these insights showed that it was worth resuming my campaign to increase researchers' awareness of search data sources. With the Bing downloads, Sophie's data from AnswerThePublic and the older Hitwise data set, the *Coronavirus Tech Handbook* had a burgeoning 'infodemiology' chapter. I decided to start spreading the word.

I emailed academics who had previously published research that used Google Trends data to answer public health questions, telling them about the data sets in the handbook. One of the first to reply was Bill Lampos, a computer scientist at University College London. It turned out that he was working on a model to forecast new Covid-19 outbreaks based on Google searches. Starting with Italy, where the outbreak was most advanced, Bill and his team had figured out which symptom-related searches best predicted the spread of the disease. It was early days, but in seven other countries the model was successfully predicting case numbers seventeen days in advance of official statistics. It was clear that in the context of limited testing capacity, Bill's model had huge potential.

We started swapping notes about the most striking things we were seeing in search data. We had both noticed a sharp increase in searches for anosmia – the loss of smell – that seemed to substantiate anecdotal reports from people who believed they had Covid-19, and were experiencing changes to their sense of smell and taste. By this time it was mid-March, and government guidance was still focused on a persistent dry cough and a high temperature as the key indicators of infection, but Bill's model was showing that loss-of-smell searches were much more predictive of actual cases. A week later, doctors Claire Hopkins and Abigail Walker at Guy's and St Thomas's Hospital in London reported that they had seen a massive increase in the number of patients presenting at ENT clinics having suddenly lost their sense of smell. Unlike a cough or a fever, smell loss is very unusual, and from a clinical perspective they were sure it was an unrecognised Covid-19 symptom. The search data and the medical experts agreed.

At around the same time, I came across Coronasearch. live, an interactive tool that visualised coronavirus searches by Chinese internet users in real time. Not only did it show search term variations, it also plotted the searches on a map of China and provided demographic information about who the searches were from. Better still, it was built using Google Data Studio, which meant the data was openly available for anyone to download. The data was much richer and more granular than what was available from Google Trends, and I wanted to find out how it had been sourced. I mentioned it to Sophie, and she sent me links to the previous projects of Patrick Berlinquette, the creator of Coronasearch.live. They involved using Google Ads in creative and socially useful ways. By bidding in Google's auction for search terms such as 'where to find heroin' and 'I want to shoot up my school', Patrick aimed to redirect people who were on the verge of doing something harmful, and also to generate data that could help decide where public health interventions were most needed. Now he was applying the same approach to coronavirus, making available Google data that would normally only be accessible to advertisers.

I was also very interested to learn that Patrick wasn't an academic researcher. Like both Sophie and Eeva Koutaniemi, who had used search data to forecast the incidence of domestic violence, he was a digital marketer. He owned an agency in New York that ran campaigns for commercial clients. Expertise in Google Ads combined with a desire to apply his skills for public good meant he had come up with a completely original search data methodology.

I got in touch with Patrick to tell him that I had added Coronasearch.live to the handbook, and it turned out he had also been tracking anosmia searches, following a *New York Times* op-ed by Seth Stephens-Davidowitz about the potential for Google symptom search data to be used to identify new Covid-19 hotspots. Patrick showed me a new tool he was working on, that heat-mapped loss of smell searches in 250 US cities. It would later correctly predict the resurgence of Covid-19 in the Sun Belt states after lockdown restrictions were eased. But I was even more excited by the potential for Patrick's methodology in countries where health infrastructure and testing capacity is weaker.

I had been reading reports from Tanzania, where the government appeared to be in denial about the seriousness of the pandemic. As well as actively encouraging mass gatherings, the country's president, John Magufuli, had publicly ridiculed the ineffectiveness of Covid-19 tests, claiming that a goat and a pawpaw had tested positive. But at the same time, video footage shared on social media showed overflowing hospitals and coffins being buried at night by men wearing military uniforms and personal protective equipment. Three members of the Tanzanian parliament had died suddenly. Meanwhile, Google Trends showed that Tanzania had more searches for anosmia per capita than anywhere apart from Ecuador, where a devastating Covid-19 outbreak was underway.

I suggested that Patrick try building a version of the tool for Tanzania. We weren't sure that it would work – Google usage in Tanzania is lower than in the US, and Swahili is more widely spoken than English – but the results were very powerful.

On 9 May, the Tanzanian government stopped reporting Covid-19 statistics, with the official number of cases at 509. Shortly afterwards, John Magufuli declared that the virus had been defeated. And yet in that week, Patrick's data was showing that roughly 130 people were googling loss of smell symptoms every day, in English. With help from Evarist Chahali,

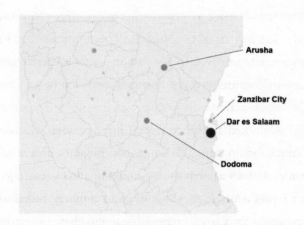

Anosmia Google searches in Tanzania, seven days to 13 May 2020.

a Tanzanian political consultant who spoke Swahili, Patrick
estimated that the total volume of anosmia searches was more
than 1,500 per day. We could also see that outbreaks were not
confined to Tanzania's largest city, Dar es Salaam. The highest
per-capita searches for loss of smell were coming from Zanzi-
bar, the northern city of Arusha and Dodoma – the country's
capital, where the three MPs had mysteriously died. As well as
producing data that could be used by public health agencies
and relief organisations in future, Patrick's tool for Tanzania
highlights another strength of search data: unlike official statistical sources, it can't be falsified by governments to serve their
own political agendas.

To make these findings accessible to a wider audience,
I began writing blogs for the Bennett Institute for Public
Policy, and two important questions about search data kept
being asked. Firstly, people wanted to know how we could be

sure that searches for symptoms weren't simply the result of people's curiosity or hypochondria. There had been a lot of media coverage of the calls for loss of smell to be recognised as a Covid-19 symptom, and that had indeed driven a spike in Google search activity. My reply was that there are different ways of dealing with this problem. Bill had used a statistical technique called autoregression in his model, which adjusted the forecasts in a way that took account of the biasing effect of media reports. Patrick, meanwhile, had simply excluded broad search queries from the Google Ads campaigns he was using to generate the data, as well as queries that contained coronavirus related keywords. As a result, searches for 'I can't smell', 'lost my sense of smell' and 'when you can't smell' were within the scope of his tool, but searches for 'anosmia' and 'loss of smell coronavirus' were not.

Secondly, people who remembered the failure of Google Flu Trends wanted to know why things would be different this time. Launched in 2008, it was the first infodemiology tool, and it's still the most widely known. Built by data scientists at Google, it used search data to predict flu cases in the US, two weeks ahead of reporting from the Centre for Disease Control (CDC). It worked spectacularly well, until in 2013 it began predicting far higher volumes of flu cases than the CDC was seeing in reality, and Google wound it down.

Why was this? An academic review published in *Science* suggested several reasons. One factor was changes in people's search behaviour over time, many of which were driven by the tweaks Google continually makes to its search algorithm in order to provide more helpful results. For example, in 2011 Google rolled out the first version of the 'People also ask' feature, which suggests related searches that Google users might want to try. That meant the Google Flu Trends model wasn't stable, because Google search was in constant flux. Another reason was what statisticians call 'overfitting' – making a model too complex in an attempt to explain all the variations in a data set. In earlier versions of Google Flu Trends, the data scientists used searches for high school basketball in their model, because in previous years such searches had strongly correlated with flu case numbers from the CDC. However, there was a simple explanation for this: like the flu, high school basketball reliably happens at a particular time of year. As the *Science* article puts it, Google Flu Trends 'was part flu detector, part winter detector'. Flu cases may have correlated with basketball searches, but they weren't causing them.

This critique might seem like a damning indictment of search data; indeed, posting on Twitter about using search data in research invariably leads to sceptical or dismissive replies that mention Google Flu Trends. So does that make Bill and Patrick's attempts to use search data in tracking the spread of Covid-19 doomed? Not at all. In my opinion, the most helpful conclusion to draw from the failure of Google Flu Trends is not that search data analysis is unreliable, but that it should be a *complement* to traditional methods rather than a *replacement* for them. As the authors of the *Science* article say, 'by combining Google Flu Trends and lagged CDC data ... we can substantially improve on the performance of Google Flu Trends or the CDC alone.'

In other words, even the most prominent critics of Google Flu Trends believe that adding search data improves the CDC's models. Searches for anosmia and other symptoms may not be the best basis for a predictive Covid-19 model in the long term, but that is hardly a reason not to make use of search data now, when the need to triangulate with other data sources is acute and the stakes are exceptionally high.

At the time of writing, Bill's model has been adopted by Public Health England and appears in its weekly reporting. He has also teamed up with researchers at Microsoft to build a model that predicts outbreaks at a UK local authority level using the Bing data – something the traditional methods used to monitor infectious disease outbreaks are unable to do because of the prohibitive cost.

Weekly Coronavirus Disease 2019 (COVID-19) Surveillance Report
Summary of COVID-19 surveillance systems

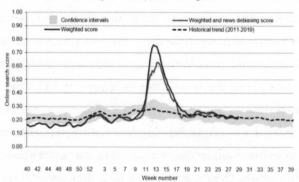

The output of Bill Lampos's Google search-based model in Public Health England's Covid-19 report.

Search data also reveals that lockdowns during the corona-virus pandemic have not been as bad for our wellbeing as was widely feared. As the first UK national lockdown dragged on into late May, concerns about a looming mental health crisis were often cited as a reason for easing restrictions. After a heatwave in early spring, the weather had got worse and participation in the Thursday night 'Clap for Our Carers' was dwindling. However, I had noticed something surprising in Google Trends data: searches relating to depression in the UK seemed to be 20 per cent lower during the lockdown period than at the same time in 2019. Intrigued, I sent this finding to my colleagues at the Bennett Institute, the political scientist Roberto Foa and the economist Mark Fabian, who are experts in measuring wellbe-ing statistically.

Aware of the pitfalls of relying on search data alone, Roberto went looking for tried and tested data sources to validate what Google Trends was showing. It turned out that YouGov had been asking a representative sample of around 2,000 people about their mood every week since June 2019. Although the survey was limited to Great Britain, if its data revealed the same patterns, we could confidently draw conclusions from Google Trends data about the mental health impact of lockdowns in other countries.

We started by comparing the data for each of the mood states YouGov had asked about with the corresponding topics in Google Trends, to see how well they correlated. We found that Google Trends wasn't much use for measuring positive moods like happiness, contentment, energy, inspi-

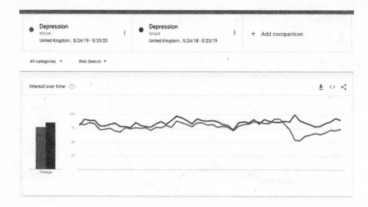

Google searches for depression: 24 May 2019–23 May 2020 (light grey line), compared to 24 May 2018–21 May 2019 (dark grey line).

ration and optimism, and reviewing the search terms that Google's machine learning algorithms associated with those moods explained why. There were a lot of false positives, with Google suggesting that searches for 'happy meal' and 'happy birthday' implied happiness. But when it came to negative moods, Google Trends worked very well. Searches for stress, boredom, frustration, sadness, fear and apathy were all highly correlated with the YouGov data. And when we compiled the negative moods into an index, the match between the survey data from YouGov and the search data from Google Trends was almost exact.

All our data pointed to the same unexpected conclusion: overall, lockdowns were *good* for people's wellbeing. Mark realised that previous studies had conflated the mental health effects of the coronavirus pandemic with the mental health effects of lockdown – because they didn't have data to tell them about

Figure 4: Comparison of Survey and Google Trend Series, June 2019 to June 2020.

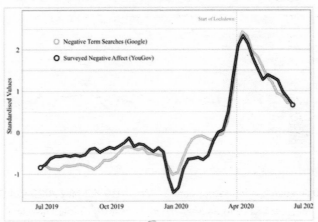

Comparison of YouGov survey data and Google Trends
search data on negative moods.

the period between the onset of the pandemic and the start of
lockdown. By contrast, our analysis of a year's worth of data
revealed the true sequence of events: people's mental health had
declined sharply during February and March 2020, as coronavirus outbreaks emerged all over the world and the number of
Covid-19 deaths began to escalate. But as soon as lockdowns
were implemented, people's mental health began to improve,
recovering almost all the way to its pre-pandemic baseline before
lockdown easing even started. When we looked at negative
mood in the UK, both the YouGov and the Google Trends data
showed a peak just three days after the national lockdown was
announced on 23 March, followed by a rapid fall. The Google
Trends data showed the same pattern in country after country,
from Canada and India to Australia.

Figure 5: Negative Affect Search Index and Lockdowns: Cross-Country Comparisons.

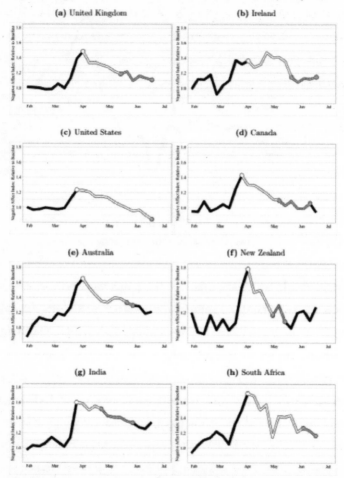

Notes: Cross-country comparisons on the negative affect Google Trends index. All countries set relative to their pre-pandemic baseline period (15 January to 15 February). Full lockdown indicated by white lines; partial lockdown indicated by grey lines. Dates of lockdown, partial easing, and return to work listed in Appendix Table A.2.

Google Trends search data on negative moods with lockdown
(white and grey lines) and without it (black line).

Using search data to complement traditional research methods, we had shown that while there might be good reasons to avoid implementing lockdowns in response to future coronavirus outbreaks, concern about mental health was not one of them. And like Citymapper and Opportunity Insights, our research would not have been possible without data openness.

Chapter Five
IT'S NOT ALL ABOUT 'US'

In 1994, I spent a month in Zimbabwe with my school cricket team. Our final game was at a festival in Harare, against a school called Plumtree. Their star player was one Henry Olonga, a fast bowler who the following year would become the first black player to represent Zimbabwe at Test level. He was not much of a batsman by professional standards, but he still managed to score a century against us, smashing our hapless attack for boundary after boundary. His bowling was something else entirely. I remember watching the Plumtree team take the field and wondering why their wicketkeeper was standing halfway between the stumps and the boundary. When he was joined by a slip cordon, I realised that was where they were expecting to be able to take the ball. All I saw of Olonga's first delivery was a puff of dust from the pitch, before the ball hit the keeper's gloves with a thud a fraction of a second later. He was seriously fast.

As I learned when I went out to bat, it wasn't just his pace you had to worry about. The ball moved – off the pitch, but also in the air. Facing my first ball, I shaped to play a forward defensive just outside off stump, but it swung away from me and the keeper had to dive to take it on the leg side. A couple of wider deliveries kept moving after passing the bat – one so dramatically that it beat the keeper's left hand and sped away for four byes, to Olonga's great frustration. The final ball of the over was shorter. I got into a backward defensive position and hoped for the best. The ball flashed off the face of the bat and the next thing I knew my teammates were applauding as it raced over the third man boundary and onto the dirt road beyond. After this, Olonga decided he had had enough and took himself out of the attack.

That was the high point of my cricketing career, but Olonga was only just getting started. In the following eight years, he would play thirty Test matches and fifty one-day internationals for Zimbabwe, taking five-wicket hauls against India, Pakistan and England. He was selected for his country's Cricket World Cup squad in 1996, 1999 and 2003.

It was in the last of these competitions, played in Kenya, South Africa and on home turf, that Olonga's life as an international cricketer would come to an abrupt end. In a match against Namibia, he and his teammate Andy Flower, who would later go on to coach England, took the field wearing black armbands. They explained themselves in the following statement:

It is a great honour for us to take the field today to play for Zimbabwe in the World Cup. We feel privileged and proud to have been able to represent our country. We are, however, deeply distressed about what is taking place in Zimbabwe in the midst of the World Cup and we do not feel that we can take the field without indicating our feelings in a dignified manner and in keeping with the spirit of cricket.

We cannot in good conscience take to the field and ignore the fact that millions of our compatriots are starving, unemployed and oppressed. We are aware that hundreds of thousands of Zimbabweans may even die in the coming months through a combination of starvation, poverty and AIDS.

We are aware that many people have been unjustly imprisoned and tortured simply for expressing their opinions about what is happening in the country. We have heard a torrent of racist hate speech directed at minority groups. We are aware that thousands of Zimbabweans are routinely denied their right to freedom of expression. We are aware that people have been murdered, raped, beaten and had their homes destroyed because of their beliefs and that many of those responsible have not been prosecuted. We are also aware that many patriotic Zimbabweans oppose us even playing in the World Cup because of what is happening.

It is impossible to ignore what is happening in Zimbabwe. Although we are just professional cricketers, we do have a conscience and feelings. We believe that if we remain silent that will be taken as a sign that either we do not care or we condone what is happening in Zimbabwe. We believe it's important to stand up for what is right.

We have struggled to think of an action that would be appropriate and that would not demean the game we love so much. We have decided that we should act alone without other members of the team being involved because our decision is deeply personal and we did not want to use our senior status to unfairly influence more junior members of the squad. We would like to stress that we greatly respect the ICC and are grateful for all the hard work it has done in bringing the World Cup to Zimbabwe.

In all the circumstances we have decided that we will each wear a black armband for the duration of the World Cup. In doing so we are mourning the death of democracy in our beloved Zimbabwe. In doing so we are making a silent plea to those responsible to stop the abuse of human rights in Zimbabwe. In so doing we pray that our small action may help restore sanity and dignity to our Nation.

To criticise the authoritarian regime of Zimbabwe's president Robert Mugabe so directly and publicly was an act of great bravery that brought serious consequences. At thirty-four, Flower was nearing the end of his international career and already had a contract with Essex County Cricket Club in the UK, but Olonga was only twenty-six and had no plans to leave Zimbabwe. Immediately ostracised by the country's cricket establishment, he was barred from even boarding the team bus. He began to receive death threats. The minister of information, Jonathan Moyo, publicly called him an 'Uncle Tom' with 'a black skin and a white mask'. The secret police let it be known that they were sending plain-clothes officers to Zimbabwe's final game of the World Cup, with the intention of arresting Olonga. They hinted that he would be charged with treason, which carried the death penalty, or 'taken care of' in some other way. With only a sports holdall and the cricket gear he was wearing, Olonga went into hiding in South Africa, before fleeing to the UK on a plane ticket gifted to him by a sympathetic stranger. He had escaped with his life, but would never play international cricket again.

What does this have to do with data and digital technology? I want to highlight how different the stakes can be depending on where someone happens to grow up. In many respects, Henry Olonga and I had similar childhoods. We both had professional parents who divorced when we were children. We both went to Christian boarding schools with great facilities and staff who valued and rewarded achievement in sport, theatre, art and music. We were sufficiently alike for our paths to cross on that cricket field in Harare in 1994. However, what was completely different about us was our relationship to the state.

At the time of Olonga and Flower's protest, I was living in a small town in Buckinghamshire and working in the digital marketing department of a bank. I'd recently been put at risk of redundancy, along with several hundred colleagues. I wasn't sure whether I wanted to relocate for a job elsewhere in the company, or accept a severance payment and move on. On the one hand, I disliked uncertainty; on the other, the economy was booming, my skills were in demand and the redundancy package would give me some savings. I was considering joining the staff union, and was weighing up whether the advice I'd get was worth the cost of membership. It wasn't the best of times, but I was cautiously optimistic about the future.

Some possibilities didn't ever enter my mind. It didn't occur to me that hyperinflation might render my redundancy package worthless overnight or that the job market might suddenly collapse, leaving me with nowhere to work. I never imagined a scenario in which I'd be blacklisted for joining the union or forcibly evicted from my home by armed police. Similarly, when I'd spoiled my ballot in the previous general election to make a point about the shortcomings of the first-past-the-post system, not once did I consider that I might be threatened or harassed at the polling station.

That was because where I lived there were a lot of basic freedoms, guaranteed by the state, which I took for granted: personal autonomy, freedom of the press, freedom of association, the rule of law, fair elections, and so on. I suspect most people reading this book are in a similarly fortunate position, but coming of age in Zimbabwe, Henry Olonga could not count on these freedoms at all. At the time, the power of the state was being wielded by Mugabe's party, ZANU-PF, in a very different way – not to expand freedom, but to exert control. On the pretext of land reform, farmers were driven from their property by government-backed militias. When the courts ruled that this expropriation was illegal, their powers were checked and judges were replaced. Political opposition by the Movement for Democratic Change, led by the trade unionist Morgan Tsvangirai, was suppressed and its supporters were persecuted and detained. Despite hyperinflation, mass unemployment, frequent power cuts, food shortages and the failure of the drinking water supply, not to mention international opprobrium, Mugabe's position was never threatened. ZANU-PF controlled the army, the security services and the media, which combined with its willingness to use violence, made it incredibly effective at crushing dissent.

However, digital technology has begun to change things. The proliferation of mobile phones and the advent of social media has equipped Zimbabweans with tools to organise protest and mobilise support, as well as a space to express political grievances and demands that is beyond the government's reach. In 2003, Henry Olonga and Andy Flower needed the spectacle of the Cricket World Cup, as well as connections to foreign journalists, to spread their message. But by 2016, Evan Mawarire was able to instigate a mass movement, #ThisFlag, with a four-minute video filmed on his phone and shared on Facebook. In it, the pastor and activist spoke directly to camera, reflecting on the values represented by the flag's colours, and the ways in which they had been betrayed by the actions of Zimbabwe's rulers. It went viral on social media, quickly building an online following for Mawarire that he used to campaign against government abuses. He and his supporters petitioned for corrupt officials to be dismissed, organising a general strike that brought the country to a standstill. A counter hashtag created by the government failed to gain traction, forcing them to resort to shutting down the internet. Mawarire has been repeatedly arrested and his

family threatened, but the movement he initiated is not dependent on him: inspired by his example, student activists have used
Twitter, Facebook and WhatsApp to co-ordinate marches on
parliament under the banner #ThisGown, protesting against the
government's failure to deliver on promises of job creation.

The same technologies also enable more unruly forms of resistance. Baba Jukwa, an anonymous blogger who claims to have
been a ZANU-PF insider, has turned their Facebook page into a
space where Zimbabweans can openly criticise the government,
contest propaganda, mock the ruling elite and defy repressive
laws on public speech. It has exposed ZANU-PF plots to assas-
sinate political opponents and rig votes, as well as mobilising
'twitchfork' mobs against politicians. By the time of the 2013
general election, Baba Jukwa had more Facebook followers than
any Zimbabwean politician and almost three times as many as
Mugabe. The government has arrested and charged individuals it suspects of being connected to Baba Jukwa, to no avail
– digital technology means the strategies of coercion ZANU-PF
relied on in the previous decade are no longer viable.

Zimbabwe is not the only place where this story is unfolding.
During the Arab Spring, Facebook groups, Twitter hashtags and
YouTube citizen journalism were instrumental in overthrowing
authoritarian rulers in Tunisia, Egypt, Libya and Yemen. It's
also not the only story about shifts in the balance of power
which digital technology has enabled. In China and Ethiopia,
citizens' internet activity is monitored to pre-empt organised
dissent and consolidate governments' power. At the same time,
well-meaning online movements can backfire, as happened with

#BringBackOurGirls in Nigeria; the campaign tried to force Boko Haram to release schoolgirls it had kidnapped, but ended up raising the terrorist group's profile and strengthening its negotiating position with the country's government.

Nevertheless, the politics of Zimbabwe is a helpful reminder that digital technology is not all about 'us'. If we keep that country in mind, we might moderate the language we use when we discuss how the user interface design of devices and apps 'makes us less free'. As Henry Olonga wrote about the impact of the armband protest, 'maybe for others yet we challenged their own world view in a way that they could reflect on their own lives and revel in the freedoms they enjoy.' What has happened in Zimbabwe should also make us think more rigorously about the technology policy solutions that are currently being proposed, and the critique surveillance capitalism theory makes of digital advertising-based business models.

For example, there are calls for tech companies to act more assertively against online harms like trolling and cyberbullying and insist that all users verify their identities. However, advocates of this can't have thought about the implications for dissent in places like Zimbabwe, where the use of pseudonyms can be a matter of life and death. Without the ability to conceal one's identity, speaking out against the Zimbabwean government on social media would carry risks as serious as those that were faced by Henry Olonga and Andy Flower.

There are also calls for big tech companies to be broken up on anti-monopoly grounds. This is an issue that we'll discuss in more detail in Chapter Eight, but for now let's observe that its proponents don't seem to have considered the benefit for political organising of social media companies holding dominant market positions. Facebook Groups is not the only tool you can use to arrange events and communicate with a closed community, and nor is WhatsApp the only free, easy-to-use, end-to-end encrypted messaging service accessible to anyone with a mobile phone and an internet connection. However, they're the best solution for organising in countries like Zimbabwe precisely because they have by far the largest number of users. As Zeynep Tufekci points out in her book *Twitter and Tear Gas: The Power and Fragility of Networked Protest*, 'Facebook is crucial to many social movements around the world, and there is no real alternative because of its reach and scope'.

Calls for the digital advertising-based business models of Google, Facebook and Twitter to be banned persist, but the commentators and politicians arguing for such a ban forget that most of their users don't live in affluent Western liberal democracies. For example, only two of Facebook's top ten country markets by user numbers are in the West; its largest market by this measure is not the United States (210 million users), but India (300 million users). The Facebook population of Brazil (130 million) is more than three times that of the UK (40 million). And the Philippines (75 million) has significantly more Facebook users than France (33 million) and Germany (31 million) combined. If there was such a thing as 'the average Facebook user', their daily life would look more Zimbabwean than British.

Looked at in a global context, the effects of Facebook's advertising-based business model are highly progressive – they transfer value away from the richest users and towards the poorest. All Facebook users receive identical services, but there are huge differences in the value of their attention and clicks. The result is that in 2018, $25.5 billion of value was effectively transferred from Facebook users in Europe, the US and Canada to users elsewhere in the world, as the below analysis of the company's financial results demonstrates.

	Annual Revenue (billion)	Average Monthly Active Users (million)	Average Revenue per User	Transfer of Value per User	Total Transfer of Value (billion)	
US & Canada	$27.0	242	$111.88	-$87.11	-$21.0	**-$25.5**
Europe	$13.8	377	$36.59	-$11.82	-$4.5	
Asia-Pacific	$9.6	908	$10.56	$14.20	$12.9	**$25.5**
Rest of World	$5.4	729	$7.45	$17.31	$12.6	
Worldwide	$55.8	2,255	$24.76	$0	$0	$0

Transfer of value between Facebook users
in different world regions in 2018.

In the language of political philosophy, this is a form of distributive justice. It satisfies two principles set out by the influential liberal philosopher John Rawls – that inequalities should only be permitted when they most benefit the least advantaged, and that people living under unfavourable political conditions should be assisted by people who live under more favourable ones.

Imagine what would happen if targeted digital advertising was outlawed and Facebook charged users a flat fee for access to its services. The amount that would be required from each user to match Facebook's 2018 advertising revenues is about $25. If the annual subscription price was set at that level, hundreds of millions of people in the Global South would be priced out of the platform – it would effectively be thirty-four times more expensive for the average Indian than for the average American. In practice, Facebook might vary its subscription pricing by country as Netflix does, with annual charges ranging from $38 in Turkey to $148 in Denmark, but the breakdown of Netflix users by region suggests that Facebook usage outside the West would still plummet. In short, if Facebook has to move away from advertising to a subscription model, it will become like

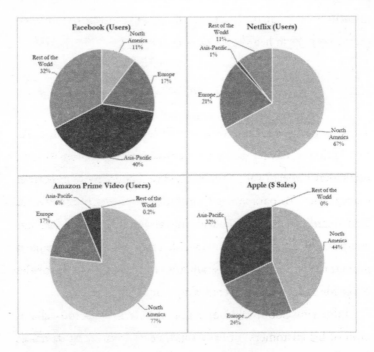

Comparison of Facebook, Netflix, Amazon Prime and Apple by region.

Netflix, Amazon Prime and Apple – a platform for the affluent. And that would be bad news in countries like Zimbabwe.

Another suggestion is that Facebook should adopt a so-called 'freemium' model. In this scenario, Facebook would continue to provide their current services for free, but would also make premium versions of the Facebook and Instagram apps available. Users would be able to opt out of ads and the associated data collection and targeting – subject to their financial resources, of course. Provided that the subscription revenue from the premium service subsidised the free services, the current benefits of redistribution would be preserved. However, such an arrangement would clearly be less egalitarian, reinforcing existing economic inequalities just as private alternatives to universal public services in healthcare or education do.

Apple's Supply Chain

There is another serious problem with these policy proposals. In addition to having unintended consequences for non-Western users, they neglect issues of global justice that are more important than privacy. To paraphrase Cambridge politics professor David Runciman, it's as if the moralising about data-driven ads has created a thick fog around policymakers. Not only does it make it more difficult for them to see what is really going on, it provides cover for those with an agenda they want to conceal.

Take Tim Cook, CEO of Apple. He is a vociferous champion of his customers' privacy rights, even contesting demands from the FBI and the courts to decrypt mobile phone data for use in criminal investigations. At the same time, in presentations to investors and interviews with journalists, he is an outspoken critic of Facebook and Google's business model and leadership decisions. It is, of course, his job to talk Apple up and its competitors down, but what issues do Cook's claims of his company's superiority regarding privacy distract attention from? What gets obscured by the fog?

The answer is Apple's supply chain, which Cook built up in his previous role as chief operating officer. Although Apple is an American company with its headquarters in Cupertino, California, the assembly of its devices is outsourced – primarily to the Taiwanese company Foxconn. Before being shipped to Europe and North America, the majority of iPhones are put together in Foxconn's gigantic factory in Longhua, Shenzhen, which employs more than 200,000 workers. By Western standards, conditions are harsh. Shifts typically last twelve hours, and tasks on the assembly lines require both precision and speed: workers fastening motherboards have a quota of 600–700 iPhones per day; for those polishing screens, it may be as high as 1,700. Performance management is based on on-the-spot fines and public shaming for substandard productivity. The demands of the work and the cruelty of the culture takes its toll: in 2010 alone, there were fourteen suicides on the premises. Nets were attached to Longhua's high-rise dormitory buildings to catch falling bodies; when the journalist Brian Merchant bluffed his way through the security perimeter in 2017, they were still there.

Electronic components come to Longhua from other factories, like Pegatron's 50,000-worker facility on the outskirts of Shanghai. In 2013, an NGO listed eighty-six labour rights violations there, in areas ranging from discrimination in recruitment to abuse by management, and from inadequate pay to poor safety standards. The following year, an undercover BBC reporter for the investigative documentary series *Panorama* was forced to work eighteen days in a row making MacBook parts, despite repeatedly asking for a day off. Another reporter, whose shifts lasted up to sixteen hours, was billeted with eleven other workers in an eight-person dormitory. Despite commitments by Apple to improve conditions, in 2016 the majority of Pegatron workers were still working more than a hundred hours of overtime per month.

Minerals and metals are integral to the manufacture of electronic components, and these come to Pegatron's factory in Shanghai from mines across the Global South. The BBC found an illegal tin mine in Bangka, Indonesia, where twelve-year-old children were digging ore from twenty-metre-high sand and mud walls, at risk of being buried alive by a landslide. A worker at the mine told journalists that the tin was sold to smelters on Apple's approved supplier list. Around 70 per cent of Indonesian tin comes from small mines similar to the one in Bangka, and it is practically impossible for Apple to be sure that its components don't use the products of child labour.

Other iPhone and MacBook parts also require minerals and metals. Rechargeable lithium-ion batteries need cobalt, which has to be extracted before being shipped to refineries in China and Scandinavia. Approximately 60 per cent of it originates in the Democratic Republic of Congo's Katanga province, where 35,000 children, some as young as six, work in appalling conditions in so-called 'artisanal' mines. For wages of less than $2 a day, they risk poisoning from toxic dust, and serious injury or death from tunnel collapses. Capacitors, meanwhile, require tantalum sheet, which is made from coltan ore. Around 80 per cent of the world's coltan reserves are in the eastern part of the DRC. Despite efforts by Western governments to outlaw 'conflict minerals', much coltan extraction and transportation is still controlled by independent militias and factions of the Congolese army that are notorious for perpetrating forced labour, systematic rape and mass killings.

None of this is to suggest that Apple does not care about the wellbeing of workers at its suppliers, or about child labour and violent conflict. In 2018, it audited more than a thousand suppliers in forty-five countries for compliance with its supplier code of conduct, and it can point to many examples of educational initiatives that it has sponsored to improve the wellbeing and prospects of workers at its suppliers. Nor is it to suggest that Google and Facebook are not implicated in the same injustices: after all, they make devices like the Nexus phone and the Portal video calling display. The point is that it suits Tim Cook for public discourse to focus on issues of data and privacy, while hardware supply chain issues fade into the fog. If we are honest with ourselves, it suits us too. Righteous indignation about how our data is being used is easy; recognising the ways in which our own everyday use of digital devices makes us complicit in the exploitation of so many people is not.

A key element of Shoshana Zuboff's argument in *The Age of Surveillance Capitalism* is the idea that digital technology companies have invented a 'rogue capitalism'. However, attending to the material reality of how digital devices are made reminds us that extraction, coercion, violence and inequality have been persistent features of conventional capitalism for hundreds of years. It highlights the continuity from slavery and indentured labour on colonial plantations, through the hazardous chemical factories and garment sweatshops that blighted twentieth-century globalisation, to the cobalt mines of Katanga and the assembly lines of Longhua in our own time. We mitigate the ills capitalism produces with laws, regulations and standards, but most of all with scrutiny from civil society. And for this scrutiny to be effective, we must be able to see clearly.

Moderation in All Things

What other issues is the fog obscuring? Despite concerns about the harmful effects of social media, most Western users' experience of platforms like YouTube, Twitter and Facebook is generally free from graphic violence, propaganda, pornography, scams, spam and hate speech. Contrary to what big tech companies like to imply, this is not all down to their machine learning algorithms; it's because 100,000 people around the world work full-time to moderate online content. Like the miners, smelters and assembly line workers behind the iPhone, most of these people are not employed by the tech companies themselves. Instead, they work for specialist suppliers like TaskUs, or IT outsourcers like Accenture.

With a high proportion of English speakers and cheap labour costs, Manila in the Philippines has become the world's capital of content moderation. Its new recruits are often recent graduates, paid between $1 and $3 per hour to review the worst words, video and imagery on the web, before deciding what is in violation of the platforms' community standards and should be removed. As at Longhua, expectations of productivity are high and tolerance of mistakes is low: Twitter moderators review up to 1,000 items a day, while making three errors in a month while moderating Facebook is enough to get you fired. But the work can also be psychologically traumatising: some moderators who review footage of terror attacks report paralysing fears of public places; others who review images of sexual abuse report damage to relationships; others find themselves tempted to recreate acts of self-harm they have witnessed. Little counselling support is available.

While young Filipinos bear the emotional costs of keeping our social media feeds clean, they also suffer a consequence of tech companies' assumption that American free speech norms are universal: the rule of president Rodrigo Duterte. Duterte's signature policy has been wiping out the trade in crystal meth. Many reasonable people might be sympathetic to that objective, but it is Duterte's methods which have seen him condemned by the European Union, the United Nations and even the Roman Catholic Church. His repeated incitements of violence against suppliers and users of meth have led to the unlawful killing of as many as 29,000 Filipinos by the police, contract hitmen and vigilante gangs. Social media was key to his election victory in 2016 and remains at the heart of his communication strategy; his team uses a network of volunteers, celebrity influencers and inauthentic accounts to distribute propaganda, smear political opponents, denounce journalists and harass critics of his government on Facebook, Twitter, Instagram and YouTube.

Social media has also been used to persecute a minority in Myanmar. Since 2016, Facebook and Facebook Messenger have been used to spread hate speech about Rohingya Muslims, building popular support for a brutal campaign of ethnic cleansing. Villages have been burned to the ground by the Burmese army and tens of thousands of Rohingya have been raped and murdered, while hundreds of thousands more have been forced to flee into neighbouring Bangladesh.

These urgent issues have nothing to do with data-driven targeting or advertising-based business models. And yet, groping around in the fog, data and ads are the only things policy-makers seem able to get hold of. It isn't horrific ad copy that scars content moderators in Manila, and Duterte's government and the Burmese military aren't using sophisticated ad targeting techniques to win support. Instead they rely on the core features of digital platforms – groups, pages, channels, hashtags and encrypted messaging. These, of course, are the exact same freely-available digital tools that are so important for resisting authoritarianism in places like Zimbabwe, meaning that forcing tech companies to pull out of politically volatile countries can't be the answer, either.

Although they may not realise it, tech companies also provide a way in which abuses like those occurring in Myanmar and the Philippines can be investigated. This is the work of the open-source intelligence community, a network of journalists, human rights workers and volunteers who verify the authenticity of videos and images shared on social media that appear to document human rights violations. Using openly available tools like Photo Sphere on Google Maps and the Facebook search function, they first aim to establish whether the footage shows what it purports to; then they work out where it was recorded and the identities of the people in it, building the evidence needed to bring perpetrators to justice.

In July 2018, a video of women and young children being executed by firing squad somewhere in rural West Africa began circulating on social media. In the online comments, some people insisted that the footage was staged, while others claimed that soldiers from Cameroon's army were responsible – a suggestion angrily dismissed by its government as fake news. There was also speculation that the killers were Boko Haram militiamen in Mali, dressed in army fatigues to mislead observers. Using open-source intelligence techniques, analysts from the Digital Verification Corps at Amnesty International were able to uncover the truth. Visible in the background of the video were terraced crops, low-growing vegetation and a distant mountain range: by triangulating the footage with satellite pictures from Google Earth, they were able to place it in the Far North Region of Cameroon, close to an army outpost. They identified the weapons carried by the killers as an unusual type of Serbian rifle, known to be used by Cameroon's army. Searching Facebook, they found images of Cameroonian soldiers wearing uniforms that matched those in the video, and even the profile page of one of the gunmen. Presented with this evidence, the country's government reversed its position and arrested seven of its soldiers.

Open-source intelligence is particularly helpful where it is difficult for human rights organisations to gather evidence on the ground – war-torn Syria being a good example. But like the search data analytics we discussed in the last chapter, open-source intelligence is in danger of becoming collateral damage in the backlash against big tech. Social media companies are under pressure to be more proactive in removing harmful content from their platforms and in mitigating risks to their users' privacy. Pressure to remove content glorifying terrorism led YouTube to take down thousands of mobile phone videos of the conflict in Syria, which NGOs had archived to help with human rights investigations. Pressure to do more to protect users' profile data led Facebook to deprecate Graph Search – the feature enabling all public content on Facebook to be searched, which the Digital Verification Corps had used to corroborate reports of a hospital bombing in Idlib in Syria and compile evidence that senior Burmese officials had directly ordered atrocities against the Rohingya people. Such decisions put 'our' user experience and concerns about being targeted with ads ahead of justice for the murdered and oppressed.

This brings us back to the Philippines. That evidence of abuse is being assiduously deleted from social media in a country where open-source intelligence might be the best hope of holding perpetrators to account is darkly ironic. And while advances in artificial intelligence might bring some respite to Manila's content moderators, they would also bring unintended consequences. To quote Sam Dubberley from Amnesty International, 'In the worst-case scenarios, algorithms will be able to remove these videos almost as quickly as human rights defenders can post them, with possibly devastating impact for investigators. We can't ask for a video to be reinstated or used to build a case against a warlord if we never knew it was there in the first place.'

* * *

By now, you'll probably have realised that I think many current policy proposals on data and tech are short-sighted. We'll consider alternative policies in Chapter Eight, but for now I hope it's clear why we should broaden the debate beyond the concerns that seem most pressing in the West.

In case you're wondering what happened to Henry Olonga, he built a career as a commentator and public speaker, and continued to play cricket for the celebrity Lashings XI, until he was forced to retire through injury. He married Tara Read, an Australian PE teacher he had met while training at a cricketing academy in Adelaide – where they now live with their young family. In 2019, Henry, who is also a fine operatic tenor, made it through to the battle rounds of *The Voice Australia*. It would have been a nice coincidence for this book if will.i.am had been one of the judges, but he'd been replaced in that series by Boy George.

PART III

POWER

Chapter Six

TAKING OVER THE PANOPTICON

The time has come for us to meet Jeremy Bentham, one of the most influential philosophers of the modern era. He's been waiting in the wings of this book – in fact, David Runciman's metaphor of "moral fog", which was so important in the last chapter, has its origins in Bentham's writing. Now we can invite him to take centre stage.

Bentham lived from 1748 to 1832, through times of great political, social and technological upheaval. He was born shortly after Bonnie Prince Charlie went into exile, and shortly before the start of the Industrial Revolution. He was about twenty years younger than Adam Smith and twenty years older than Napoleon Bonaparte. The French Revolution happened in the middle of his life and the Regency happened towards the end of it.

Although he never used the term himself, Bentham is best known as the founding father of utilitarianism – the theory of ethics that says we should decide what is right based on what brings the greatest happiness to the greatest number of people. In case you think that's not relevant to a discussion of twenty-first-century technology companies, consider this: when the German government set rules for autonomous vehicles in 2017, it insisted that their software operate on utilitarian principles. When a collision involving a self-driving car is unavoidable, the car must minimise casualties – even if that means sacrificing the lives of its own passengers.

Bentham's commitment to utilitarian principles expressed itself in ways that show him to have been remarkably ahead of his time. He believed women were equal to men, and argued that they should be given the right to vote more than 100 years before suffrage was finally granted in 1918. And in 1785 he wrote the first documented argument in favour of decriminalising gay sex. As far as Bentham was concerned, since it harmed no one and gave pleasure, prohibiting it was simply wrong.

On the other hand, some manifestations of utilitarian thought make Bentham seem wildly eccentric. Wanting to undermine what he saw as sentimentality about the human body, he specified in his will that his corpse should be publicly dissected, then preserved and used as a decoration. As a result, you can see him on display in a glass case at University College London. Well, you can see parts of him – the mummification technique used on his head went wrong, so it was replaced with a wax version, which sports a wig made from his hair.

Bentham's thinking about infanticide was even more challenging. Utilitarian philosophy told him that there were two reasons why murder needed to be prohibited: because it robbed people of the pleasures of being alive and because if murder was permissible, everyone would live in constant fear of being killed. It seemed to him that neither of these reasons applied to newborn babies. They were unaware of their own existence, so couldn't be troubled if it was taken away from them; and they hadn't yet learned to experience fear, so couldn't be afraid of being killed. On the other hand, parents who smothered their newborn children out of desperation would suffer the terror of being put on trial and condemned to death; Bentham thought it caused pointless suffering for infanticide to be treated in the same way as murder, when social opprobrium was punishment enough.

Bentham's eccentricity is to the fore in the Panopticon, his innovative design for a prison that profoundly shapes how we think about power in the era of big tech. From the 1970s onward, academics increasingly used it as a metaphor for state-run electronic surveillance. More recently, it has become popular as a metaphor for social media – in fact, if you search 'panopticon' now, alongside scholarly articles you'll find long reads from the *Guardian* and *TechCrunch* discussing Facebook and Google. The intriguing story of how that came to pass will unfold throughout this chapter, but first we need to take a virtual tour of Bentham's imaginary prison and see how it works.

The first thing to notice about the Panopticon is that it is circular. On each of its six floors, rows of cells run all the way around the perimeter, surrounding a cavernous atrium. In the centre of the atrium is a tower with large windows that are covered with venetian blinds: this is the inspector's lodge. Stepping inside the lodge, it becomes clear that the windows provide a view into every cell in the prison. The higher windows are accessed via a spiral staircase, and a trapdoor enables the inspector to come and go without being seen.

The next stop on the tour is an empty cell. The partitions separating it from the adjacent cells carry on for a few feet beyond the grating, limiting our view. The only cells in our field of vision are across the atrium, far away. By contrast, the lodge, looming overhead, is impossible to ignore. However, the position of the blinds and the fact that it is dark inside the tower prevents us from seeing inside. At this very moment, the inspector might be watching us; or she might be observing a cell on the other side of the prison; or she might have slipped through the trapdoor and gone for a tea break. There is no way of telling. The genius of Bentham's design starts to dawn on us: as the prisoners in the Panopticon know that they might be under observation by the inspector at any given moment, the rational thing for them to do is to behave at all times. In other words, the Panopticon makes them self-discipline.

The Panopticon wasn't just a concept; it was a business plan. Bentham's intention was to persuade the British government to pay for the construction of a Panopticon and appoint him to run it on what we would now call an 'outsourcing contract'. He saw it reducing prison staff costs: the lodge would only need to be occupied some of the time, so he could employ fewer inspectors, while self-disciplining prisoners would need fewer guards to control them. What's more, he could save money on shackles and chains, as even the most boisterous prisoners would quickly realise that getting up to mischief was futile. He even wondered whether it would be possible to raise extra revenue by offering tourists entry passes to the inspector's lodge. He was a prisons entrepreneur – like an eighteenth-century version of the security companies G4S in the UK or CoreCivic in the US.

Unfortunately for Bentham, the government, though initially enthusiastic, never struck a deal with him. And while many prisons have since been built on panoptic principles, Bentham made little money from the idea. Would he have been consoled to know how frequently the Panopticon would be invoked in discussions of Google and Facebook? Or would that knowledge have had no value to him, since it would not have improved his material circumstances? To mull over that question is to use what Bentham called *felicific calculus*: adding up the amount of happiness caused by something and subtracting the amount of unhappiness to determine whether it's a good thing. We touched on this idea in Chapter One when we considered the trade-offs involved in implementing legislation like GDPR which affects everyone, and it will be particularly important in this part of the book.

Is Facebook a Panopticon?

What do critics of Facebook mean when they claim that it's a Panopticon? Most straightforwardly, it means that everything we do on Facebook is *visible*. It's obvious that posting a status update or liking an article shared by a friend is visible – that's the point of doing it. It is somewhat less obvious that the activities we might prefer to keep to ourselves – like track-ing down the profile page of a new colleague or looking at an ex-partner's photos – are also in some sense visible. They are not visible to other Facebook users, but they are logged in Facebook's databases and visible to its algorithms, and there is a possibility that they might be looked at in encoded form by a Facebook engineer in the course of their work. Integra-tion with other websites makes some of our online activity elsewhere on the web visible to Facebook in the same tech-nical sense – its algorithm can 'see' that you browsed that mattress but never placed an order, for instance. Now, it isn't true that everything in Facebook's network is visible – encrypted messages on Messenger and WhatsApp can only be seen by the sender and the recipient – but if you think it's meaningful to talk about algorithms 'seeing', it makes sense to talk about Facebook being panoptic, with a small "p".

However, a Panopticon is a prison as well as an observa-tory. To say that Facebook is – in the words of *Newsweek* – an 'online panopticon' is to say that its users are prisoners, and that a form of authority is exerting control over them. Control in the Panopticon involves the physical constraint of cell walls, but its defining characteristic is self-discipline produced by the prison-ers' awareness of constant surveillance. In *Nineteen Eighty-Four*, George Orwell brought this idea vividly to life through the all-seeing figure of Big Brother. Conceived in the aftermath of the Second World War, in the context of Stalin's totalitarian rule in the Soviet Union, Orwell's version of the Panopticon is elec-tronic rather than architectural. A network of CCTV cameras in homes, workplaces and public spaces gives the state's security services total visibility of its population:

> There was of course no way of knowing whether you were being watched at any given moment. How often, or on what system, the Thought Police plugged in on any individual wire was guesswork. It was even conceivable that they watched everybody all the time. But at any rate they could plug into your wire whenever they wanted to. You had to live – did live, from habit that became instinct – in the assumption that every sound you made was overheard, and, except in darkness, every movement scrutinised.

Surveillance-driven self-discipline makes dissent and resistance to the state impossible. Not even writing a journal can be concealed, never mind political organising. Although the hero of *Nineteen Eighty-Four*, Winston Smith, can leave his flat, go to the office, visit an antique shop and take a daytrip to the countryside, he is still effectively a prisoner because he knows Big Brother is watching. Just as the inspector's lodge in Bentham's Panopticon did not depend on any individual inspector, Big Brother is not an individual leader or official, but rather a technological system of control.

That brings us to another hugely significant figure in the history of ideas: Michel Foucault. If Bentham appears to be an English eccentric, Foucault – shaven-headed, wearing oblong glasses and fond of a turtleneck – is the epitome of French intellectual cool. His academic influence in sociology, history, psychology, philosophy and political theory has been so great that it's hard to exaggerate. Foucault was fascinated by power, and much of his writing tries to explain what power is and how it works. Bentham's Panopticon resonated with him because it demonstrated how disciplinary mechanisms could be used to exercise power over a large number of people in a highly efficient manner. It seemed to Foucault that the design principles of the Panopticon were applicable not just to prisons, but to schools, factories, job centres, asylums and hospitals. If they know they might be being watched, pupils won't copy each other's home-work; assembly-line workers won't attempt to form a union; patients with symptoms of a contagious disease won't break social distancing rules. In fact, Foucault argued, if you closely examined the way any modern institution worked, you would find the same dynamics of inspection and self-discipline. And if you thought of inspection not as literally watching people but as gathering data to measure, benchmark and classify them, the model was scalable to entire national populations. We live, he wrote, in 'the disciplinary society'.

If Facebook is a Panopticon, as many of its critics claim, its power must operate in a way that Bentham, Orwell or Foucault would recognise as disciplinary. Control must be being exerted over users in a way that undermines our freedom, putting us in the same position as prisoners, pupils, oppressed workers or patients. That control doesn't need to be exerted by a particular individual like Mark Zuckerberg; it can be exerted by a system – an inspector's lodge, a Big Brother or a set of algorithms. If there are personnel involved, they can change without compromising the system: inspectors can wander in and out of the lodge, and there can be turnover in the ranks of the Thought Police, or among teachers, doctors, supervisors and developers at Facebook's Menlo Park headquarters. Facebook isn't a state, so the objective of this control is not to maintain political order; as a multinational corporation, its objective is to maximise profits. It follows that the behaviours Facebook wants from us are the ones that drive up its revenues – spending time on Facebook-owned apps, clicking on ads and giving up data that can be used in targeting or optimisation.

It probably won't surprise you to learn that I don't find this presentation of Facebook as a digital Panopticon very persuasive. Firstly, power in a Panopticon is based on a massive asymmetry of knowledge. The inspectors can see everything that the prisoners do, but the prisoners can see nothing of the inspectors. However, Facebook isn't like that at all. Anyone can go to Mark Zuckerberg's Facebook page and see that he is a fan of the musical *Hamilton*, or view Sheryl Sandberg's page and see that she likes coffee, grapefruit and frozen yoghurt. Anyone can follow Facebook's head of virtual reality, Andrew 'Boz' Bosworth, for the inside track on development of the new Oculus headset, or watch Instagram Stories by the division's CEO Adam Mosseri. Of course, Facebook executives could, if they wanted to, use their internal systems to see more of us than we can see of them, but they are not concealed; if they are inspectors, their quarters have windows that the prisoners can see through.

Secondly, in a Panopticon, power only flows in one direction. The inspectors exert it over the prisoners, who must submit to it. Panoptic accounts of Facebook often associate targeted advertising with this one-sided power dynamic, as we saw earlier in the book. In this telling, the inspector's lodge is the Ads Manager software, built and maintained by Facebook, but occupied and used primarily by its advertiser clients. Looking out of its windows, observing the characteristics and behaviour of the prisoners, inspector-advertisers can decide which groups they would like to target and place their ads on the cell walls.

The trouble with this version of the Panopticon story is that it assumes an essential difference between a Facebook advertiser and a Facebook user. But this difference doesn't exist: you have to be a Facebook user to advertise, and Facebook's advertising tools are accessible to all 2.5 billion users. Running an ad campaign on Facebook doesn't require any special skills; the tools are remarkably easy for anyone to use. Let's look at what would be involved in targeting Mark Zuckerberg with a Facebook ad. While it isn't technically possible to target individuals or groups of fewer than 100 people, we can use publicly available information about Zuckerberg to build a campaign that we could expect to reach him. As you can see from the below screenshots from Ads Manager, it is easy to target an advert at men aged thirty-five who are located in Menlo Park, hold liberal political views, have children under the age of five, work in computation and mathematics, and like the musical *Hamilton*. All you'd need to do it right now is a credit card and a budget of at least $1.

Jeremy Bentham would not think much of a Panopticon in which prisoners were allowed to be inspectors and where every prisoner had access to the inspector's lodge – he might think it was rather missing the point. Similarly, it would have detracted from the nightmarish vision depicted in *Nineteen Eighty-Four* if the proles had been able to plug in to the wires of the ruling elite at will. For Foucault, meanwhile, one of the reasons the Panopticon makes it possible 'to perfect the exercise of power' is because it 'reduce[s] the number of those who exercise it'. By contrast, Facebook has *increased* the number of people exercising power: there are now more than seven million Facebook advertisers. Power can't be flowing only in one direction when there are seven million inspectors moving between the lodge and their cells.

Targeting people like Mark Zuckerberg with Facebook Ads Manager.

The accessibility and widespread usage of Facebook ads is not the only evidence that power is flowing in multiple directions. A Panopticon is supposed to make organised resistance impossible, but we saw in the last chapter that Facebook features can be used by the weak against the powerful – in Evan Mawarire's #ThisFlag protest against the repressive government of Zimbabwe, for example. There have even been occasions when these features have been turned against Facebook itself. In 2007, the company rolled out a programme called 'Beacon' that automatically posted Facebook stories about users' purchases on participating third-party websites. There was nothing technologically remarkable about it, but what was significant was the co-ordinated resistance that was mobilised against it – *on Facebook*. Objecting to Beacon on privacy grounds, the advocacy organisation MoveOn petitioned Facebook to withdraw it, using a Facebook group. In a matter of days, the group attracted tens of thousands of members, and a class action lawsuit against Facebook followed. Mark Zuckerberg admitted that Facebook had made a mistake, and Beacon was shut down in 2009.

The final reason I don't think Facebook is a Panopticon is that characterising the way we behave on social media as 'self-disciplining' seems at odds with practical experience. Think about the time you spend on Facebook or Instagram. Are you constantly aware that you might be being observed by someone much more powerful than you? Do you scroll through your feed or react to a news story shared by a bad-tempered uncle because it's what Facebook expects of you? Do you modify your behaviour to align with what Facebook wants, to avoid punishment? Me neither. Scholars who think we live our digital lives inside a Panopticon might say that we're in a state of *false consciousness*, meaning that we've internalised the system of control to such an extent that we are no longer aware of our real motivations. Whether or not you're persuaded by this claim will depend on how well you think you know your own mind, and how capable you think you are of making your own choices, a question we will return to shortly.

If you want to see self-discipline in action, think about your experience of living under lockdown during the Covid-19 pandemic. In the UK, the government stipulated that we could only leave our home to buy food, collect medicine or exercise. The chief enforcer of this mass house arrest was not the police, but the general public. Some people reported their neighbours to the authorities for going running more than once a day, some chastised 'non-essential' businesses like ice cream vans for continuing to trade and others photographed people sitting too close together in public parks. It marked a resurgence of an old form of peer-to-peer surveillance, often associated with the Stasi's network of informers in East Germany during the Cold War, but traced as far back as Calvinist communities in sixteenth-century Holland by the sociologist Philip Gorski. Its effect is that people regulate their own behaviour, weighing up how their actions will be judged by observers so they can avoid provoking disapproval and risking punishment.

Is Google a Panopticon?

Is the Panopticon more effective as a metaphor for Google? It's obvious that much of our online activity is technically visible to Google – not just because Google Search, Gmail, YouTube and other Google products are so embedded in our everyday lives, but because its technology is used to trade the advertising space on more than two million websites through its 'partner network', and to measure traffic on another 30 million websites through Google Analytics. However, as we've seen, in addition to visibility, there needs to be knowledge asymmetry, power needs to flow in one direction only and we need to be able to describe Google's users as self-disciplining.

As with Facebook, Google executives can see things about us that we can't see about them if they access our Google histories. But they themselves aren't hidden – in fact, exposing information about public figures is a function of Google Search. That it reveals more about Google's CEO than about you or me somewhat redresses the power imbalance – see what Google suggests if you type 'Sundar Pichai' into the search box (opposite).

At the same time, power on Google platforms clearly flows in many different directions. It's harder and more expensive to set up and run campaigns on Google than on Facebook, but there are still four million Google Ads advertisers. Of the 31 million people who have their own YouTube channel, around 16,000 have more than a million subscribers each, double the circulation of the *New York Times*. Finally, self-discipline is an overcomplicated way of explaining why Google's services are so

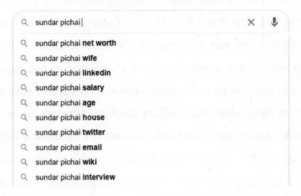

How Google Search makes Google CEO Sundar Pichai visible.

widely used – that they are incredibly effective and mostly free seem like more straightforward reasons.

To sum up, the power relations of Facebook, Google and other tech platforms are not like those of the Panopticon. But if the Panopticon is the wrong model for how we should think about power in the era of big tech, what is the right one?

Cambridge Power

Foucault explored a different type of power in the last ten years of his life, after he had written about the Panopticon in *Discipline and Punish*. In academic literature, this type of power is generally referred to as 'structural' or 'constitutive power', but I've never found those words very intuitive. So I will call it 'Cambridge power', and use a story from Cambridge to bring it to life.

The story begins on a bright, cold day in November 2018, in the History Faculty Building. I was standing in a basement corridor outside a classroom, waiting for a lecture to begin. I had spent a fruitless hour in the library, unable to concentrate on reading because of a draught on the back of my neck that seemed to pursue me wherever I chose to sit. Designed by James Stirling, after whom the RIBA Stirling Prize is named, the History Faculty Building is a Grade I-listed classic of modern architecture, so I couldn't understand why it was always so uncomfortable. On my phone I found an *Architectural Review* essay about it from 1968, which explained that the controls for heating and ventilation were complicated to operate. The author predicted that they were likely to get 'fouled up through mismanagement' as 'most of the occupants of the building will be humanities-oriented, and therefore likely to fall below the national average in mechanical literacy and competence'. In other words, if I was cold, it was my own fault.

Before arriving in Cambridge I'd looked through the lists of lectures for the term and noted down the ones I wanted to go to – either because they were relevant to the politics course I was taking or because I thought they would enrich my understanding of the world. I had imagined feasting on ideas from history, sociology, philosophy and English literature, and even contemplated signing up to learn modern Greek. However, five weeks into my life as a mature student, I had already given up on that project. The required readings for my course – journal articles, chapters or even the entirety of academic books – averaged over 500 pages a week. On top of that were three two-hour seminars and a mandatory class on social science research methods at 9 a.m. on a Monday morning. Finally, I was supposed to be making progress with my research thesis, as my supervisor would soon be uploading a progress report about it to the student administration system. Another habit I had imagined before moving to Cambridge was going for a long run by the river every morning. In practice, I was managing a short loop of Midsummer Common and Jesus Green two or three times a week – a joyless hurrying before the day's labour began. More keenly than at any point in my career, I felt like there was no time to do anything apart from work.

The lecture that day was the first in a series about our friends Jeremy Bentham and John Stuart Mill, who we will meet in the next chapter. It was aimed at second year undergraduates, meaning that I was waiting in the corridor with students roughly half my age. Some wore college boat club hoodies and tracksuit bottoms; others had bleached hair and turned up jeans. Some were skittish; others subdued. When the hour came round, the door to the lecture room opened and there was a sudden melee. Trooping in, I was vividly reminded of being at school: long rows of wooden desks and stackable polypropylene chairs faced a whiteboard; I could smell the inside of my old pencil case – HB pencil shavings, blotting paper suffused by blue-black Parker ink. I went to the back corner of the room – ostensibly to be close to a socket where I could plug my laptop in, but really because I felt like an outsider who should be kept apart from the other students. A young man sitting on the row in front warily passed me a photocopied handout. Striking up a conversation seemed impossible; basic social skills had deserted me.

Eventually the lecture began and I quickly became absorbed in stories of Bentham's life. It was only when the lecturer started outlining the themes of the following week's lecture that I realised an hour had passed, remembering with a jolt that I was due in a seminar on comparative politics and religion five minutes later. I packed away my things and hurried out of the building and across the campus.

Unlike lectures, seminars involve small groups and require active participation. On the surface they look like the sort of progress meeting you might have if you work in an office; participants generally sit around a table with a senior person chairing the discussion. But they are different in several respects. Firstly, there isn't much chit-chat: there tend not to be ice-breakers to put people at their ease, or jokes to provide light relief from difficult conversations. Secondly, facilitation is the sole preserve of the seminar leader. If you want to say something, you put your hand up and wait until they invite you to speak. Thirdly, the default mode of a seminar is critique. Comments on the readings tend to probe their weaknesses rather than celebrate their strengths. It's not really the done thing to offer other people encouragement or praise for what they have said: better to point out a flaw in their argument. As a result of these conventions, seminars are usually serious affairs, with a rather negative energy.

For me, participating in seminars meant switching off the instincts about how to interact in groups that I'd built up over the previous eighteen years in my professional life. Sometimes I would arrive brimming with enthusiasm about the week's readings, only to feel my excitement ebb away as I realised the format wouldn't allow the kind of sparky, collaborative discussions that I enjoyed so much. At other times, I would turn up feeling useless and underprepared – either I had been too lazy to read the articles and chapters closely enough, or I was too stupid to grasp them. On this occasion, I asked a question about different meanings of secularisation and made a point about the entanglement of national and religious identity. I had no idea whether the contributions I was making had any value. There was a moment of silence, and then the seminar leader addressed the room: 'So what's at stake here?' What was I to make of that? Should I feel embarrassed? Ashamed? I became terrified of saying the wrong thing, getting butterflies when I even thought about raising my hand. I longed for the banal reassurances of normal working life – for someone to say something like, 'I agree, Sam, that's such a great point,' or even 'Picking up on what Sam said earlier...'

It was three o'clock by the time the seminar finished and I hadn't eaten anything since breakfast. I was too hungry to think straight. Marks and Spencer was on the way back to my flat, so I went in and bought a tub of hummus and a sliced white loaf. I took my meagre shopping back to the basement kitchen, and ate while staring into space. I had turned all the radiators up as high as they would go, but my study-bedroom refused to warm up. I made a cup of tea and settled down at my desk to spend three hours on the readings for the next seminar. It was already getting dark.

Later, I went out to the pub to meet Alex, my old colleague Helen's brother-in-law. A philosophy professor at Boise State University in Idaho, he was in Cambridge for a year on study leave, researching a book. Both on sabbatical at the same stage of life, and with a shared love of real ale, we had quickly become friends. I had planned to ask him about Bentham and Foucault, but I realised what I really needed was to moan to someone about what a miserable time I was having. I moaned about the workload, the seminar format and the absence of feedback. I moaned about the gulf between what I had expected my year in Cambridge to involve and the drab and gruelling reality – about the lectures I was missing, the runs I wasn't going on, the sports teams I hadn't joined, the cloisters I wasn't lingering in, the candlelit choral concerts, formal dinners and wine tastings I wasn't attending. I summed up: 'I'm just not having the Cambridge experience.'

'Hang on a minute.' Alex took a sip of his beer. 'You just told me you've spent most of the week cold and alone in your room, worrying that all your endeavours are worthless. That *is* the Cambridge experience.'

How is the rapid change in my personality during my first term at Cambridge best explained? Was it more evidence that I was having a midlife crisis, as the old colleague I mentioned at the start of this book suspected? Or did I simply 'lose my confidence'? Alex put his finger on an alternative explanation: I was experiencing the psychological, emotional and physical effects of Cambridge power.

Cambridge power was everywhere. It had got under my skin and worked on me all the time. But it wasn't being deliberately exerted by seminar leaders, by the university vice-chancellor or by a carefully designed system of control. It just *was*. It emerged mysteriously from the interaction of architecture, climate, bureaucracy, social norms, memory, pedagogical practice, commerce and who knows what else. It structured and constrained the actions I could perform, the words I could use, the choices I could make – even the possibilities I could imagine. Under its spell, I was re-constituted as a different sort of person.

Many of the social ills that tech companies are blamed for are, in my opinion, better understood as effects of Cambridge power – or, to return to the academic language, 'structural' and 'constitutive' power. In no time at all, the proliferation of smartphones has changed the everyday habits of billions of people: seven out of ten Americans sleep with their phones on the bedside table, in bed with them or in their hand; for four out of ten people in the UK, checking their phone is the last thing they do before going to sleep at night and the first thing they do when they wake up in the morning. It can be hard to remember what people did when using public transport before there were smartphones to look at. At the same time, the emergence of social media has encouraged people to expose more of themselves than ever before, and to perform idealised versions of their own lives. The ubiquitous phenomenon of the selfie is one product of these shifts. More than 90 people die every year taking selfies, typically falling off cliffs or being run over by vehicles. Selfies now account for more deaths than lightning strikes, shark attacks and train crashes combined. In death as in life, we have become different sorts of people.

None of this was willed by tech entrepreneurs. Steve Jobs didn't mastermind a plan to make people so obsessed with their iPhones that they can't bear to be separated from them. Kevin Systrom and Mike Krieger didn't found Instagram with an elaborate theory of how they would get people to document their breakfast, and they didn't invent the selfie. Rather, they noticed some of the ways human life was being mysteriously reshaped, and responded to them. These responses – iOS notifications or the Clarendon filter, for example – had a shaping effect of their own. Tech companies benefit from and contribute to structural and constitutive power, but they aren't the source of it. As a result, it's no more possible to identify the app that caused trolling, cyberbullying or online self-harm than it is to locate the person responsible for the woes of my first term in Cambridge. It's no more appropriate to blame big tech for your wasted screen time than to blame 'big coffee' for your daily flat white, an expensive habit that you somehow find yourself in thrall to.

What are we to do about this type of power? It might not originate with any individual, product or company, but it still has major effects on us. For Foucault, the answer lay in practices of self-care. The power that compels us to touch our phones thousands of times a day, check WhatsApp during a family dinner, or rage-tweet a public figure can't be escaped, but we can win a measure of freedom by training ourselves to resist it. With digital technology as with artisan coffee or being a mature student, that training starts with noticing the strange ways power is operating and making conscious choices in spite of it.

Market Power

Another type of power that can help us understand power relations in the age of big tech is more straightforward: market power.

Unlike structural and constitutive power, market power is held and deliberately wielded by tech companies to advance their interests.

Many manifestations of market power are obvious, like the lobbying of governments, and here, there is no essential difference between tech companies and other large corporations. Between them Apple, Amazon, Google and Facebook spend roughly the same as the major players in financial services, defence and the car industry on lobbying in Washington, DC (some $55 million in 2018, in case you were wondering). For better or for worse, lobbying is just a thing big companies do.

An insatiable appetite for acquiring competitors is another obvious and familiar manifestation of market power. However, comparisons between big tech and other industries are complicated by the fact that consolidation in the tech industry does not tend to lead to consumers paying higher prices. Since the 1970s, consumer welfare – understood narrowly as what is in people's short-term financial interests – has been the main factor competition regulators have considered when deciding whether to approve mergers and acquisitions. A single player in the automotive industry would not be allowed to own four of the top six global car brands, because that would enable it to increase its profit margins at consumers' expense. By contrast, Facebook's ownership of four of the top six social media apps, enabled by its multi-billion-dollar acquisitions of Instagram and WhatsApp, is acceptable because it doesn't appear to make consumers financially worse off – in large part because the services are free.

Nevertheless, the use of market power by tech companies to increase their market share is a cause of concern for scholars, commentators and policymakers. In the West, we tend to be instinctively suspicious of concentrations of power, and I think it's this suspicion that leads people to give so much credence to the idea of digital Panopticons and to surveillance capitalism theory: powerful tech companies don't appear to be ripping us off, so they must be exploiting us in some other more sophisticated and covert way.

However, there is a category of people who suffer the effects of tech companies' market power: business owners. Take brothers Mike and Matt Moloney, whose business FilterGrade provides a marketplace for photographers to buy and sell digital photo-editing tools. The FilterGrade website contains a great deal of useful original content that helps photographers use these tools and learn new techniques – Mike and Matt use search data to understand what their users are looking for, and create content to serve these needs. As a result, Google rewards them with prominent positions in its search listings. However, Google also does something else: it extracts words and images from the FilterGrade website and uses them to enrich its search results with so-called 'featured snippets'. In some contexts, having a featured snippet can be a huge blessing for a business – if you google 'What does dog insurance cost?', you'll see how it helps Bought By Many. But where Google has monetisation opportunities, it can be a curse.

In April 2020, Mike found that Google was populating a featured snippet for the search '35mm film stocks' with content from the FilterGrade website (pictured opposite). However, because of the user interface design of the search results page, there was almost no chance that a user would click through

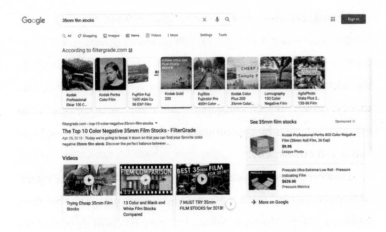

A 'featured snippet' on Google's results page
which uses FilterGrade's content.

to FilterGrade's website – instead, the links in the image and video carousels funnelled users towards ads in Google Shopping and YouTube.

Although this particular piece of user interface design has since been deprecated, Google has a history of exercising its market power in similar ways. It once acquired a financial price comparison platform and integrated it into search results for loans, credit cards and mortgages, earning commission income from clicks that otherwise would have gone to third-party websites. It did the same thing in the flight comparison market by acquiring the company ITA Software for $700 million and turning it into Google Flights. Search for 'flight to San Francisco' on Google, and a Google Flights integration will take up as much of your screen as links to third-party websites like Kayak and Skyscanner.

These exercises of market power are made possible by *vertical integration* – that is, the control of different parts of the value chain in an industry by the same company. It's a strategy that goes back 130 years to Andrew Carnegie, the Scottish-American steel magnate who owned mines, ships and railways as well as steel mills. As a result, he had more market power than his competitors, who depended on the transport infrastructure he controlled. If he wanted to drive them out of the steel business, all he needed to do was increase freight prices until their profit margins disappeared. In our own time, vertical integration isn't particular to Google – it's a feature of all the big tech companies. At the time of writing, Amazon is under investigation by the EU Competition Commission, having been accused of exercising market power to the detriment of third-party sellers on its Marketplace platform. Amazon operates Marketplace while simultaneously acting as a merchant, listing its own products alongside those of its advertiser clients. It appears to have used sales data gleaned from its role as Marketplace operator to decide what products to sell in its role as a merchant. Similarly, Apple operates the App Store, meaning it has the ability to give apps built by its own developers preferential treatment.

Market power is less exciting to read about than the disciplinary power of the Panopticon, meaning there's a danger that it will get lost in the fog – like the supply chain and content moderation issues we discussed in Chapter Five. What's more, preventing the misuse of market power requires us to scrutinise boring and often technical details about how tech companies act in relation to smaller businesses, many of whom are their clients. Too much concern with 'our' data can be an obstacle to such scrutiny as well as a distraction from it. Remember the US Congress investigation into anti-competitive practice in Google search, mentioned in Chapter Four? To quantify the impact of Google's vertical integration on businesses like FilterGrade, we need data that shows the number of users clicking on links in Google results. But because of privacy concerns about Jumpshot compiling anonymised records of people's internet behaviour, such data is no longer available. As the saying goes, we have cut off our nose to spite our face.

Reach Power

The final type of power that can help us make sense of digital power relations is newer and more distinctive. It is also less well theorised – in fact, it doesn't even have a name. Let's call it *reach power*.

Market power is concentrated with a small number of companies, and is tractable in nature – it can be deliberately exercised to advance an agenda. The more mysterious structural/constitutive power is diffused throughout society, but is intractable – it can be tapped into, but not used as a tool in the same way that market power can. Reach power, on the other hand, is a type of power that is both tractable *and* diffused throughout society.

I'm calling it reach power because it enables you, me and everyone else with a reliable internet connection to reach billions of other people. It's the power to document, network, broadcast, convene, celebrate, endorse, cajole, influence, persuade, agitate,

insult, harass and incite – on a global scale. Reach power is channelled through an incredibly sophisticated array of hardware
and software, ranging from mobile phone video cameras to the
Facebook Lookalikes algorithm. It is so widely distributed that
it could be described as even more democratic than democracy
itself: unlike voting rights, it has no minimum age, and it's available in the fifty-nine countries around the world that are ruled by
authoritarians. It can be harnessed in profound or trivial ways,
for political purposes or for commercial ones, for good or for
evil. Many of this book's examples of reach power attest to this
duality. I used the reach power of targeted ads to recruit diabet-
ics and pug owners to early Bought By Many groups; Dominic
Cummings used it to persuade people to vote Leave. WorldStores
used the reach power of Google search to corner the market in
trundle beds; Patrick Berlinquette used it to track the spread of
Covid-19. Evan Mawarire used the reach power of social media
to disseminate messages of protest against the failures of Robert
Mugabe's government; supporters of Rodrigo Duterte used it to
legitimate extrajudicial killings. MoveOn used the reach power
of Facebook pages to petition Mark Zuckerberg to shut down
his Beacon programme; Burmese army officers used it to incite
the Rohingya ethnic cleansing.

This duality of reach power explains many of the contra-
dictions of the digital age: why we see the same technologies
creating both freedom and oppression; stirring up both compas-
sion and hatred. Returning to the idea of the Panopticon, we
live in a world in which the inspector's lodge – the privileged
position from which power can be wielded in any direction –

can be occupied by literally anyone. It's so democratic as to be anarchic: it's a free-for-all. We saw in Chapter Two that it is the absence of controls on who can use Facebook's targeting technologies that causes political problems rather than the technologies themselves. The same is true of the other instruments of reach power, from YouTube channels to Twitter hashtags and WhatsApp groups. The question is, how can we curb the abuses of reach power without also losing its socially beneficial effects?

Chapter Seven
TECH CEO HUBRIS

In Greek mythology, King Minos of Crete commissions the master craftsman Daedalus to build a subterranean labyrinth in which he can keep the Minotaur – a human-bull hybrid, born to his wife. Once its construction is complete, the king imprisons Daedalus and his son Icarus in a tower so that he can keep the existence of the labyrinth secret. Planning their escape, Daedalus makes wings from feathers held together with string and wax, and teaches Icarus to fly. As they get ready to take off, Daedalus reminds his son not to fly too low over the sea in case the spray saturates the feathers, or too high in case the sun melts the wax. Icarus, of course, ignores him. So enraptured by the experience of flight that he forgets his own mortality, he soars into the sky; the wax holding the wings together melts and he plunges to his death.

The story of Icarus can be read as a warning of the dangers of *hubris*: excessive pride that leads to over-reaching, and ends with a disastrous fall to earth. It is commonly used in writing about tech company founders and CEOs; Elizabeth Holmes and Adam Neumann are two recent examples.

Holmes's company Theranos promised revolutionary blood tests that could be administered with a single finger-prick. Just a few drops of blood would be enough for a Theranos lab to screen for hundreds of medical conditions, from STDs to diabetes to cancer. After raising some $700 million from investors including Rupert Murdoch, Carlos Slim and the Walton family, Theranos spent ten years developing its blood tests in great secrecy. It did not publish papers about its research in peer-reviewed journals. Demonstrations were only given to people who were prepared to sign a non-disclosure agreement and be accompanied to the toilet when visiting its Palo Alto headquarters. Upstairs, Holmes' conference room was modelled on the Oval Office, with the same configuration of furniture and bullet proof windows. She had a private jet and a detail of bodyguards who referred to her by the code name 'Eagle One'.

In 2015, forty Theranos testing centres opened in branches of the pharmacy chain Walgreens in Phoenix, Arizona. The company appeared to be on the verge of realising its vision to make comprehensive blood screening available at a fraction of the usual cost. The trouble was, the tests didn't work. Investigative journalism revealed that Theranos hadn't succeeded in developing new screening technology after all; instead, they had resorted to diluting their tiny blood samples and analysing them using standard equipment manufactured by Siemens. The test results were highly unreliable as a result, which led to Walgreens customers who used Theranos's service being wrongly advised to stop taking medication they still needed, or to have medical procedures that weren't necessary. The company, valued at $10 billion, collapsed, and Holmes was indicted on multiple counts of fraud.

While Adam Neumann has not committed fraud, he has destroyed significantly more shareholder value than Holmes as co-founder and CEO of upscale office rental company WeWork. Early in 2019, Japan's SoftBank ploughed $2 billion into WeWork at a valuation of $47 billion, with the expectation that it would IPO at a valuation of between $60 and $100 billion later that year. For context, $47 billion is almost double the market capitalisation of Tesco or Barclays Bank at the time of writing. Barely a year later, after failing to IPO, WeWork is wholly owned by SoftBank, which now values it at $2.9 billion – $44 billion less than previously.

Neumann was renowned for his personal charisma and eccentricity. It took him only twenty-eight minutes to persuade SoftBank to make its initial $4.4 billion investment in WeWork in 2016. He served tequila shots after redundancy announcements and smoked weed on a rented Gulfstream jet, leaving a spare portion on board for the return journey, stashed in a cereal box. He personally trademarked the term 'We', and then sold it back to the company for $5.9 million. WeWork's IPO paperwork recorded the company mission as being 'to elevate the world's consciousness' – a tall order for a serviced office business, even if it does offer its tenants free flat whites.

Unlike Holmes, Neumann didn't mislead anyone about his company's product or capabilities. But he did convince investors that there was something magical about WeWork that meant it belonged alongside companies with proprietary technologies. Tech companies' valuations are predicated on their marginal costs being close to zero: creating a million new Twitter accounts or a million new copies of Microsoft Office is basically free. As a result, the only practical limit on the growth of a tech company is demand. WeWork, however, is completely different: satisfying more demand means leasing and fitting out more buildings. By 2017, it had used five million kilograms of aluminium to create the office dividers in its 253 locations; it bought a million square metres of white oak flooring in that year alone. It is hard to soar into the sky when you are carrying all that weight.

Tech CEOs' desire to defy gravity can be literal as well as metaphorical; the goal for Elon Musk's SpaceX is to reach, geo-engineer and colonise Mars, as he finds the thought of a future in which we are not a 'multiplanet species' 'incredibly depressing'. The same goes for their desire to transcend mortality. Musk's vision of living forever involves brain-computer interfaces that will enable people to upload their minds to the cloud; other tech CEOs, including Jeff Bezos of Amazon, Google founders Larry Page and Sergey Brin, and PayPal's Peter Thiel have invested in cryogenic facilities, stem cell treatments, experimental blood transfusion procedures and anti-ageing drugs. Their underlying assumption is that humanity's planetary and biological limitations are engineering problems that can be methodically solved.

What is it about the tech sector that seems to encourage hubris? It may have something to do with being remarkably successful at a young age. Steve Jobs was a billionaire at forty;

Jeff Bezos at thirty-five; Bill Gates at thirty-one; Larry Page at thirty. Mark Zuckerberg and Evan Spiegel both reached the milestone before their twenty-sixth birthday. If you achieve so much at such an early stage of life, perhaps it's not surprising that you think you can do literally anything.

Their hubris must also be to do with their forgetfulness or ignorance of history. The basis of all the world's largest tech companies is massive US government investment during the Cold War: the work of the Defence Advanced Research Projects Agency (DARPA) laid the foundations for the internet, on which Apple, Amazon, Microsoft, Google, Facebook, Snap and every other big tech company has been built. And yet it is rare to hear tech CEOs credit the government in their own origin stories – they are more likely to express libertarian views, even while their accountants work to maximise subsidies and minimise corporation tax bills. To return to the myth that began this chapter, we might think of DARPA as Daedalus: once Icarus has taken off, he forgets all about his father the master craftsman, instead attributing the miracle of flight to his own genius.

There are many more examples of hubristic technological visions, ranging from Musk selling 20,000 flamethrowers to help Americans defend themselves in the event of a zombie apocalypse, to Thiel's support for "seasteading" – the plan to build new, privately owned city states on concrete barges in the ocean. It's enjoyable to poke fun at them and to experience schadenfreude when their plans come crashing down to earth. However, their hubris also has a less spectacular and much more serious side.

The hubris of tech CEOs gives us a world in which the role of the state and intergovernmental organisations is increasingly subsumed by private foundations – a system sometimes referred to as 'philanthrocapitalism'. Bill Gates is sympathetic to the account of inequality laid out by the economist Thomas Piketty, who in his hugely influential book *Capital in the Twenty-First Century* shows that return on capital always exceeds economic growth, leading to socially damaging concentrations of wealth. Nevertheless, Gates opposes Piketty's proposal of a global wealth tax to address inequality. As Linsey McGoey writes, we can only conclude that Gates believes that he and his co-trustees of the Gates Foundation, Melinda Gates and Warren Buffett, are better than governments and international agencies at spending money to alleviate poverty, feed the hungry, raise educational attainment and promote health. He must also believe that the results achieved by private foundations justify their lack of transparency and accountability, and the damage they do to popular support for government spending on public services.

This is not to criticise the work of the Gates Foundation – its endowment is clearly a more socially beneficial use of $47 billion than, say, buying all the shares in WeWork. Rather, I want to highlight Gates's hubris in determining that his personal goodwill is an acceptable substitute for political systems. In the event that the world's governments manage to implement a wealth tax, surely he should pay up like the rest of us.

The hubris of tech CEOs also leads to a world in which norms of corporate governance are dissolving. One example is the prevalence of dual-class stock structures, which give some shareholders voting rights that are disproportionate to their equity holding. At an early stage of a company's life, having different classes of shares can protect founders with long-term visions from being forced to take a direction they disagree with by investors with short-term financial motivations. This was certainly a consideration for us at Bought By Many. We were trying to address longstanding deficiencies in insurance, and didn't want investors to be able to make us charge higher prices or cut investment in product development. In the event, we managed to keep more than 50 per cent of the equity in the company for long enough that we never needed extra protection, but creating a different share class that gave founders outsize voting rights would have been helpful if we had needed to raise more capital. However, dual-class structures are now being used to entrench founder control at a much later stage, when companies are preparing to float on the stock market.

At WeWork, a dual-class stock structure gave Adam Neumann twenty times the voting rights of ordinary shareholders. Furthermore, its IPO papers gave his wife and business partner Rebekah Paltrow Neumann the exclusive right to choose his successor in the event of his death. Incredibly, Adam and Rebekah even intended future generations of Neumanns to retain a controlling stake in the company. Speaking to WeWork employees in 2019, Neumann said: 'It's important that one day, maybe in 100 years, maybe in 300 years, a great-great-granddaughter of mine will walk into that room and say, "Hey, you don't know me; I actually control the place. The way you're acting is not how we built it."' Neumann's assertion was that only his biological descendants would be capable of holding the company to its consciousness-raising mission.

WeWork's dual-class structure is not an outlier: Pinterest's founders receive twenty votes for each one vote by a holder of ordinary shares, Snap issued non-voting shares at its IPO in 2017 and Larry Page and Sergey Brin still control more than 50 per cent of the voting rights at Google. But the most significant example of all is Facebook. Not only is Mark Zuckerberg both chairman and CEO; he also holds a majority of the voting stock. He can, at his discretion, complete an acquisition, merger or disposal that Facebook's other shareholders unanimously oppose, or block one that they support. He can appoint or remove members of Facebook's board at will, but cannot himself be dismissed. His management of the company is therefore completely unchecked – he is accountable only to himself. Even Facebook's own filings with the US Securities and Exchange Commission refer to this arrangement as one of 'concentrated control'. When he dies, control will pass intact to whoever he has nominated.

How does Zuckerberg justify 'concentrated control'? He claims that as Facebook is what he calls 'a controlled company', it can resist 'the whims of short-term shareholders' and instead 'serve our community' by making 'decisions that don't always pay off right away', such as the rejection of take-over approaches, investments in security that adversely impact profitability or the acquisition of Instagram. He does not argue that Facebook's mission of 'giv[ing] people the power to build community and bring the world closer together' justifies extraordinary means, but claims that 'concentrated control' is a superior form of corporate governance. He appears to believe that conventional governance does nothing more than promote the immediate material interests of shareholders at the expense of a company's users. Like Bill Gates, Zuckerberg also makes a philanthrocapitalist argument in favour of 'concentrated control': Facebook's dual-class stock structure enables the vast majority of his personal wealth to be channelled into third-sector and charitable initiatives that promote education, public health and social justice.

The irony of Zuckerberg's attachment to 'concentrated control' is that he is otherwise a quintessential *liberal*. I am not using the word loosely, as a synonym for 'progressive', but to denote a particular political ideology that emerged in the seventeenth and eighteenth centuries, and is still dominant in the West. Historically, liberalism is associated with thinkers like John Stuart Mill, Alexis de Tocqueville and Jeremy Bentham, while its more recent sages are philosophers like John Rawls and Martha Nussbaum. While there is much debate among political theorists about what liberalism is and isn't, one of the things they all agree on is that liberals can't stand absolute power, because of the danger it poses to human freedom. Whenever they see power being concentrated, liberals become suspicious and instinctively want to constrain it though laws and systems of checks and balances. Otherwise impeccably liberal, Zuckerberg seems blind to the fact that his 'concentrated control' of Facebook is an illiberal affront. And that's hubris.

However, it is when hubris is combined with liberal politics that Facebook is at its most dangerous. To understand how it has enabled authoritarian repression and ethnic cleansing, we need to understand what I will call 'Zuckian liberalism'.

Zuckian Liberalism

When looking for a synthesis of Zuckerberg's politics, commentators have generally referred to a 5,700-word post called 'Building Global Community', which he published in 2017. In it, Zuckerberg articulated the role he wanted Facebook to play in the liberal cause of 'spreading prosperity and freedom, promoting peace and understanding, lifting people out of poverty and accelerating science'. His critics were unimpressed: John Naughton dismissed the post as 'astonishingly naïve', while Shoshana Zuboff regarded it as a smokescreen for Facebook's version of surveillance capitalism.

But there is much more to Zuckerberg's thought than this post. In fact, a team at Marquette University in Milwaukee has collected more than 1,000 transcripts of things he has said or written since 2004 in a comprehensive digital archive called 'The Zuckerberg Files'. It's from mining this resource that I draw my conclusions about Zuckerberg's liberal ideology and his commitment to Facebook's stated mission. Over the course of the next few pages, I will outline why you should believe him when he says he wants to give power to people and bring the world closer together.

So what exactly is Zuckian liberalism? The easiest place to start in answering that question is by saying what it's not. Although it takes for granted that freedom of economic exchange across borders is a good thing, Zuckian liberalism is not the same as neoliberalism – the ideology of deregulation and free markets developed by Friedrich Hayek and later embraced by Margaret Thatcher and Ronald Reagan. Nor is it the libertarianism associated with figures from Silicon Valley counterculture like John Perry Barlow, which rejects the usefulness of government and advocates utopian experiments like the Burning Man festival and seasteading. Instead, Zuckian liberalism is a more classical version, which would be recognisable as liberalism by the ideology's canonical thinkers. It's based on four interlinked ideas:

1. Humans have a plurality of values.
2. They are also rational.
3. Therefore, encouraging freedom of expression...
4. ...leads to greater mutual understanding and progress.

Using Zuckerberg's own words, we can elaborate these ideas. Technology is 'a huge lever for improving people's lives', so Facebook has a 'moral responsibility' to provide universally accessible 'social infrastructure' that enables 'meaningful connections' and 'meaningful interactions', offline as well as online. In a world of 'wildly different social and cultural norms', Facebook must be 'a platform for all ideas' that 'gives every person a voice', 'helping promote diversity and a plurality of opinions' while avoiding judgements about what constitutes acceptable speech. So fundamental is the importance of freedom of expression, that even the speech rights of 'people who deny that the Holocaust happened' must be defended. Since 'most people are pretty open-minded' when engaged in a dialogue, this will ultimately 'build common understanding', allowing problems such as Islamophobia to be overcome through a focus on 'what unites us'. Once 'all people have the power to share their experiences, the entire world will make progress' towards becoming a 'global community that works for everyone'.

Zuckerberg's perspective is intimately related to the history of liberal thought. The view of the past as the story of human progress can be traced back to the German liberal philosopher Hegel (1770–1831), although Zuckerberg's Facebook posts suggest his immediate influences are books by modern-day admirers of Hegel, like *The Better Angels of Our Nature* by Steven Pinker and *Sapiens* by Yuval Noah Harari. The idea that connections between people of different nationalities contribute more to world peace than international relations between states appears in the writing of the liberal political theorist Benjamin Constant (1767–1830) and the radical liberal politician Richard Cobden (1804–65). The mutual interdependence implied by Zuckerberg's 'global community' echoes what New Liberals like L. T. Hobhouse (1864–1929), J. A. Hobson (1858–1940) and Herbert Croly (1869–1930) called 'organicism'. Influenced by advances in biology, organicism saw political communities as living organisms, meaning that if one part of the 'body politic' was injured or diseased, it would inevitably harm the whole – an idea that provided intellectual justification for public health reforms and the introduction of state pensions and unemploy-ment benefits in the early twentieth century.

What's more, Zuckian liberalism emphasises the value of 'offline' community, as seen in clubs, associations, town hall meetings and so on. In doing so, it draws on two classic liberal texts: Alexis de Tocqueville's *Democracy in America* (1835), which celebrated civic culture, and Robert Putnam's *Bowling Alone* (2000), which lamented its decline. Zuckian liberalism is also pluralist, meaning it affirms that people with diverse values, beliefs and lifestyles can peacefully co-exist. Pluralism is rooted in the liberal philosophy of Isaiah Berlin (1909–97), Martha Nussbaum (1947–) and John Rawls (1921–2002), who is clearly a direct influence on Zuckerberg. In *A Theory of Justice*, Rawls proposed a thought experiment called the 'Original Position', asking the reader to imagine themselves before birth, without any awareness of their gender, race, nationality, abilities or preferences – and then to consider what sort of political system they would want to be born into. (Spoiler: you are meant to realise that liberal democracy is the fairest system of all). Zuckerberg has described using Rawls's thought experiment as a tool to help him make decisions, as has his long-time lieutenant Andrew 'Boz' Bosworth, who used it to explain to staff why Facebook would not be fact-checking ads or posts by candidates in the 2020 US presidential election. Another core Zuckian concept is 'enough common understanding', a paraphrase of Rawls's 'overlapping consensus' – the idea that it's possible for groups with very different values to agree on common principles as the basis for political institutions. Essentially, Zuckian liberalism claims that if 'enough common understanding' is built between Facebook users, Facebook can form the basis of a global political community and divisive nation-states can wither away.

Finally, the Zuckian liberal case for freedom of expression is a version of the arguments made by John Stuart Mill in *On Liberty*, one of the most important texts in the history of liberalism. Mill argues that people are 'improved by free and equal discussion', and that 'the collision of adverse opinions' enables those involved in a lively debate to get progressively closer to the truth. As a result, it's critical that people have 'absolute freedom' of 'expressing and publishing' 'opinion and sentiment on all subjects', without fear of being censored or punished. For Mill, it is particularly important to protect minority perspectives, so that 'the tyranny of prevailing opinion and feeling' can be avoided. Under Zuckerberg's leadership, Facebook has sought to enshrine these liberal principles for the digital age.

For many readers of this book, these ideas will sound eminently sensible; Western cultural norms are so permeated by liberalism that they may seem self-evident. But here's the rub: the arguments presented in *On Liberty* are from 1859. The mid-nineteenth century was liberalism's youthful and optimistic heyday. At that point, when schooling was not yet compulsory, when just one in five men – and no women – had the vote and when urban poverty was widespread, there was every reason for liberals to believe that state education, the expansion of political and civic freedoms, and advances in material prosperity would bring an end to social ills like prejudice, intolerance and sectarianism.

But it was not to be. By the first decade of the twentieth century, there was already a 'Crisis of Liberalism'; a 1902 essay of that title by Célestin Bouglé wondered how far liberals should tolerate freely-chosen racial and religious bigotry before using the state's power to suppress it. Hobson's 1909 book of the same name argued that liberals were losing a struggle with conservative and reactionary forces – or, to put it in today's terms, a 'culture war'. Even with the Battle of the Somme, Hiroshima and countless other modern atrocities still in the future, the limitations of classical liberalism were already apparent.

The digital age has underlined these limitations. Mill's notion of 'harm' was narrow: it encompassed physical injury and being dispossessed of property, which is not sufficient in a world where people may be harmed by cyberbullying, trolling, revenge porn or livestreamed violence. Mill thought the collision of opinions revealed the truth because it helped the 'disinterested bystander' see things more clearly. But in our own time, social media feed algorithms filter out the debates in which we would be 'disinterested bystanders', meaning we see only the ones we are already engaged participants in. Mill was ahead of his time, rejecting convention in his personal relationships and speaking up passionately in favour of equality for women, but it's a mistake to assume his ideas about free speech are timeless truths that can be applied today without re-evaluation.

I believe that Zuckian liberalism is needed to explain many of Facebook's actions; the imperatives of capitalism aren't sufficient by themselves. Let's consider the $19 billion acquisition of WhatsApp as an example. Shoshana Zuboff attributes it to Facebook's desire to control 'the gargantuan flows of human behaviour' that 'pour through' the application. I don't find that explanation convincing: end-to-end encryption of WhatsApp means that most of this data is not accessible to Facebook; furthermore, WhatsApp contains no media inventory and therefore generates no advertising revenue. Explaining the rationale for the acquisition, Zuckerberg situated it within the context of Facebook's goal to 'connect the entire world' and 'build the infrastructure for global community', which is consistent with the argument he makes in texts that appear in The Zuckerberg Files. It is worth noting that when he made these remarks, Zuckerberg's audience was composed of investment analysts from banks such as UBS, JP Morgan and Nomura Securities. If Zuckian liberalism is a smokescreen or a decoy, it would serve no purpose in such an overtly capitalist setting. Instead, its presence demonstrates that it is Facebook's guiding ideology. That the company's vice-president of global affairs, Sir Nick Clegg, and its vice-president of public policy in the EMEA region, Lord Allan of Hallam, are both former Liberal Democrat MPs is not a coincidence.

Zuckian liberalism is also the key to understanding why Facebook is so indiscriminate in its distribution of reach power, the distinctive new form of power wielded by ordinary users of digital technology. Many of the worst unintended consequences of Facebook's actions stem from the Zuckian liberal conviction 'that on balance people are good, and that therefore amplifying [their capacity with technology] has positive effects'. It seems that when one is ideologically committed to the idea of human goodness and progress, one fails to imagine how the Graph API might 'amplify the capacity' of app developers with sinister intent, how Lookalike Audiences might enable marginal political parties to grow as rapidly as e-commerce start-ups or how encrypted group WhatsApp messaging might be used to incite and co-ordinate violence.

Presented with evidence of these unintended consequences, Zuckian liberalism is remarkably durable. In a post on Facebook's role as a channel for disinformation during the 2016 US presidential election, Zuckerberg reaffirmed his faith in human virtue and progress, concluding, 'In my experience, people are good, and even if you may not feel that way today, believing in people leads to better results over the long term.' Despite earning negligible revenue from Myanmar and incurring significant reputational costs, Facebook continues to operate there. Even in acknowledging that the business he created had facilitated the ethnic cleansing of the Rohingya, Zuckerberg returned to his liberal optimism about human progress, finding it 'heartening' that millennials 'identify the most with not their nationality or even their ethnicity... [but] as a citizen of the world'. His conclusion is not that he must reckon with the consequences of Facebook's indiscriminate distribution of reach power, but that the rise of a younger generation of enlightened global citizens will enable humanity to transcend national and ethnic conflict. For Zuckian liberals, human cruelty is like the colonisation of Mars or mortality: an engineering problem waiting to be solved. As a result, we should expect that Facebook's products will continue to be used to inflict suffering.

Karpian Realism

The hubris of tech CEOs makes a potent cocktail when it is mixed with a different kind of politics. While Mark Zuckerberg wants to transcend the nation-state, other tech CEOs want to entrench it. For them, the world isn't a place where humanity comes together to make progress; it's the arena of ceaseless competition between great powers. In international relations, this view is known as realpolitik or realism. While liberals believe that co-operation yields the best results, realists play a zero-sum game that can only end with winners and losers, and in which you have to pick a side.

For realist CEOs, the proper role of American tech companies is to advance American strategic interests. At times, that may be aligned with liberal values – for example, when America's foreign policy agenda includes promoting democracy and free trade – but at other times, it may be in tension with them. During the so-called 'War on Terror', many tech companies appear to have made their peace with helping the US government illiberally monitor the private communications of its own citizens, as the NSA whistle-blower Edward Snowden later revealed. At a time of intensifying economic and geopolitical competition with China, the former Google CEO and executive chairman Eric Schmidt is in a new job as chair of the Pentagon's Defence Innovation Board. There, he warns that it would be a strategic mistake for America and its allies to allow Huawei to build 5G infrastructure for them – not because of the risk of being spied on by the Chinese state, but because it would allow a Chinese company to consolidate its advantage over Western rivals in a critical emerging technology.

Google seems to have taken a more liberal turn since Schmidt's departure. In 2018 it withdrew from Project Maven, a Pentagon initiative that used artificial intelligence to analyse aerial imagery. In an open letter to the CEO Sundar Pichai, Google employees expressed concern that Maven would be used to improve the accuracy of drone strikes, asserting that 'Google should not be in the business of war' – perhaps forgetting that Google owes its existence to DARPA. Luckily for the US government, the CEO of Palantir Technologies, Alex Karp, took a different view and was more than happy to step up to the plate.

Founded in the wake of 9/11 with seed investment from the CIA's venture capital fund, Palantir is often referred to as a 'big data' company, but that's slightly misleading. Unlike Google or Facebook, Palantir doesn't collect data itself – instead, it provides software tools and analytical consulting services to help organisations get insights from their own data. Having initially focused on US defence and national security, it has since diversified into other branches of government like immigration and law enforcement, and into industries like financial services, manufacturing and pharmaceuticals. It turns out that the same tools and techniques used to predict the locations of roadside bombs in Iraq and uncover international cyber espionage networks can forecast fraudulent benefit claims and detect insider trading at investment banks.

Palantir's critics regard this as another example of technology and data being 'weaponised': products developed to fight America's adversaries are being turned against American citizens, on American soil. In addition to Project Maven, a particularly controversial example is their involvement with so-called 'predictive policing' – the use of big data analytics to deploy law enforcement personnel in anticipation of crimes being committed. Eerily reminiscent of the film *Minority Report*, predictive policing can lead to self-reinforcing cycles of racial and class discrimination. A further example is Palantir's work building the software that enables US Immigration and Customs Enforcement (ICE) to identify illegal immigrants and compile the evidence needed to deport them. Data from a variety of sources including the FBI, the Drug Enforcement Administration and private security contractors is pooled on Palantir's platform, empowering ICE agents to do their case work more effectively.

This is very different from the use of Facebook Lookalike Audiences to recruit supporters to far-right groups, or of encrypted WhatsApp messaging to incite racial hatred. Better-targeted bombs, higher numbers of arrests and faster deportations are not unintended consequences; they are the kinds of outcomes Palantir expects its technology to achieve. So how does Karp justify this? If we scrutinise public statements he has made in interviews and presentations, what we find is realism. He describes Palantir's business as 'tech that saves lives and protects lives' by 'finding people who are up to … bad things'. These 'bad things' might be 'in the anti-terrorism area, in cyber' or they might be 'in financial malfeasance [or] mortgage fraud', but it is the 'mission impact of our government work' that makes Karp 'most proud'. It seems to infuriate him that many tech company CEOs see Silicon Valley as an 'island' rather than recognising that it is 'part of the United States proper ... part of a larger whole that made your company possible, that's protecting you against terror' – a fight that they 'ought to be involved in', so that 'Western values win'. Terrorism is not the only threat to these values. Like Schmidt, Karp sees Chinese technology as undermining American hegemony and wants American tech companies to set aside their moral qualms and 'bring our A game' to the contest.

For Karp, Adam Neumann's talk of 'elevating the world's consciousness' or Mark Zuckerberg's of 'building global community' is dangerous mumbo jumbo. The world is a battleground. There are winners and losers, and you are either with us or against us.

Unlike most of Palantir's critics, I don't think the company's products are morally objectionable per se – I can see no essential difference between them and those of Palantir's competitors in the boringly named business intelligence (BI) software category. When I hear Karp describe the process of integrating different sources of data to identify 'bad people', it sounds functionally identical to the 'single customer view' projects that were all the rage when I worked in retail banking nearly twenty years ago. Along with telephone and utility companies, the banks built their IT systems in silos, based on account types. That meant it was easy to see the customers who had a specific type of account, but almost impossible to see the types of account held by a specific customer – as you will know if you ever tried asking the same customer service agent about your credit card and mortgage at that time. BI software companies like Tableau and SAP evolved in response to this problem, along with products like Microsoft's Power BI. Today, these companies pitch for the same contracts as Palantir.

With that context in mind, objections to Palantir's involvement with Project Maven, predictive policing and immigration enforcement start to look like objections to the policies the technology is being used to implement, rather than to the technology itself. And of course, accountability for those policies rests with political representatives, who can be petitioned by their constituents and kicked out of office at the ballot box. Palantir is the wrong target.

There are other reasons to be sceptical of claims that Palantir's software is immoral. Unlike Facebook ads, Gotham, its product for finding 'bad people', abounds with controls. There are features to ensure that data collected for one purpose can't be appropriated for different purposes or viewed without the right permissions, and that users can be held accountable for the analysis they conduct. Karp also likes to draw attention to another Palantir product, Foundry. In the manufacturing, automotive and aerospace sectors, it helps technicians use big data to determine the best time to replace engine parts before they fail (among other things). Unlike most applications of machine learning by tech companies, Karp claims, Foundry doesn't displace American jobs – it protects them, by enhancing workers' capabilities.

For the foreseeable future, humans will remain far superior to robots and algorithms at performing most tasks, meaning that the greatest productivity gains will come from humans and AI working in concert – not from trying to automate people's jobs out of existence. So instead of accentuating the concentration of wealth in Silicon Valley at the expense of everywhere else, Palantir improves the economic prospects of America's industrial heartlands, reducing geographic inequality.

Karp might be exaggerating the robustness of Gotham's controls and Foundry's positive social impact. But even if he is, I still don't think big data analytics is delegitimated by Palantir's work for the Pentagon, US police departments or ICE, any more than geodemographic targeting is delegitimated by Cambridge Analytica. After all, these same techniques give us less annoying interactions with our banks, in addition to projects like Opportunity Insights (discussed in Chapter Four), where the benefits to society are clear. I also don't think Palantir produces the form of digital power that should concern us most – reach power. While Facebook distributes power indiscriminately, Palantir only amplifies the capacities of the already powerful: commercial enterprise clients, not to mention the governments of the United States and its allies. That's not straightforwardly a good thing, but it's much less likely to produce disastrous unintended consequences.

Does that mean we shouldn't be concerned about tech companies like Palantir that aim to work in the national interest? Unfortunately not. In contrast to most of the tech CEOs we have met in this chapter, Karp and Schmidt are not like Icarus. To understand them, we might imagine Icarus has an obedient and dutiful brother – let's call him Aleric. Aleric is fully aware of the opportunities his father Daedalus has given him; he is profoundly grateful, and proud to offer his service in return. Ethical questions are moot for Aleric; if his father says something must be done, it must be done – whatever it takes. Aleric may not always agree with his father, but filial loyalty is a higher good. People who oppose Daedalus' agenda, meanwhile, are plain wrong – at best they inadvertently aid the enemy; at worst they are evil. In this way, Aleric acts as Daedalus' proxy.

For Americans and citizens of America's allies who are generally supportive of American hegemony, tech companies taking their lead from the American government may not be so alarming. But what about people who are on the receiving end of American hard power and don't have any democratic leverage – undocumented immigrants from Mexico, for example, or families displaced by the conflict in Syria? And what happens when the American presidency stops promoting settled liberal norms like press freedom and the rule of law and instead deliberately undermines them, snubbing democratic leaders and praising authoritarian ones? During the early stages of the coronavirus outbreak in the UK, the NHS chose Palantir Foundry to support a 'single customer view'-type project, drawing criticism from privacy campaigners and parliamentarians. The argument made by groups like No Tech For Tyrants was twofold: firstly, that the bar for allowing a private company to analyse highly sensitive health records should have been set much higher; and secondly, that it was simply wrong for the UK government to work with a business whose products were implicated in the oppression of migrants and ethnic minorities. However, awareness of the realist politics of Alex Karp points us in a different direction.

It is not unthinkable that an American president might see a benefit in having NHS data covertly analysed – to gain advantage in a post-Brexit trade negotiation over pharmaceuticals, for example. If Palantir were asked to undertake that analysis in service of the national interest, there is plenty in Karp's public statements to suggest that he would comply. The hubris of the son can be in obeying the instructions of the father, as well as in ignoring them.

If Zuckian liberalism is predisposed to underestimate the evil in the world, Karpian realism is primed to exaggerate it. A broad definition of 'bad guys' as 'everyone who threatens America's interests' already puts disgruntled employees, people who lie on loan application forms and residents of deprived neighbourhoods into a category with enemy combatants, foreign intelligence agents and mass murderers. The presidency of Donald Trump shows how easily a populist take on those interests can include judges, journalists, civil servants and political opponents in the same category. It's clear that for the power created by digital technology to be channelled in the most socially beneficial way, we need something more than the political ideologies of tech company CEOs, whether they are liberals or realists.

PART IV

PROPOSALS

Chapter Eight
DIGITAL LEGITIMACY

I began this book by challenging the claim made by surveillance capitalism theory that digital advertising-based business models make companies like Google and Facebook 'fundamentally illegitimate'. Calling something 'illegitimate' suggests that its power is unacceptable and must not be tolerated – like a government that gained power through a coup d'état or by rigging an election. But as we've seen, data-driven targeting isn't as sinister as it seems and can even promote global equality – so if Google and Facebook *are* illegitimate, advertising can't be the reason. But that leaves us with the bigger question unanswered: are they legitimate or aren't they? And what about Apple, Microsoft, Amazon and other tech companies with models in which advertising doesn't play much of a part – should we tolerate their power, or contest it?

To be able to answer these questions, we first need to explore legitimacy as a concept. In political theory, the language of legitimacy is used when talking about the acceptability of power. There are two types: input legitimacy and output legitimacy. When something has secured its power through a means that is widely accepted, it has input legitimacy. The most obvious example is a government that wins power through an election run in accordance with constitutional principles. In fact, in recent decades, elections have been such an effective way of achieving input legitimacy that even anti-democratic rulers have embraced them, leading to a new category of 'competitive authoritarian' regimes in countries such as Zimbabwe, Tanzania and Peru. But elections are not the only source of input legitimacy for governments: it can also come from abroad. During the Cold War, the backing of the USA and the Soviet Union provided input legitimacy for the governments of some of their allies. More recently, had the Venezuelan politician Juan Guaidó succeeded in displacing Nicolás Maduro as president, whatever input legitimacy he would have enjoyed would have come not from the ballot box but from the support of the Trump administration.

By contrast, output legitimacy isn't based on how power was obtained, but on how it is wielded. Governments can gain output legitimacy through recognition that their power is being used appropriately and in the public interest. A ruler might violently seize power in a military coup but then improve healthcare and educational provision; in that case, they would have output legitimacy but not input legitimacy. Conversely, a democratically elected government might rule disastrously, burning bridges with its closest allies, implementing policies that increased inequality and ruining the economy. Such a government might not have any output legitimacy, but it would still have input legitimacy.

These examples draw attention to an important point about legitimacy, which is that most thinking done about it has related specifically to the power of states. Ever since Thomas Hobbes wrote *Leviathan* in the late seventeenth century, the discussion of legitimate power has centred around the acceptability of states being able to make their citizens obey them – with the exclusive right to use violence if needed. Although these theories have also been applied to intergovernmental organisations like the UN and the EU, applying them to companies is a bit of a stretch. There are some respects in which Facebook, say, is state-like: its market capitalisation is greater than the GDP of 163 countries, and you could think of its 2.5 billion users as a 'population'. Mark Zuckerberg has even said that he thinks it is 'more like a government than a traditional company'. However, there are many more respects in which Facebook is not at all like a state. It doesn't raise taxes, maintain an army or control territory – unlike historical precedents of powerful multinational corporations, like the East India Company. It might have monopolies, but a monopoly on the use of violence is not one of them. And Facebook users have much greater freedom to leave and go elsewhere than the citizens of states.

One response to this would be to say that companies don't need to be legitimate; they just need to serve the interests of their shareholders, within the bounds of the law. However, recent research by the political theorist David Ciepley has shown that in the early years of the American republic, corporations were only chartered by the government if they promised a clear public benefit. Even if one disagrees with Ciepley's argument that all companies should have a legal responsibility to act in the public interest, the particular features of big tech companies mean that we can't reject the concept of legitimacy as irrelevant. At the time of writing, the world's seven largest corporations by market capitalisation are all tech companies (China's Tencent and Alibaba are the two that might not come to mind immediately), which gives them incredible market power to acquire competitors, squeeze suppliers, exploit employees, lobby governments, avoid tax and evade regulations. But as we saw in Chapter Six, tech companies also produce reach power. Because this is a new form of power, different to that of companies in the oil, financial services or pharmaceuticals sectors, it demands we think differently about legitimacy.

What are critics getting at when they say big tech companies are illegitimate? Surveillance capitalism theory mainly contests the input legitimacy of tech companies that collect, compile and monetise personal data (as we saw in the introduction). Its claim is that the power of Google, say, is illegitimate because it has been gained by untransparent means that no reasonable person would assent to if they understood them. Other critics place more focus on the *consequences* of tech companies' power: for example, the phenomenon of radicalisation through YouTube, or Facebook's role in Rodrigo Duterte's 'war on drugs'. To do this is to question tech companies' output legitimacy. Some critics go so far as to say that input illegitimacy accentuates or even produces output illegitimacy, making tech companies doubly illegitimate.

While I think surveillance capitalism theory's charge of input illegitimacy misses the mark, I agree that there are things about tech companies that detract from their input legitimacy. Dual-class stock structures enable control to be concentrated with founders in a similar way to constitutional reforms implemented by 'competitive authoritarian' rulers so they can cling on to power beyond their allotted term in office. At the same time as getting rid of these illiberal features of their governance, tech companies could take positive actions to increase their input legitimacy. There have already been some helpful experiments. From 2009 until 2012, Facebook involved users in policy decisions, both through consultation processes and through votes that were binding if at least 30 per cent of users participated. This arrangement added to Facebook's input legitimacy, because it required the company to seek democratic approval for changes to policies affecting its users. Some scholars have suggested that the turnout requirement was unrealistically demanding, since some 300 million users would have needed to participate for a vote to be binding. However, this criticism commits what political theorists call the 'exercise fallacy', muddling the capacity to do something with whether or not that capacity is used. What mattered for Facebook's input legitimacy was that its users had the ability to accept or reject decisions by its management – not whether they chose to exercise it.

In 2020, Facebook made good on a commitment to establish an independent oversight board. With a remit to review appeals from users regarding Facebook's content moderation decisions and make recommendations on the company's content moderation policy, the board exists beyond the sphere of Mark Zuckerberg's 'concentrated control', and its decisions are both public and binding. Commentators may be sceptical about how influential it will be, or about whether its ultimate aim of protecting freedom of expression on Facebook is the right one. But from the perspective of input legitimacy, that is beside the point: Facebook's input legitimacy can only be enhanced if it is answerable to an independent body.

What about output legitimacy? I agree with Siva Vaidhya-nathan, Zeynep Tufekci and John Naughton when they say that tech companies' output legitimacy is undermined by the disastrous social and political outcomes they are implicated in. However, their output legitimacy is at the same time boosted by the benefits to users of being able to communicate with friends and family, grow businesses, build networks and so on – partic-ularly as poorer users in the Global South benefit most. Rather than being causally related to the advertising-based business model, the thing which is said to most diminish tech companies' input legitimacy, I think the negative outcomes flow from the political ideologies of tech company CEOs, as we discussed in the last chapter.

If we consider Facebook, the Cambridge Analytica scandal, the proliferation of misinformation during elections and the incitement of the Rohingya ethnic cleansing, they can all be traced back to the Zuckian liberal conviction 'that on balance people are good, and that therefore amplifying [their capacity with tech-nology] has positive effects'. When Facebook has enhanced its output legitimacy, it has generally been by taking a less rose-tinted view of human nature. The first version of the Graph API – the pipe that gave Cambridge Analytica access to the Facebook user data it needed to build its psychographic targeting model – was closed in 2015. Data available through the current version of the API is more restricted, and stronger assurances are required from app developers that their use of it is compliant and benign. The 'Page Transparency' feature puts information on the management and provenance of every Facebook fan page into the public domain, while the Facebook Ad Library provides an open, searchable archive of all advertising run on the platform, with details on the expenditure of political ads. Meanwhile, message-sharing on WhatsApp has been limited to slow the spread of disinformation.

Tech companies, governments and intergovernmental organisations might yet take other kinds of output legitimacy-enhancing actions. Mark Zuckerberg has set out proposals for internet regulation that encompass harmful content, electoral integrity, data portability and enhancements to data privacy. In the UK, the Department of Digital, Culture, Media and Sport Select Committee has proposed a legally enforceable code of ethics for tech companies and the reform of electoral communication law. However, these are backward-looking actions that mitigate the risk of known unintended consequences reoccurring in the future – not the risk of as-yet-unknown ones emerging. Speculative fiction like Dave Eggers's novel *The Circle* and Charlie Brooker's TV series *Black Mirror* show what some of these might be, from social media credit-scoring to Internet of Things-enabled vigilante justice. Others are beyond imagining.

In this context of rapid technological change and uncertainty, tech companies must adopt a more austere political ideology in order to maintain output legitimacy. One option is what the philosopher Judith Shklar called the 'liberalism of fear'. The claims of output legitimacy made by Zuckian liberal-type ideologies offer us assurances of tech CEOs' moral convictions and benign intentions. Confronted with the terrible political and social consequences of pursuing utopia by distributing reach power to all and sundry, the best they can offer is what Tufekci memorably termed a 'fourteen-year apology tour': repeatedly saying sorry, promising to do better and expressing blind optimism that things will be different in future. However, what is needed is an acknowledgement that people are often violent and unreasonable, and a credible strategy for mitigating the worst manifestations of those regrettable human characteristics.

By prioritising the avoidance of cruelty and other harms over the pursuit of utopia, the liberalism of fear would require tech companies to abandon their default mode of 'permission-less innovation' and take a more cautious approach to their development of new products. In terms of Facebook's notorious early mantra, this view regards it as more important *not* to break things than to move fast. The development of existing applications, geographic expansion and the roll out of products linked to augmented reality, virtual reality, cryptocurrency and voice-enabled devices would therefore proceed slowly and after much consideration of the potential unintended consequences. At the same time, by seeking to secure 'freedom from the abuse of power and intimidation of the defenceless' ahead of freedom of speech and freedom to advertise, Shklar's liberalism of fear would insist on faster and more assertive action against social media users expressing hostility to minorities, and on robust approval processes for all advertising. 'When in doubt,' Zuckerberg has written, 'we always favor giving people the power to share more.' The liberalism of fear makes the opposite demand.

The Theory

If we put all this together, we can construct a toolkit to help us make judgements about the acceptability of tech companies' power. A theory of 'digital legitimacy' is important if we are to move beyond the polemical arguments of tech companies' critics and the ideological assertions of their CEOs. Beginning with David Ciepley's political theory of the corporation, it goes like this.

Like all corporations, the authority of a tech company to provide services to the public ultimately derives from the state via the corporate charter. This authority is conditional on the tech company promoting public good.

Not all corporate power requires legitimation; the question of digital legitimacy only arises when a tech company's power is such that many millions of individuals are significantly affected by it.

Digital legitimacy can be assessed along five dimensions, which reflect current public concerns about tech companies. The input legitimacy dimensions are the transparency of the tech company's business model and its corporate structure and governance arrangements. The output legitimacy dimensions are the distributional consequences of the company's activities, the extent to which its services empower its users and the controls it applies to prevent its services being abused.

When we want to ask whether or not a tech company is legitimate, we can consider whether it is doing well or badly along each of these dimensions. A company that was doing badly on transparency would conceal how it made money and only respect data privacy as far as the law required. If it was doing adequately, we'd expect its business model to be comprehensible to its users, and for data privacy controls to be available to users that chose to activate them. If the company was doing well on transparency, how it made money would be self-evident, and users' data privacy would be assured as a default.

On governance, a company that was doing badly would concentrate control with its executive management, and users' access to its services would be entirely at its executives' discretion. A company doing adequately would apply current governance norms, with non-executive board directors or independent ombudsmen able to hold the executive management to account. If a company was doing well, users would have both the legal right to access the company's services and a means of influencing decisions that affected them.

Turning to the output legitimacy dimensions, if a company was doing badly in terms of distributional consequences, its activities would transfer resources from the less advantaged to the more advantaged, increasing inequality. If it was doing adequately, its activities would have little or no impact on how resources were distributed, but if it was doing well, it would be transferring resources from the more advantaged to the less advantaged, reducing inequality.

On user empowerment, a company doing badly would offer products that were harmful to its users or failed to serve their stated purpose. Conversely, a company doing well would amplify the capacities of its users, while a company doing adequately would offer products that did 'what they said on the tin', but no more.

Finally, a company doing badly in terms of controls on abuses would allow its products to be used to inflict significant harm, while releasing new products and features without considering how they might also be exploited. A company doing adequately would impose robust controls that bad actors could only overcome with great effort, and it would have a process for assessing the risks posed by new products before they were introduced. For a company to do well, its controls would need to evolve in anticipation of future threats, and it would need to proceed cautiously with the development of new products.

Once we have considered each of the dimensions in turn, we can look at the overall picture, to assess a tech company's overall legitimacy. If we were to apply the theory to Facebook, what would we conclude? We would probably say that it is doing adequately on transparency, because it offers choices over how users' profile and behavioural data is used in advertising, and it isn't hiding the fact that it's in the ad business. It's doing badly on governance, because its corporate structure gives Mark Zuckerberg absolute control over the company – everyone's ability to use the Facebook app,

Messenger and WhatsApp depends on his goodwill. In terms of distributional consequences, Facebook is doing well; using an advertising-based business model to fund universally available free services most benefits the least advantaged – poorer users in the Global South. It's also doing well on user empowerment, thanks to its wide distribution of power that can be mobilised by anyone. But Facebook is doing badly on controls on abuses; the inadequacy of controls on powerful tools such as Lookalike Audiences means that its features can be exploited for illegitimate political purposes and to inflict harm.

Overall, the theory suggests that when it comes to legitimacy, Facebook is doing adequately. It doesn't pass with flying colours, but nor is it a total write-off. It has realistic opportunities to put its legitimacy beyond doubt, by reforming its governance and implementing stronger controls to prevent the malevolent use of its features.

With a theory of digital legitimacy now established, we are in a better position to consider the specific policy proposals that have been made in relation to how big tech companies might be reformed.

Should Digital Advertising-based Business Models be Outlawed?

While there are plenty of calls for it, I believe that banning targeted digital advertising would diminish Facebook's legitimacy rather than enhancing it. Close examination of the role played by user data in Facebook advertising shows that the means by which it is monetised is less opaque than surveillance capitalism theory suggests, while the data's economic value is dependent on many other factors.

There are also good reasons to reject the suggestion that there are extreme power imbalances between Facebook users and advertisers on the platform. Facebook isn't like Jeremy Bentham's imaginary Panopticon, where inspectors could see everything from the lodge while prisoners were trapped in their cells. Instead, the barriers to entry for Facebook ads are so low that more or less everyone who is on Facebook can use them. The same is true of other digital advertising platforms, like Google Ads and Microsoft's Bing Ads. Although they are harder and more expensive to get to grips with than Facebook ads, they are still far more accessible than pre-digital forms of targeted advertising like geodemographics. It is clear that when it comes to targeting, today's platforms level the playing field rather than tilting it further in the direction of the already-powerful.

More importantly, the redistributive effects of advertising-based business models are a major source of output legitimacy for companies like Facebook. Zeynep Tufekci celebrates the way Facebook provides an enabling toolset for political protest and resistance (admittedly with some important caveats) but deplores its business model. However, the two things are inextricably linked: advertising targeted at Facebook users in the West means that Facebook's array of product features can be made freely available to 1.6 billion users in the Global South. If we consider the difference in income between 'the West and the rest', it is clear that a move away from advertising to a paid subscription model would have negative consequences for users in poorer countries. Fewer people would be able to access social networking services, and it would become harder to co-ordinate opposition to repressive governments.

This argument about the beneficial consequences of advertising for equality also applies to other big tech companies with global user bases and advertising-based business models, like Google, Twitter and Snap. The opposite argument can be made about Apple, whose CEO Tim Cook is a vociferous critic of advertising-based business models. Cook claims input legitimacy for Apple on the basis that it charges for its devices and software, meaning that the firm's interests are aligned with its users' interests on issues of privacy. But this misses something important: Apple's choice of business model means that it only serves the global middle class. Furthermore, the injustice within its supply chain resembles something from the colonial era, with precious raw materials being extracted from mines in the Congo, and iPhones being assembled by migrant labourers in the factories of Shenzhen. The benefits that Apple's products offer to affluent Western users derive from the struggles of workers in the Global South.

In short, business models where users pay for products and services don't have an inherent legitimacy that advertising-based models lack. And in my opinion, the output legitimacy generated by the way in which ads on Facebook and Google redistribute resources outweighs the input legitimacy of Apple's more transparent business model.

Is More Privacy the Answer?

For advocates of surveillance capitalism theory, mandatory enhancements to privacy would be an acceptable alternative to banning data-driven digital advertising. This might include the end-to-end encryption of all electronic communications between private individuals, putting them beyond the scope of state and corporate monitoring. In fact, Facebook has already signalled its intention to make all its apps fully encrypted.

However, while this so-called 'pivot to privacy' might generate input legitimacy, it could well damage output legitimacy. Facebook ads are not the only Facebook product which has been exploited for nefarious ends: the sharing and groups features of WhatsApp and Messenger, which are already encrypted, have too. In addition to the Myanmar case, where messages inciting violence against the Rohingya minority were spread through one-to-many sharing, WhatsApp groups were used during the 2018 Brazilian presidential election for the mass distribution of Jair Bolsonaro campaign materials to lists of phone numbers that had been obtained illegally. They were also used during India's 2019 general election to disseminate disinformation about the success of airstrikes in Pakistan. As Mark Zuckerberg himself acknowledges, encryption makes hate speech, propaganda and other harmful content much harder to detect and remove; implementing it may be regarded as an abdication of moral responsibility by Facebook. The liberalism of fear, which I have proposed as an alternative to Zuckian liberalism, would make this argument; encryption increases the potential for cruelty to be inflicted, in exchange for the comparatively modest benefit of less invasive advertising.

So, the gains in input legitimacy from privacy enhancements could easily be offset by losses on the 'controls on abuses' dimension of output legitimacy. Facebook employees suggested to me during interviews that the decision of Chris Cox, Facebook's chief product officer, to leave the company in 2019 was motivated by concerns about the social consequences of greater encryption. In my opinion, a subscription version of Facebook, with all applications end-to-end encrypted, would have less, rather than more, overall legitimacy. The same would be true of a paid-for, privacy-preserving version of Google Search and end-to-end encrypted versions of Gmail and YouTube.

A final drawback of privacy enhancements is that they reduce the amount of aggregated and anonymised data in the public domain, where researchers and entrepreneurs can put it to use. If tech companies make less of this data available, it will reduce their output legitimacy.

Should Social Media Companies be Regulated as Publishers Rather than Platforms?

Facebook's output legitimacy would be enhanced if it assumed greater responsibility for the content published on its platform. It already moderates content at massive scale, using both artificial and human intelligence to comply with the law and enforce its own 'Community Standards'. Despite claims to the contrary, these efforts keep most users' experience of Facebook applications free from violent or pornographic imagery, as well as spam and hate speech.

Until very recently, Facebook has neglected its responsibility for the truth of claims made in advertising on the platform. Initiatives such as Page Transparency and the Facebook Ad Library are meaningful steps that increase the accountability of advertisers by making information about their campaigns freely available. However, at the same time as these features are being rolled out, fact-checking partnerships with expert third parties like Snopes are lapsing. If Facebook had to answer to regulators when it allowed untruthful ads to run, or if it had a legal liability for them, it would have incentives to implement stricter rules and make its processes for authorising advertisers and approving their ads more rigorous.

It's possible that this would give an advantage to large advertisers over their smaller competitors, as they would be better able to absorb the costs of complying with new rules and processes. However, in my opinion, that would be a price worth paying in order to establish the same norms and standards that make it very difficult to spread untrue claims through direct mail or TV advertising campaigns. In terms of the theory of digital legitimacy, this would involve trading off some 'user empowerment' to do better on the 'controls on abuses' dimension, making Facebook more legitimate overall. In its moral fog, the company conflates the freedom to advertise on Facebook with freedom of speech, but the first of these things can be limited without damaging the second.

The case for making Facebook legally liable for the content published by users, however, is less clear. It seems likely that it would result in the sort of artificial intelligence-powered censorship that prevents users from publishing messages and posts containing banned keywords on the popular Chinese social media app WeChat. It might help increase legitimacy on the 'controls on abuses' dimension – for example, if any keywords used to describe Rohingya were prevented from being shared – but it would be detrimental to 'user empowerment' if Facebook introduced similar restrictions on keywords that they were worried might implicate them in civil lawsuits.

The same arguments also apply to Twitter and Snapchat, both of which allow any user with a credit card to set up and run targeted campaigns; stronger controls would enhance their legitimacy. As we saw earlier, barriers to entry on Google Ads and Bing Ads are higher, and checks on advertising copy are more rigorous. On the 'controls on abuses' dimension, Google and Microsoft currently have greater legitimacy than Facebook.

Should We Break Up Big Tech?

Tech companies' power over their competitors, clients and suppliers has not been this book's main focus, but anti-monopoly proposals designed to constrain this power also have a bearing on ordinary users.

Facebook clearly has a monopoly among social networking services: it owns four of the top six social media applications by active user numbers. The Facebook 'blue app', Messenger, Instagram and WhatsApp all have well over a billion users. Consistent with Peter Thiel's advice to monopolists, Facebook's defence of its position is to obfuscate by defining its consumer market very broadly as the market in 'tools for communication', where there are 'new competitors coming up every day', while pointing out that it only has a 6 per cent share of the global advertising market.

A less disingenuous position would be to admit that Facebook is indeed a kind of monopoly – a natural one. Another concept we can thank John Stuart Mill for, a natural monopoly occurs when the most efficient way for a market to operate is with a single provider. Historic examples include the telegraph and domestic energy markets, where the fixed costs of building the physical infrastructure were very high. Facebook's case is different: the costs of building a new social networking service are negligible. There are, however, obvious benefits to users in a provider of social networking having a monopoly: the more people are in the same network, the more useful that network is. Breaking up the main Facebook app and the integrated Messenger app into, say, four new networks each a quarter of the size would greatly reduce their usefulness. I would argue that this legitimates Facebook's monopolistic position, and even passionate critics of Facebook such as Jaron Lanier and Jonathan Taplin seem to agree. It is worth noting, however, that historical precedents of natural monopoly have been assertively regulated to avoid consumers being taken advantage of.

It is less clear whether the divestment of WhatsApp and Instagram from Facebook would be to the detriment of users. The question turns on the user benefit created by these apps being integrated with the main Facebook app, which at the time of writing is still unclear.

The argument in favour of natural monopoly is applicable to other tech companies whose products deliver value to their users through network effects – for example, Twitter, Snap and Microsoft-owned LinkedIn. However, it does not apply to the search, e-commerce or video-streaming markets and therefore can't be used to legitimate the monopoly positions of Google, Amazon and Netflix.

It seems to me that the best reason to consider anti-monopoly action against big tech companies is to prevent them from controlling multiple links in the same value chain – so-called 'vertical integration'. This is what allows Amazon to take business from the merchants who use its Marketplace platform and Google to divert search clicks away from third-party websites to its own properties, detracting from their legitimacy. Those sorts of hustles are sufficiently familiar from the era of Andrew Carnegie and the 'robber barons' that regulators such as the EU Competition Commissioner Margrethe Vestager already have them in their sights.

But vertical integration also has other, less obvious problems. A key difference between digital ads and older forms of targeted advertising is that in the former, everything happens in one place. Geodemographic segmentation in the direct mail campaign for 1980s electronics we imagined in Chapter Two would have required input from a data provider like Experian, a marketing agency, a printer and a mailing house. All those parties had professional codes of conduct to comply with and reputations to worry about, giving them incentives to uphold standards of truthfulness and decency. The ad copy and creative would be subject to multiple sign-offs – not to mention rigorous challenge if it was in poor taste or made controversial claims. By contrast, running a targeted campaign through the Google Display Network or Facebook Ads Manager is completely different: the role of data provider, agency, printer and mailing house is collapsed into a single piece of self-service software, and it's rare for either copy or creative to be reviewed by a human before it's published and distributed. Breaking tech companies apart along vertical lines – forcing Google to divest YouTube or Facebook to sell Instagram, for instance – does little to address problems of vertical integration. Although it would be complicated to execute, a better approach might be to separate tech companies' targeting and publishing functions into different organisations – similar to the way in which TV programmes are often produced by one company but broadcast by another.

Should Dual-class Stock Structures be Reformed?

Although Mark Zuckerberg owns less than 20 per cent of Facebook's shares, he controls approximately 60 per cent of its voting stock, as a result of the company's dual-class structure. The value that 2.5 billion people derive from Facebook therefore depends entirely on his goodwill. Regardless of the legality of the situation, it's hard to think of a credible argument for its legitimacy.

A range of remedies have been proposed to tackle the increasing prevalence of such structures. Some argue for an outright ban or for delisting offending companies from major stock market indices; others have suggested 'sunset' clauses that dissolve the additional voting rights of founders' shares a specified number of years after an IPO. Unless legislation is passed, Zuckerberg must himself decide to reduce the extent of his control over Facebook. Ceding voting rights, stepping down as chairman, appointing an ombudsman or reviving mechanisms to secure democratic approval for policy changes from Facebook's users would help make it more legitimate. Another possibility would be to replace the banal statement of Facebook's purpose in its corporate charter – 'to engage in any lawful act or activity for which corporations may be organized' – with its espoused mission: 'To give people the power to build community and bring the world closer together.' That would create fiduciary duties for its executives, in place of Zuckerberg's personal good intentions.

These arguments are also relevant in the many other technology companies where founder control is exerted through multiple classes of stock that confer different voting rights, including Google, Snap and Pinterest. As Microsoft, Apple and Amazon all have conventional stock structures, they are more legitimate in terms of governance. Meanwhile, Amazon's ongoing reinvestment of its profits into new initiatives undermines Zuckerberg's claim that he needs personal control to prevent shareholders from forcing him into prioritising short-term financial performance over what's best for Facebook's users.

Should We Allow Big Tech Companies
to Control Internet Infrastructure?

The power that tech companies have over nation-states has not been a focus of this book, but the implications of their increasing control of internet infrastructure are worth noting briefly. In addition to operating the Free Basics programme, which offers free internet access to hundreds of millions of people in the Global South, Facebook owns significant stakes in undersea fibre optic cables and has also experimented with beaming internet access from drones into regions with little or no connectivity. In July 2020, a fleet of high-altitude balloons was dispatched by Google's sister company Loon to bring more 4G coverage to Kenya. Noting that control of the infrastructure for sending telegrams helped nineteenth- and twentieth-century empires maintain power over their subjects, critics of Facebook and Google have accused them of perpetrating a new form of colonialism. Indeed, Facebook board member Marc Andreessen appeared to confirm that the company understood its role in imperial terms with a tweet in response to the banning of Free Basics in India: 'Anti-colonialism has been economically cata-strophic for the Indian people for decades. Why stop now?'

Providing internet connectivity against the wishes of govern-ments reduces tech companies' input legitimacy because it's from the state that the authority to build infrastructure derives. It might also reduce their output legitimacy by undermining the social contract between states and their citizens – after all, why should you pay taxes to a government if the infrastructure you need is being provided unilaterally by a private company? Even when internet connectivity is provided with the co-operation of the state, it undermines the tech companies' legitimacy if they become the gatekeepers of internet access for hundreds of millions of people. Microsoft and Amazon have also invested in internet infrastructure; the same questions need to be asked about them.

* * *

I began this chapter by observing that existing theories of legitimacy aren't suitable for analysing the power of tech companies, because the kind of power they have is so different from the power of states. As a result, my proposed theory of legitimacy makes some new demands of commentators, academics and policymakers. Because tech companies' activities seem complex, people rely on metaphors of resource extraction and surveillance when describing how their power operates. However, as we've seen, these metaphors are morally loaded and can obscure as much as they reveal. If we want to make tech companies more legitimate, we first need to understand the details of how their products and business models really work. Then we need to consider the ways in which policy proposals intended to increase legitimacy in one way might simultaneously detract from it in another. Only then can we decide which of their powers we should tolerate, which ones we should add conditions to and which ones we should curb.

Chapter Nine
DATA ETHICS
FOR BIG TECH

Big companies have self-interested reasons to care about legitimacy – not least because when governments decide they are too powerful, they tend to be fined, regulated, broken up or even nationalised. But do companies have moral responsibilities, that their executives should pay attention to even when there is little prospect of government intervention? Neoliberals don't think they do; for them, companies' only duties are to act in the interests of their shareholders and to obey the law. Talk of 'business ethics' is nonsensical.

That might be a valid position in principle but in practice it's untenable, for the simple reason that big companies' share prices are affected by the ethical concerns of the public. It's common for journalists, NGOs and activists to highlight issues such as the poor treatment of workers and environmental degradation, while tax avoidance and regulatory arbitrage are increasingly

regarded as unethical, irrespective of their legality. And historically, the involvement of corporations in catastrophes has
materially damaged shareholder value. This isn't just a matter
of financial losses from reduced sales or from paying compensation for fatalities and injuries; when a company's management is
perceived to have been responsible for lapses in safety, there is a
long-term negative impact on its share price that can amount to
billions of dollars.

In 1982, seven people died of cyanide poisoning in Chicago,
after taking capsules of the painkiller Tylenol that had been
tampered with. Shares in the drug's manufacturer, Johnson &
Johnson, lost 10 per cent of their value almost immediately, and
a further 8 per cent over the next four months. Following the
1989 oil spill from the Exxon Valdez tanker, the company's share
price followed the same trajectory: it was 15 per cent down fifty
days after the spill, and 18 per cent down after six months. And
Union Carbide, the chemical company responsible for the toxic
gas leak at Bhopal in 1984, which caused up to 16,000 deaths,
lost 29 per cent of its value in the same time frame.

The implication is that ethics is important for all big companies, whether they like it or not. So what should the CEOs
of big tech companies pay particular attention to? The short
answer is a new field called 'data ethics'. Between the 1970s
and the 2000s, technology ethics tended to be discussed either
at the level of computers or of their human designers and users.
The term data ethics has been coined to reflect the fact that in
the digital era, many ethical questions need to be discussed at
the level of data. As part of a recent project with my Cambridge

agents (21) algorithmic (42) analysis (20) approach (28) artificial (33) case (18) challenges (34) communication (28) computer (65) data (220) design (44) development (24) digital (49) ethics (263) games (18) health (19) human (30) ict (20) information (112) intelligence (25) internet (33) introduction (19) issues (31) machine (19) media (23) moral (74) networking (24) online (27) personal (21) perspectives (25) politics (21) practices (29) privacy (85) protection (17) public (26) research (46) responsibility (35) robots (50) science (36) social (79) software (18) study (19) surveillance (24) systems (28) technology (98) towards (18) trust (25) value (41) virtual (26) world (23)

Word cloud visualisation of all the article titles in my database of academic literature on data ethics, with frequencies shown in brackets.

colleagues, I compiled a database of 953 peer-reviewed journal articles on data ethics, and used the 'data photography' technique I described in Chapter Three to reveal what those questions are.

If you stare at the visualisation for long enough, you can see the key themes of data ethics emerge. We've examined some of them already, including privacy, surveillance and software user interface design. But now it's time to touch on some of the others.

Bias, Discrimination and Injustice in Algorithmic Decision-making

Like targeted advertising, the use of algorithms – rather than humans – to make important decisions is not a new phenomenon. Ever since the 1980s, financial services companies have used automated scoring to decide whether to accept or reject applications for loans, credit cards, car finance plans and mortgages. Drawing on data held in credit bureaus, scorecards had supplanted bank managers as the chief decision makers on the extension of credit by the turn of the century, while similar models were adopted by direct-to-consumer insurance brands to automate their underwriting decisions.

Prior to the subprime mortgage crisis in 2008, the use of algorithmic decision-making in financial services wasn't widely regarded as an ethical issue. However, the proliferation of data and advances in machine learning have enabled algorithmic decision-making to be extended to other domains, including criminal justice and policing – often facilitated by tech companies like Palantir, as we saw in Chapter Seven. In the criminal justice system, algorithms that predict the likelihood criminals will reoffend are used in sentencing and parole decisions, while 'predictive policing' models are used to determine where law enforcement personnel should be deployed in anticipation of potential crimes.

However, researchers have demonstrated that the unconscious biases of algorithm designers and their models' reliance on historic data can reproduce racial, ethnic and gender discrimination. In her excellent book on the subject, *Weapons of Math Destruction,* Cathy O'Neil gives the example of LSI-R, an algorithm used by courts in some US states to estimate the likelihood that prisoners will reoffend. One of the data points the algorithm uses relates to involvement with the police at a young age. 'Involvement' might mean committing a crime, but it also encompasses being on the receiving end of a stop and search encounter, which is far more likely to happen to young men of colour. In New York City, Black and Latino males aged between fourteen and twenty-four account for less than 5 per cent of the population, but more than 40 per cent of those stopped and searched by the police. As a result, LSI-R makes parole and sentencing recommendations that are informed by human police officers' perception that people of colour are more likely to commit crimes.

So far, tech companies' efforts to mitigate the risk of such injustices have come in the form of resources for algorithm developers. Facebook has an internal tool called 'Fairness Flow' that measures how algorithms affect specific groups; Google has released the 'What-If Tool', which is intended to help developers identify biases in data sets and algorithms. IBM has gone a step further with AI Fairness 360, an open-source toolkit that is designed to check for and mitigate unwanted biases embedded in algorithms and the data used to train machine learning models. These are all steps in the right direction, but tech companies might also need to accept that they have a moral responsibility to make their algorithms transparent and explainable – not just to lawmakers, but to the individuals who are most affected by them.

Artificial General Intelligence as an Existential Risk to Humanity

In the view of a large number of AI experts surveyed by researchers in 2017, there is a 50 per cent chance that AI will outperform humans in all tasks by 2060. Although there is disagreement among the experts about how imminent this situation is, its severity is more certain: human intelligence is constrained by the information-processing limits of biological tissue, but machines are not subject to the same limits. According to Nick Bostrom and his colleagues at the University of Oxford's Future of Humanity Institute, AI poses an existential threat to human survival.

This threat can be illustrated with a simple thought experiment, borrowed from Jamie Susskind's *Future Politics*. Imagine a machine superintelligence was given the objective of calculating Pi. Optimising towards its goal, it could be expected to channel all the world's resources into building a planet-sized supercomputer; and since humanity serves no useful computational purpose, we could expect to be wiped out entirely or instrumentalised (think of *The Matrix*, where people are used as batteries). Bostrom therefore stresses the importance of ensuring that the objectives of AI systems are both aligned with human values and rigorously specified.

Many tech companies have set up AI ethics boards in recent years, with executives' personal views on existential risk often providing the motivation. Elon Musk has tweeted that he thinks AI is more dangerous than nuclear weapons, while the founders of DeepMind made the creation of an AI ethics and safety board a condition of their acquisition by Google.

However, there are reasons to be sceptical of this trend. The sudden proliferation of ethics boards at tech companies has led to accusations of 'ethics washing' – the disingenuous engagement with ethics as a PR strategy, similar to the 'greenwashing' that companies with poor environmental records have undertaken in the past. As the AI researcher Meredith Whittaker points out, even Axon, which manufactures taser weapons, surveillance drones and AI-enhanced police body cameras, now has an ethics board, the establishment of which is clearly not a sufficient response to the ethical issues raised by the company's business activities. Unless ethics boards have the authority to veto product decisions and hold executives to account, they are no more than 'ethics theatre'. The same is true of moves by tech companies to publish ethical principles and appoint chief ethics officers: without tangible evidence that they are driving ethical actions, they are likely to lack credibility.

Salesforce is a good example. The company states that it has 'a broader responsibility to society ... to create technology that ... upholds the basic rights of every individual'. In 2018, it appointed Paula Goldman as chief ethics and humane use officer, with a remit to understand the impact of the company's products on the world, create an ethical internal culture and product design process, and advance the field of data ethics through dialogue with stakeholders. However, that hasn't stopped Salesforce facing the same ongoing criticism as Palantir over its contract with the US Customs and Border Protection Agency, which implicates it in alleged inhumane treatment of migrants at the US southern border.

Similarly, in 2019, Google's AI ethics board closed a week after launching, amidst criticism over the appointment of a board member who had illiberal views on minority rights. This suggested significant gaps in Google's thinking on AI ethics – not least their failure to realise that algorithmic injustice is more of a clear and present danger than machine superintelligence.

Job Displacement from
Machine Learning and Robotics

In 2013, research by the economists Carl Benedikt Frey and
Michael Osborne suggested that 47 per cent of American jobs
were at high risk from computerisation. Their paper precip-
itated a wave of reports and studies on 'the future of work',
receiving over 5,000 academic citations. Longer-term prospects for jobs appear even more bleak: the survey of AI experts
mentioned earlier suggests there is a 50 per cent chance that
machines will have displaced all human jobs by 2140. So
central is work to our sense of identity, that job displacement is
an existential question, as well as an economic one. It has been
suggested that tech companies which prosper from automation
have a moral duty towards the workers whose livelihoods it
puts at risk.

Tech CEOs seem somewhat sympathetic to this view. The
Partnership on AI, a non-profit think tank founded by Amazon,
Facebook, Google, Microsoft and IBM, has addressed questions of job displacement in its research. Consistent with his
hypothesis about the pace of advancement in AI, Elon Musk
has supported calls for a universal basic income, as have Pierre
Omidyar, founder of eBay, and Sam Altman, who runs the
influential Silicon Valley start-up accelerator Y-Combinator. At
a 2017 meeting of the World Economic Forum in Davos, the
Microsoft CEO Satya Nadella remarked that 'We should do our
very best to train people for the jobs of the future,' while his
counterpart at Salesforce, Marc Benioff, spoke of his fear that

AI would create 'digital refugees'. However, while job displacement may be a concern of tech company CEOs and a focus for conference speeches and philanthropic activity, so far there has been little tangible action by tech companies to mitigate it.

Reconciling Differences in the World's Ethical Traditions

One complication for big tech companies in thinking about data ethics is the existence of different ethical traditions in the countries where they operate. The world's main ethical traditions include the Islamic tradition, the Confucian tradition, the Indian tradition and the Buddhist tradition, as well as the Western or Judaeo-Christian tradition.

Even in this far-from-exhaustive list, there is significant divergence on matters of business ethics. Trust-based relationships may be viewed as more or less important than legal contracts. Favouritism towards family members may be regarded as a virtue or as a vice. Furthermore, there is also divergence *within* ethical traditions. For example, America emphasises the virtue of self-reliance, while Europe emphasises the duty to look after the needy. In the Islamic tradition, law is interpreted based on local context, which leads to variations in ethical conduct.

However, there are also significant points of convergence. Fulfilling duties and treating people as you would wish to be treated are universal virtues. This 'Golden Rule' is familiar to readers of the Bible, but it also appears in *The Analects*, the collection of Confucius' sayings and ideas.

At the same time, harming people, stealing, telling lies and committing fraud are universally regarded as vices. As a result of these points of convergence, it has been possible to determine universal minimum ethical standards for multinational business activities – more or less everyone believes in respecting human dignity and basic rights. As a result, minimum ethical standards include ensuring products, services and workplaces are safe; upholding individuals' rights to education and an adequate standard of living; and treating employees, customers and suppliers as people with intrinsic value rather than as a means to an end. Similarly, it's generally accepted that companies should support essential social institutions like the education system and work with governments to protect the environment.

These standards were developed with industries such as pharmaceuticals, oil and chemicals in mind, and following disasters like the Tylenol poisonings, the Exxon Valdez oil spill and the Bhopal gas leak. As we've seen, digital technology raises new questions, and it is unrealistic to expect that they can be fully addressed by applying existing ethical standards. However, I'm optimistic that an 'overlapping consensus' on data ethics can be achieved, and the story of Shanghai Roadway brings this idea to life.

Shanghai Roadway was a Chinese subsidiary of the American data company Dun & Bradstreet, which provides data and analytics to around 90 per cent of the companies on the Fortune 500. Until it was bought out by private equity investors in 2019, Dun & Bradstreet was listed on the New York Stock Exchange; in 2017, it had revenues of $1.7 billion. It acquired Shanghai Roadway in 2009 as part of a strategy to expand in the Chinese market. Like many other divisions of the company, Shanghai Roadway marketed data about businesses and consumers to lenders and other commercial clients, generating revenues of $23 million in 2011.

However, Shanghai Roadway's data collection practices were to result in controversy. In common with the business model of other data companies such as Experian, Shanghai Roadway sourced data on individuals to populate its databases through commercial relationships with banks, insurance companies, real estate agents and telemarketing companies. The company held personal information, including income levels, jobs and addresses, on approximately 150 million Chinese citizens, with records from this database sold for around $0.23 each to companies as marketing and sales leads.

In September 2012, the Shanghai District Prosecutor charged Shanghai Roadway and five former employees with illegally obtaining private information belonging to Chinese citizens. The court fined the company the equivalent of $160,000 and sentenced four of the former employees to two years in prison. The basis for the decision was a 2009 amendment to the criminal law, which made it illegal for companies in the financial services, telecommunications, transport, education and healthcare industries to obtain or sell a citizen's personal information. Following the judgment, Shanghai Roadway ceased trading and Dun & Bradstreet reported itself to US regulators. In April 2018, Dun & Bradstreet agreed to pay a $9 million fine to resolve charges under the Foreign Corrupt Practices Act, relating to payments made to third-party agents who had procured data on Shanghai Roadway's behalf, and to the bribery of government officials by another Chinese subsidiary of Dun & Bradstreet to facilitate access to personal data.

The significance of the Shanghai Roadway case is that it demonstrates an 'overlapping consensus' on a real-life question of data ethics. Chinese and US prosecutors agreed that Shanghai Roadway had acted unethically and sanctioned Dun & Bradstreet accordingly, but they did not agree on what aspect of Shanghai Roadway's conduct was unethical. In China, it was its business model of collecting and selling personal data without informed consent, while in the US, it was the practice of making off-book payments to intermediaries and government officials. The former is ethically acceptable in the US – indeed, there is a $2.6 billion industry, digital lead generation, devoted to it. And in the context of Chinese norms around gift-giving, the latter can be perceived as an honourable way of investing in a long-term business relationship, rather than an unethical instance of bribery.

Beyond the Trolley Problem

Of course, religious traditions aren't the only basis for ethics. The recent development of self-driving cars by big tech companies like Google, Tesla and Uber has put philosophical ethics in the spotlight.

Globally, road traffic accidents accounted for 1.4 million fatalities in 2016. While developers of autonomous vehicles claim they will have a net favourable impact on road safety by reducing human error, it's inevitable that their adoption will lead to fatal accidents. Indeed, at the time of writing, Tesla's automated driving system has already caused five deaths, and Uber's has caused one. This raises an ethical question about the software used to determine how a self-driving car should react in the event of a probable collision. Programmers are presented with a version of the ethical dilemma famously framed by the philosopher Philippa Foot as 'the trolley problem'.

The trolley problem is a thought experiment involving an out-of-control train that's heading towards five people, who are unable to move and will be killed in the collision. Imagine you are standing next to a set of points between the runaway train and the people. By pulling a lever, you could divert the train onto a second track, killing one person instead. Should you pull the lever?

The problem captures the divergence of views between two of the main schools of philosophical ethics – utilitarianism and deontology. As we saw in Chapter Six, utilitarianism weighs up the consequences of an action to determine whether it is ethical or not. If Jeremy Bentham was standing at the points he would pull the lever, on the basis that the happiness created by saving five lives would more than offset the happiness destroyed by

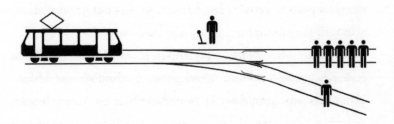

The Trolley Problem: should you divert the train?

causing one death. By contrast, the competing theory of deon-tology, which is associated with Immanuel Kant (1724–1804), says that all actions are right or wrong in and of themselves. Kant would *not* pull the lever to divert the runaway train, on the basis that it is one's duty not to kill, regardless of any extenuating circumstances.

With many human lives potentially at stake, academics have argued that the decision about which theory of ethics is encoded into autonomous vehicle software should not be left up to the programmers. It's not even a straightforward binary choice: software operating on utilitarian principles would need to know whether to prioritise the life of the passenger against the lives of pedestrians and passengers in other vehicles. And if we apply these theories to the case of Shanghai Roadway, it's hard to see how either a strictly deontological or utilitarian approach to data ethics would be feasible. Deontology requires the determination of whether actions are right or wrong in and of themselves, leaving no room for variations in norms in differ-ent regions of the world. Utilitarianism, meanwhile, requires us to weigh up the consequences of different actions, and even in the relatively simple example of Shanghai Roadway's procure-ment of personal data, it is difficult to make this calculation. What proportion of the Chinese citizens whose data was traded by Shanghai Roadway experienced harm, whether through unwanted phone calls or messages or in more serious forms? What economic benefits did Shanghai Roadway's clients gain from using the data, and how much of those benefits flowed on to their own clients, shareholders and employees? How are these harms and benefits to be quantified? More complex questions – in relation to the development of the algorithms used in the criminal justice system, for example – are even more resistant to the calculations utilitarianism requires.

Luckily, there is another theory called virtue ethics, which goes all the way back to ancient Greece and the thinking of Aristotle (c.384 BCE–c.322 BCE). For Aristotle, ethics should be less concerned with specific actions than with the character of the person or organisation who carries them out.

In the trolley problem, whether or not it is ethical to pull the lever therefore depends on the circumstances of the person faced with the choice: pulling the lever might express the virtue of bravery or the vice of megalomania. When applied to data ethics, virtue ethics suggests that tech companies should ask themselves: 'What kind of company should we be?' In the Shanghai Roadway case, Dun & Bradstreet might have asked, 'Do we want to be the sort of company that covertly gains access to personal data by making off-book payments?' Posing this question helps to identify what may be a universal virtue of tech companies: transparency. Acting transparently would have required them to both make it clear to consumers how data about them might end up in a commercially available marketing database, and to eschew extra-contractual arrangements with suppliers and intermediaries.

Cloudflare's decision to withdraw services from 8chan, a message board associated with white supremacist and neo-Nazi ideologies, offers an example of virtue ethics in practice. Cloudflare is a San Francisco-based web infrastructure company that provides cloud security, protecting websites from cyberattacks. It supports over 19 million websites for clients including IBM, Thomson Reuters and Zendesk.

Until 2019, 8chan was one of Cloudflare's clients. Historically, Cloudflare saw itself as a neutral utility service, and it didn't make judgements about its clients based on the content of their websites. This position could be justified from a deontological or a utilitarian perspective: one could argue that it is wrong for a private company to censor speech, or that removing a client like 8chan might lead, say, to pressure from governments to remove websites belonging to unfavoured minorities. However, when it became clear that the perpetrator of a mass shooting in El Paso, Texas in August 2019 had posted a manifesto on 8chan, Cloudflare's CEO Matthew Prince changed his stance and terminated their contract with 8chan. In a blog post on Cloudflare's website, he wrote:

> We do not take this decision lightly. Cloudflare is a network provider. In pursuit of our goal of helping build a better internet, we've considered it important to provide our security services broadly to make sure as many users as possible are secure, and thereby making cyberattacks less attractive – regardless of the content of those websites. Many of our customers run platforms of their own on top of our network. If our policies are more conservative than theirs it effectively undercuts their ability to run their services and set their own policies. We reluctantly tolerate content that we find reprehensible, but we draw

the line at platforms that have demonstrated they directly inspire tragic events and are lawless by design.

Cloudflare, it seems, wants to be the kind of company that upholds net neutrality as far as is possible without undermining the rule of law. It is also worth noting that by writing publicly about his decision and by giving interviews to journalists about it, Prince exhibited the virtue of transparency.

If virtue ethics is the framework that makes the most sense for big tech companies, how should they apply it? To think through this, let's consider an imaginary provider of telecoms infrastructure and hardware. Seeking revenue growth, this provider might consider diversifying into so-called 'value added services' such as messaging apps, location services, Internet of Things analytics and mobile advertising. All these services involve the collection and storage of personal data: even end-to-end encrypted messaging produces metadata that could contribute to the identification of individual users; and even business-to-business Internet of Things apps could capture data on individual employees via sensors. At the same time, storing personal data from these services creates the risk that it may be misappropriated by 'bad people' and used for harm.

In short, providing value added services risks individuals being exposed to harm. In addition, as data protection legislation typically lags behind advances in digital technology, the law cannot be relied on for guidance. One potential response might be to adopt best-practice data protection standards. These would include ensuring that individuals give informed consent for data collection and are able to withdraw it in future, and the principle of 'data minimisation', which means collecting only the data that's required for the services to function effectively.

Further issues would arise if the data produced by providing value added services was put to secondary uses, such as using location data to target advertising or packaging Internet of Things data from smart home devices as an analytics product. Since secondary uses are often unknown at the point of data collection, they are in tension with the principle of consent. Similarly, big data analytics is in tension with the principle of data minimisation, as it is based on the serendipitous discovery of correlations in very large data sets.

At the same time, the development of value added services can have unintended consequences. Location services have been used by perpetrators of domestic abuse to track down their victims. Livestreaming services have been used to broadcast footage of self-harm, suicide and mass killings. Encrypted messaging services have been used to circulate images of child sexual abuse and to plan acts of terrorism.

Do such unintended consequences imply that it would be unethical for the telecoms company to develop new products in these areas at all? And do the best practices imply that value added services can only be ethical if their scope is tightly circumscribed? I don't think so, as that ignores the benefits the services bring to large numbers of users and clients, and it forecloses on opportunities for data analytics to create public value – imagine, for example, that smart home analytics enabled major advances in domestic energy conservation that could significantly reduce carbon emissions. Instead, asking 'What kind of company should we be?' can help strike a balance between pursuing innovation, growth or profitability at any cost and the inertia that often follows when we get risks out of proportion.

The Virtuous Big Tech Company

So, what should big tech companies actually do about data ethics? Governance is a good place for them to start. Expanding the scope of their compliance function to 'ethics and compliance' would acknowledge that all companies have broader social responsibilities than simply complying with the law and mitigating regulatory risk, and that the distinctive power that tech companies have only heightens these responsibilities. If a group is established with responsibility for data ethics, it should have a formal role in the company's governance structure, including rights to veto product decisions. Without these rights, ethics boards will struggle to transcend 'ethics theatre'. At the same time, the board's scope should not be limited to AI. As we've seen, data ethics questions run broader and deeper, and many are more immediate than the threat of machine superintelligence.

Tech companies could also use ethical frameworks when evaluating whether to terminate client relationships that may be enabling unethical practices – Salesforce and Palantir's relationships with the US Customs and Border Protection Agency being a current example. These are rarely straightforward decisions, but deliberating on them in public, as Cloudflare did on 8chan, is a virtuous thing to do. Meanwhile, where practical questions of data ethics are complicated by differences in ethical traditions and norms, as was the case with Shanghai Roadway, 'overlapping consensus' may be achievable and should certainly be pursued.

Returning to the themes of previous chapters, companies also have an ethical imperative to provide transparency to individuals over how their personal data is collected, stored and used, and to offer tools enabling them to exercise control over it – like Google's Safety Center and Facebook's Ad Preference Center. Meanwhile, the suitability of 'engagement' metrics as business targets should be reviewed, as they may be misaligned – or even at odds – with users' wellbeing. And new products should be developed with due consideration for both data-related risks and potential unintended consequences, rather than by fostering a culture of 'permissionless innovation' where anything goes.

But as well as working to reduce risks of harm, a virtuous tech company would also try to maximise the good it did in the world. What positive actions might it take?

'Co-creating' the Jobs of the Future

Automation is not the only driver of disruption to work; as the emergence of the term 'the gig economy' indicates, the labour market is becoming more flexible and more volatile. Although there has been no shortage of corporate research initiatives on 'the future of work', most tangible interventions have come from start-ups and social enterprises responding to the increasing insecurity of employment. There is, therefore, an opportunity for tech companies who seek to enable human flourishing to proactively fashion the jobs of the future – jobs in which humans and machines are not in competition, but instead collaborate in a way that both enhances performance and enriches human life.

Precedents for this form of working already exist. Machine learning algorithms can be as effective as experienced doctors at diagnosing some forms of cancer, pointing to a future for medical professionals in which human clinical experience is complemented by AI's strengths in pattern recognition and data processing speed. However, opportunities also exist in less specialised types of work that employ far more people. One example is the food delivery sector, where tech companies such as Deliveroo and Alibaba's Ele.me have created high-growth businesses by combining mobile apps, logistics and casualised labour. Ethnographic research has revealed a somewhat adversarial relationship between human couriers and the algorithms used to assign jobs and plan routes. In face-to-face conversations and in WhatsApp groups, couriers collaborate in an attempt to reverse-engineer the algorithm, iteratively testing strategies to optimise their earnings. Meanwhile, isolated in a head office where they never interact with the couriers, the algorithm's developers build new features based on assumptions about their users' needs that the couriers know to be flawed.

A 'co-creation' approach offers the potential to redesign the relationship between human workers and AI to be more harmonious and more economically productive. The process involves bringing together groups of stakeholders to work collaboratively on a solution. In the case of food delivery, these stakeholders would be the couriers, the algorithm developers and users of the apps. Although co-creation is usually associated with the development of new consumer products and services, it has been proposed as an approach to help map the future of work at Mondragón in the Basque region of Spain, where automation and the need for a green transition are creating uncertainty for large numbers of manufacturing and construction workers. Tech companies could undertake co-creation processes with their own employees in fields that are at risk of technological displacement, or with people whose employability is threatened by their products. Millions of workers in fields like customer services, social media content moderation and device manufacture could benefit from new kinds of jobs designed through such initiatives.

Putting More Data into the Public Domain

Tech companies with data-driven business models tend to reject the assertion that the services they provide are worth less than the user data they monetise; as a result, they have not generally explored the idea of compensating users for data. In my opinion, there are both philosophical barriers to treating data as private property and practical barriers to paying users for data. Nevertheless, the kind of tech companies who want to enable scientific progress and social justice could consider sharing data value in a different form. Specifically, I want to propose that tech companies make a greater proportion of the data they have collected openly available for researchers, policymakers and members of the public to reuse.

What sort of data do I have in mind? As ever, internet search data provides a helpful example. The limited search data that Google already makes available through Google Trends is demonstrably valuable for academic research; in public health, it has already been used to analyse the symptoms of fibromyalgia and the seasonality in domestic violence, and to forecast transnational migration flows and the spread of coronavirus. However, Google Trends provides very little data on search term variations – the data that shows exactly what users search for when they are searching on a particular topic. It is deep search term variation data that holds untapped insights into public opinion, attitudes, preferences, needs, desires and behaviours. As much of this data has negligible value to advertisers – think of the hundreds of millions of searches for state benefits, for example – there is little commercial reason for tech companies to hoard it. It is not only search engines like Google, Baidu and Bing that are able to capture internet searches: web browsers, browser extensions, anti-virus software applications and internet service providers are, too. Making more search data openly available – in de-identified and aggregated form – is one way that tech companies can promote public good. The same argument can be made about de-identified and aggregated location data, Internet of Things data and clickstream data – behavioural data about which websites users visit and in what sequence.

Regrettably, however, this is not the prevailing trajectory. Google recently deprecated Google Correlate, which enabled researchers to see what search terms were correlated with their own time series data sets. Similar trends are apparent in relation to social media data from Facebook, Twitter and YouTube. Motivated in part by calls for stronger privacy controls in the wake of the Cambridge Analytica scandal, researchers' access to data sets is increasingly constrained – a development sometimes referred to as the 'APIcalypse'. Beyond academia, as we saw in Chapter Five, open-source intelligence organisations that rely on access to social media data for their investigations into potential war crimes and human rights violations have found their work hampered by the deletion of video archives by YouTube and the withdrawal of tools like Facebook Graph Search and Google Earth's Panoramio layer.

It seems likely that tech companies are simply ignorant of many of the beneficial uses of the data they already share and cannot imagine the uses that might be found for data they hoard. These could include scientific advances, medical breakthroughs, criminal prosecutions and public policy innovations. A virtuous tech company would seek to unlock those opportunities, not to foreclose them.

CONCLUSION

It was a sunny morning in July. The previous day, I'd given my furniture away to other students, packed up my books and clothes, and cleaned the flat. Ray, the removal man, wasn't due to arrive until one o'clock, so I found myself with a couple of hours to kill. I ambled down to the River Cam and had a flat white and avocado on toast in a café, its windows flung wide open. Cyclists trundled over the cobbles, and groups of tourists were being helped into punts. The city suddenly seemed very green, and full of birdsong. I wondered why I hadn't spent more of the year idly enjoying its simple pleasures. And then, with a wry smile, I remembered the reason: Cambridge power.

When Ray pulled up outside the flat, he was driving a new van. Business was good; he'd seen significant growth in bookings from the comparison website I'd used to find him originally, as well as demand from returning customers. As we drove along the M11 towards London, I thought I should tell him what had made me choose him rather than his competitors in the first place. The photos in all the other listings had been photos of vans: small vans and big vans; white vans and grey vans; Mercedes vans and Transit vans. But Ray's listing had had a photo of Ray. He'd looked experienced, reliable and kind. He nodded. 'You're not the first person to tell me that,' he said. 'I used to have a picture of the van, like everyone else on there. But then I thought, perhaps people care more about the driver than the type of van they've got? So I put that picture of me up instead, and I started to get more bookings.' Ray had formed a hypothesis about how people behave online, tested it and used data to evaluate the results. 'In my line of work,' I told him, 'we call that *optimisation*.'

We chatted about our summer plans. Ray was taking his dogs to his sister's place in Suffolk for a couple of weeks; I was going to the Greek islands. I mentioned I was feeling a bit guilty about my carbon footprint, and then Ray said something I wasn't expecting: 'I don't believe climate change is man-made.' I was a little taken aback. 'The way I see it,' he explained, 'the planet's always heated up and cooled down. That was happening before humans came along, so it can't be all about us now.' I was wondering what to say next when he stopped at a red light and two pugs crossed the road in front of us, giving me the perfect opportunity to change the subject.

I think climate change is a very important subject and that Ray is wrong about it. But that doesn't make him a bad person or mean that I should refuse to book removals with him in future. If anything, I should listen to him more. Putting myself in Ray's shoes, it's clear that there are different things at stake for him when it comes to climate policy. His livelihood depends to a much greater extent than mine on activities that produce carbon emissions. For similar reasons, we're bound to have different perspectives on self-driving vehicles and the algorithms used to assign jobs on gig economy platforms. That's why policymaking needs to include a wide range of perspectives – on data and technology as on climate change. Of course, being inclusive makes disagreements inevitable, so we have to abandon the idea that there is a single 'right' answer and look for 'overlapping consensus' instead.

However, that isn't how the debate about data and technology is currently unfolding. Instead, it's looking increasingly like a clash between two implacable opponents, with citizens and their political representatives on one side and tech companies on the other. To borrow the adversarial title of Jamie Bartlett's book, it's *The People vs Tech*. In this context, perhaps it's not surprising that so many people believe the conspiracy theories that claim coronavirus is a biological weapon invented by Bill Gates, or that Huawei is using the 5G network to spread it. After all, if tech companies are prepared to harm us for profit in the digital world, why wouldn't they do it in the physical world too? Meanwhile, even academics, who can usually be relied upon to be balanced, talk about tech company executives as if they are not just wrong or misguided, but evil. Mark Zuckerberg has been called 'a sociopath', and Sheryl Sandberg 'the Typhoid Mary of surveillance capitalism'.

When I hear such judgemental language being used, I'm reminded of the first time I visited Experian's headquarters in Nottingham. Before setting out, I checked Google Maps to plan my route from the station, and was surprised to see that the office had been tagged 'Shower of Bastards'. It was 2009, and 'verified listings' had yet to be added to Google Maps. As a result, anyone could drop a pin on a business and write whatever they liked about it. Perhaps it had been created by someone who objected to the Mosaic geodemographic segmentation system. Or, more likely, someone was angry about having a loan application declined, and blamed Experian for their misfortune.

Foreshadowing the sinking feeling I would experience at the *Guardian* event with Carole Cadwalladr and Christopher Wylie years later, I realised I had joined a company that was widely disliked. A couple of years later, at a World Economic Forum workshop about the future of personal data, I experienced this dislike in a different way. I was serious about finding ways to use data to benefit individuals and society, but my public and third sector collaborators at the event didn't seem to trust me, assuming I had a hidden agenda to hoover up data for Experian and increase its profits.

I remember the 'Shower of Bastards' tag every time I meet people who work at a company I dislike because of its business practices or for other ethical reasons. It reminds me that in every organisation there are people with integrity who are trying to make things better – and that instead of my judgement, they deserve the benefit of the doubt.

That's why I think it's time for the tone of the debate about data and technology to change. It's just not helpful to assume that all people who work for big tech companies are selfish, amoral or evil. This hostile attitude will drive some people away from work that could bring huge benefits to everyday life, public health, the economy, medical science and social equality. Others will think, 'Well, screw you – if all you expect of me is to pursue my own financial interests, that's what I'll do,' becoming the archetypal figures we imagined they already were. Instead, they have to be included in discussions about policies, and we need to listen to what they have to say. It also needs to be made easier for data scientists and developers to apply their skills in socially useful ways, by opening more government data, and highlighting the ways that techniques with commercial origins such as search data analytics can help address public challenges.

Employees of Chinese tech companies should also be included. Before buying into the 'realist' story that we are entering a new Cold War and need to strip out Huawei equipment and ban TikTok, we should at least make an effort to find a global 'overlapping consensus' on the governance of digital technology. A common set of norms and standards must be preferable to a 'splinternet' that deepens existing ideological divides. Global agreement on questions of data privacy may not be possible, but limiting the ways digital technology can be used to inflict cruelty is a more important goal, and a more achievable one.

Preventing cruelty should also be the priority for reform to American tech companies. In advertising, we need tighter controls on who can use machine learning tools like Lookalike Audiences, and enforceable rules on the truthfulness of claims made in digital ads much more than we need curbs on how data is used for targeting. The restriction of one-to-many sharing in encrypted messaging services and tougher action on posts that incite cruelty are much more important than additional protections for privacy and the freedom of expression. Once these checks are in place, policymakers can turn their attention to constraining big tech companies' ability to take advantage of their clients, suppliers and competitors, and to reforming the stock structures that allow founder-CEOs to maintain absolute control long after their companies have gone public.

All this will inevitably involve trade-offs: a simple tool like the theory of digital legitimacy I sketched in Chapter Eight can be used to think through them. Meanwhile, there is little policy can do to tackle 'Cambridge power', the diffuse and intractable form of power that is constantly working on us in the background. An equivalent of the Hippocratic oath for developers and designers might help, but if we are serious about reducing technology's mysterious influence on our everyday lives, committing to self-care is more important.

What about data itself? Throughout this book I've suggested that it is the lifeblood of the digital word, and that – as a general rule – it should flow freely. Governments need to open more data, but tech companies do too. Sometimes that will involve taking calculated risks to individuals' privacy – if medical records are to be used in big data analytics projects aimed at finding a cure for cancer, for example. But most of the time, aggregated and anonymised data is more than good enough, as we've seen with the community mobility and search data used to aid the fight against Covid-19. As individuals, we should stop thinking about data as our private property, and start thinking about it as a shared resource that everyone contributes to and can benefit from. From this perspective, data does not belong to us; we belong to data.

ACKNOWLEDGEMENTS

Good Data started life as an academic thesis called "Towards a Theory of Digital Legitimacy", which I wrote for my MPhil in International Relations and Politics at the University of Cambridge in 2018-19. I learned a huge amount from my teachers and classmates on the programme, and from the numerous seminars, lectures, workshops, and events that being in Cambridge gave me the chance to attend. I am particularly indebted to Professor Duncan Bell for his supervision.

After finishing the MPhil, I wanted to find a 'home' for the project of developing the thesis into a book. Professor Diane Coyle and Professor Michael Kenny offered me an affiliateship at the Bennett Institute – a community of Cambridge researchers rethinking public policy for these times of turbulence and growing inequality. I continue to be inspired by the Bennett Institute's work and proud to be part of the team.

A serendipitous conversation with Professor Alastair Beresford at a meeting of the Trust & Technology Initiative introduced me to my agent, Jonathan Conway – without whose dedication and creative input *Good Data* would not have been possible. At Welbeck Publishing, Wayne Davies bought into the book's contrarian arguments, and Oliver Holden-Rea's editing encouraged me to make them accessible to the widest possible audience.

Had I not worked in data and digital marketing for so long, I would have had little to bring to the debates *Good Data* engages with. I am grateful for many conversations and collaborations with colleagues from Bought By Many, Experian, and my wider professional network from those years. Some are mentioned by name in this book, and I thank them for humouring me.

I began writing *Good Data* in another country and a different world. Jennie Winhall's advice, encouragement, and support have been constants; I am profoundly grateful to her, as always.

– Sam Gilbert, Copenhagen, January 2021

NOTES

Introduction

The *Guardian* event was 'Newsroom: The Cambridge Analytica files'. The image is by Matt Kenyon.

Techlightenment is now called Alchemy Social. VisualDNA was acquired by Neilsen in 2017.

The term 'surveillance capitalism' first appears in Zuboff, S., 'Big Other: Surveillance Capitalism and the Prospects of an Information Civilization', *Journal of Information Technology*, 30(1), 2015, pp. 75–89.

Digital advertising-based business models are described as 'fundamentally illegitimate' in Zuboff, S., *The Age of Surveillance Capitalism: The Fight for a Human Future at the New Frontier of Power*, Profile, 2015, Kindle edition, Loc 250. It is referred to as 'illegitimate' a further twelve times (Loc 2689, 3403, 3587, 5850, 6263, 8736, 8811, 9375, 9429, 9463, 12705). For a fuller discussion of the concept of legitimacy, see Chapter Eight.

In addition to Zuboff, the claim that Facebook's business model is expropriative and extractive features in recent work by Fred Turner, including:

- Turner, F., 'The Arts at Facebook: An Aesthetic Infrastructure for Surveillance Capitalism', *Poetics*, 67, 2018, pp. 53–62.
- Turner, F., 'Machine Politics: The Rise of the Internet and a New Age of Authoritarianism', *Harper's Magazine*, January 2019, pp. 25–33.

In the second of these pieces, Turner attributes the Rohingya ethnic cleansing to Facebook (p. 26).

John Naughton attributed the mainstreaming of conspiracies to social media companies in a presentation entitled 'Computational Conspiracism: How Digital Democracy Brought Conspiracy Theory into the Mainstream' at the CRASSH event *Conspiracy and Democracy: History, Political Theory and the Internet*, 23 November 2018.

On claims that Facebook benefits financially from hate speech and bears responsibility for the election of populist leaders, see Vaidhyanathan, S., *Anti-*

social Media: How Facebook Disconnects Us and Undermines Democracy, Oxford University Press, New York, 2018, pp. 2–3, 5–6, 101, 184ff, 192–3.

On digital serfdom, see Cobbe, J., *Big Data, Surveillance and the Digital Citizen*, Queen's University Belfast, 2018, pp. 101ff.

On the user interface design ethics of Facebook and other apps, see Williams, J., *Stand Out of Our Light: Freedom and Resistance in the Attention Economy*, Cambridge University Press, Cambridge, 2018.

The description of Facebook as 'legalized crack' is from García Martínez, A., *Chaos Monkeys: Mayhem and Mania inside the Silicon Valley Money Machine*, Ebury, London, 2016, p. 228.

For examples of politicians citing surveillance capitalism theory in policy proposals, see:

- Warren, E., 'Here's How We Can Break Up Big Tech', Medium, 8 March 2019.
- Perrigo, B., 'How This Politician Put Britain at the Forefront of the War Against Facebook', *Time*, 19 February 2019.

On Twitter shaming see, Ronson, J., *So You've Been Publicly Shamed*, Picador, London, 2015.

On the market capitalisation of big tech companies, see https://ycharts.com/.

Chapter One: The New Oil?

The quotes from Senator Orrin Hatch and Mark Zuckerberg are from the *Washington Post*, 'Mark Zuckerberg's Senate hearing', *Zuckerberg Transcripts*, 998, 2018.

Chris's start-up (sadly now defunct) was called Executips.

Steve Johnston and Liam McGee's big search data analytics company Kaiasm was formerly known as Taxonomics. See https://www.kaiasm.com/.

Facebook Audience Insights can be accessed at: https://www.facebook.com/business/insights/tools/audience-insights.

You Are *Not* the Product

John Naughton's *95 Theses about Technology* are available at https://95theses.co.uk/.

Niall Ferguson's book is Ferguson, N., *The Square and the Tower: History's Hidden Networks*, Allen Lane, London, 2017, p. 356.

Zeynep Tufekci's TED Talk is called 'We're Building a Dystopia Just to Make People Click on Ads', https://www.ted.com/talks/zeynep_tufekci_

we_re_building_a_dystopia_just_to_make_people_click_on_ads. The claim appears at 22:10.

For a longer discussion of the flaws in the 'You are the product' claim, see Oremus, W., 'Are You Really the Product? The History of a Dangerous Idea', *Slate*, 27 April 2018.

The Reuters Tracking survey is Social Media Usage (2018), available at http://fingfx.thomsonreuters.com/gfx/rngs/FACEBOOK-PRIVACY-POLL/ 010062SJ4QF/2018%20Reuters%20Tracking%20-%20Social%20 Media%20Usage%205%203%202018.pdf.

Data is the New Manure
The quote by will.i.am is from 'We Need to Own Our Data as a Human Right – and Be Compensated for It', *The Economist*, 21 January 2019.

'The World's Most Valuable Resource Is not Oil, but Data' was a leader in the 6 May 2017 edition of *The Economist*. The cover image is by David Parkins.

The best source of Facebook user numbers is the company's quarterly earnings presentations, available via its investor relations portal at https:// investor.fb.com/home/default.aspx.

The statistic about average daily app usage by Facebook users is from Meeker. M., 'Internet Trends 2017', available at https://www.kleinerperkins. com/perspectives/internet-trends-report-2017, p. 114.

For the revenue per Facebook user calculation, see Chapter Five.

Chapter Two: Mind Games

The T-shirt website is https://teeshoppen.dk/. Facebook's case study of Kristian and Mads's work for Teeshoppen is at: https://www.facebook.com/ business/success/teeshoppen?__tn__=-UK-R.

Psychological Manipulation?
For a philosophical discussion of the difference between manipulation, inducement, encouragement and persuasion, see Lukes, S., *Power: A Radical View*, 2nd Edition, Palgrave Macmillan, New York, 2005, pp. 35–6.

The Christopher Wylie quote is from Cadwalladr, C., '"I Made Steve Bannon's Psychological Warfare Tool": Meet the Data War Whistleblower', *Observer*, 18 March 2018.

For Aleksandr Kogan's side of the Cambridge Analytica story, see Lewis, M., 'The Alex Kogan Experience', *Against the Rules with Michael Lewis*, 16 April 2019.

The classic account of subliminal techniques in advertising is Packard, V., *The Hidden Persuaders*, D. McKay Co, New York, 1957. For a discussion see Nelson, M. R., '"The Hidden Persuaders": Then and Now', *Journal of Advertising*, Vol. 37, No. 1, 2008, pp. 113–26.

The Dominic Cummings quote is from Ferguson (2017), p. 383.

The example from the Obama 2012 campaign is described in Stephens-Davidowitz, S., *Everybody Lies: What the Internet Can Tell Us about Who We Really Are*, Bloomsbury Publishing, 2018, Kindle edition, Loc 2566.

For the details of what is and isn't possible with Facebook Custom Audiences and Lookalike Audiences, see https://www.facebook.com/business/help/744354708981227 and https://www.facebook.com/business/help/164749007013531.

Companies selling software products which enable marketers to set up and measure optimisation 'experiments' include Optimizely, Unbounce and Visual Website Optimizer.

Facebook's experiment with users' emotional responses is described in Flick, C., 'Informed Consent and the Facebook Emotional Manipulation Study', *Research Ethics*, Vol. 12(1), 2016, pp. 14–28.

Lookalike Audiences at the Experian Museum

On the Aquila drone, see Zuckerberg, M. (2017f), 'Aquila's Second Successful Flight', *Zuckerberg Transcripts*, 939.

The image of the 1980s mail order catalogue can be found in the retro/vintage Tumblr Atomic Chronoscaph: https://atomic-chronoscaph.tumblr.com/.

For a history and detailed explanation of geodemographics, see Harris, R., Sleight, P., Webber, R., *Geodemographics, GIS and Neighbourhood Targeting*, Wiley, London, 2005. More on Experian Mosaic is available at: https://www.experian.co.uk/assets/business-strategies/brochures/Mosaic%2520UK%25202009%2520brochure%5B1%5D.pdf.

On 'Motorway Men', see Doward, J., 'Motorway Man Holds Key to General Election Victory', *Observer*, 7 February 2010.

The Trump 2016 campaign's tactics are described in 'Inside the Trump Bunker, With Days to Go', Bloomberg, 27 October 2016.

On the AfD's use of social media in political campaigning, see Privacy International (2017), 'Social Media Campaigning and targeting – the growth of the AfD', available at https://privacyinternational.org/examples/2849/social-media-campaigning-and-targeting-growth-afd and Avaaz (2019), 'Far Right Networks of Deception', available at https://avaazimages.avaaz.org/Avaaz%20Report%20Network%20Deception%2020190522.pdf, p. 18.

Facebook's rules for authorising ads in different countries are outlined at: https://www.facebook.com/business/help/167836590566506?helpref=page_content

For examples of commercially motivated disinformation, see Subramanian, S., 'The Macedonian Teens Who Mastered Fake News', *Wired*, 15 February 2017, and Barr, S., 'Jameela Jamil calls out celebrities who promote laxative "detox' teas", *Independent*, 26 November 2018.

For an explanation of the Supreme Court judgment which shapes the attitudes of American companies towards political advertising, see Lau, T. (2019), 'Citizens United Explained', *Brennan Center for Justice*, https://www.brennancenter.org/our-work/research-reports/citizens-united-explained.

On the use of Facebook ads by Chinese news sites, see 'Gaining Face: China Is Using Facebook to Build a Huge Audience Around the World', *The Economist*, 20 April 2019. Images of CGTN and China Daily ads are from the Facebook Ad Library.

The Graph API

The Graph API was originally called 'Open Graph'. For an overview, see https://developers.facebook.com/docs/graph-api/overview/#basics. On uses of the Graph API by Yelp and the *Guardian*, see Schonfeld, E., 'Zuckerberg: "We Are Building A Web Where The Default Is Social"', *TechCrunch*, 21 April 2010, and, 'Guardian Announces New App on Facebook to Make News More Social', *Guardian*, 23 September 2011.

The quote by Rohit Chopra is from Davies, R. and Rushe, D., 'Facebook to Pay $5bn Fine as Regulator Settles Cambridge Analytica Complaint', *Guardian*, 24 July 2019.

The publication Nigel and I discussed was Information Commissioner's Office, 'Investigation into the Use of Data Analytics in Political Campaigns: A Report to Parliament', 6 November 2018.

Chapter Three: Collective Consciousness

The Google usage statistics are from a compilation by SEOTribunal.com: https://seotribunal.com/blog/google-stats-and-facts/.

The 'most important data set ever collected on the human psyche' quote is from Stephens-Davidowitz, S., (2018), Kindle edition, Loc 224.

The Screwfix demand taxonomy case study is described at https://www.taxonomics.co.uk/clients/screwfix/taxonomy/.

The parrot cages story was part of Hitwise folklore, and my version almost certainly reflects the embellishments that come from multiple retellings. More objective accounts include Fiona Graham's 'Searching the Internet's Long Tail and Finding Parrot Cages' for BBC News (https://www.bbc.com/news/business-11495839) and Steph Welstead's profile of Neil Hutchinson (https://web.archive.org/web/20170927052958/http://startups.co.uk/forward-neil-hutchinson).

Sources for the quotes and statistics on WorldStores are as follows:
- Cellan-Jones, R., 'WorldStores – Searching for Retail Success', BBC News, 31 March 2011.
- Wilson, A., 'WorldStores founders build furniture megastore', Daily Telegraph, 16 October 2012.
- Casey, D., 'Dunelm swoops for £100m turnover retailer', Insider Media, 28 November 2016.

Pug Insurance

The article about Bought By Many pug insurance is Solon, O., 'Bought By Many uses crowd clout to negotiate cheaper pug insurance', Wired, 21 February 2013.

Data points about Ping An come from the 'Company Profile' section of its English-language corporate website: : https://group.pingan.com/about_us/who_we_are.html.

ArchDaily has a list of the world's tallest skyscrapers at: https://www.archdaily.com/779178/these-are-the-worlds-25-tallest-buildings.

The unusual products which were a feature of Chinese insurance until 2017 are described in articles by Will Coldwell for the Guardian (https://www.theguardian.com/travel/2014/mar/19/chinese-smog-insurance-ctrip-travel-agency-air-pollution-policies) and Don Weinland for the Financial Times (https://www.ft.com/content/bee51a52-accd-11e6-9cb3-bb820790 2122). Yuan Yang subsequently wrote about the regulatory clampdown in the Financial Times: https://www.ft.com/content/6c4e4ea6-d263-11e6-9341-7393bb2e1b51.

Sophie Loras's story for ClickZ, 'China's Ping An Leverages Social Data to Personalize Travel Insurance', summarises Bought By Many's work with Ping An: https://www.clickz.com/chinas-ping-an-leverages-social-data-to-personalize-travel-insurance/24990/.

Chapter Four: Data Abundance

Diane's book is *GDP: A Brief but Affectionate History*, Princeton University Press, Princeton, 2014.

Google Trends can be used to recreate the comparison of R and MATLAB: https://trends.google.co.uk/trends/explore?date=all&geo=GB&q=%2Fm%2F0212jm,%2Fm%2F053_x.

Sophie Coley's blogs using AnswerThePublic Data can be found at https://searchlistening.com/.

The examples from *Everybody Lies* are at Stephens-Davidowitz, S., (2018), Kindle edition, Loc 210, 1361ff, 1614.

The academic papers authored or co-authored by Nicola Bragazzi are:

- Alicino, C., Bragazzi, N. L., Faccio, V. et al., 'Assessing Ebola-Related Web Search Behaviour: Insights and Implications from an Analytical Study of Google Trends-Based Query Volumes', *Infectious Diseases of Poverty*, 4, 54, 2015.
- Bragazzi, N. L., Alicino, C., Trucchi, C., Paganino, C., Barberis, I., Martini, M., et al., 'Global Reaction to the Recent Outbreaks of Zika Virus: Insights from a Big Data Analysis', *PLoS ONE*, 12(9), 2017, e0185263.
- Bragazzi, N. L., Bacigaluppi, S., Robba, C., Siri, A., Canepa, G., Brigo, F., 'Infodemiological Data of West-Nile Virus Disease in Italy in the Study Period 2004–2015', *Data in Brief*, Vol. 9, 2016, pp. 839–45.
- Bragazzi, N. L., Tramalloni, D., Valle, I., 'The Angelina Jolie Effect and the Increase in the Breast Cancer Screening-Related Internet Activities', *European Journal of Public Health*, Vol. 25, Issue suppl_3, 2015.
- Bragazzi, N. L., 'A Google Trends-based approach for monitoring NSSI', *Psychol Res Behav Manag*. Vol. 7, 2014, pp. 1–8.
- Bragazzi, N. L., Dini, G., Toletone, A., Brigo, F., Durando, P., 'Leveraging Big Data for Exploring Occupational Diseases-Related Interest at the Level of Scientific Community, Media Coverage and Novel Data Streams: The Example of Silicosis as a Pilot Study', *PLoS ONE* 11(11), 2016, e0166051.

Eeva Koutaniemi and Elina Einiö's paper is Koutaniemi, E. M., and Einiö, E., 'Seasonal Variation in Seeking Help for Domestic Violence Based on

Google Search Data and Finnish Police Calls in 2017', *Scandinavian Journal of Public Health*, 2019.

The pre-print paper which looks at evacuation search during natural disasters is Yabe, T., Tsubouchi, K., Shimizu, T., Sekimoto, Y., Ukkusuri, S., (2019), 'Predicting Evacuation Decisions using Representations of Individuals' Pre-Disaster Web Search Behavior', *KDD*, August 2019.

For an example of search data being used to forecast migration patterns, see Böhme, M. H., Gröger, A., Stöhr, T., 'Searching for a Better Life: Predicting International Migration with Online Search Keywords', *Journal of Development Economics*, Vol. 142, 2020, 102347.

The Strange Death of Jumpshot

Privacy experts might point out that there is no such thing as 'anonymised' data and that what I mean is 'de-identified'. That's fair enough; with time, additional data sets and the right expertise, it is indeed theoretically possible to figure out someone's identity from their behavioural data. However, in practice it's a highly uneconomical thing to do, so nobody does it – except to prove the point that it's possible.

On the events surrounding Jumpshot's closure, see Koebler J., 'Avast Antivirus Is Shutting Down its Data Collection Arm, Effective Immediately', *Vice*, 30 January 2020.

For a discussion of the Jumpshot closure, including the implications for other analytics companies and antitrust action against Google, see Rand Fishkin's blog 'Avast's Shutdown of Jumpshot Will Harm the Web and the World', at https://sparktoro.com/blog/avasts-shutdown-of-jumpshot-will-harm-the-web-and-the-world/.

Avast publicly discussed the privacy implications of its acquisition of Jumpshot in its user forum (https://forum.avast.com/index.php?topic =171725.0) and blog (https://blog.avast.com/2015/05/29/avast-data-drives-new-analytics-engine/).

The Ben Thompson and James Allworth quote is from Episode 148 of their podcast *Exponent*, 'Facebook Fatigue', 22:39.

On organ donation rates by country, see Arshad, A. et al., 'Comparison of Organ Donation and Transplantation Rates between Opt-Out and Opt-In Systems', *Clinical Investigation*, Vol. 95, Issue 6, 2019, pp. 1453–60.

Open Banking

For more examples of open banking apps, see Warwick-Ching, L., 'Open Banking: The Quiet Digital Revolution One Year On', *Financial Times*, 10 January 2019.

Open Data

Many of the open data examples are drawn from the Open Data Handbook (https://opendatahandbook.org/value-stories/en/business-and-open-data/), and the Open Data Institute's 'Knowledge & Opinion' resource, where the quote from Citymapper appears: https://theodi.org/article/citymapper-exec-utive-to-governments-open-more-data-so-we-can-improve-your-cities.

Citymapper statistics are from Arianne Cohen's profile of Azmat Yusuf, 'The Guy Making Public Transit Smarter', *Bloomberg Businessweek*, 26 March 2018.

There is more about the role of open data in Cambodia in Pilorge, N., Yeng, V. and Eang, V., 'Think of Cambodia Before You Add Sugar to Your Coffee', *Guardian*, 12 July 2013.

Properati's plane tree app can be downloaded from https://blog.prope-rati.com.ar/properati-tools/, and the Buenos Aires tree census data it draws on from https://data.buenosaires.gob.ar/dataset/arbolado-publico-lineal.

Opportunity Insights' interactive tools, data sets, reports and video lectures are available via https://opportunityinsights.org/. The process Raj Chetty and Emmanuel Saez went through to get access to tax record data is described by Jeff Mervis in an article for *Science* magazine: https://www.sciencemag.org/news/2014/05/how-two-economists-got-direct-access-irs-tax-records. Other Opportunity Insights data points come from:

- Matthews, D., 'The Radical Plan to Change How Harvard Teaches Economics', *Vox*, 22 May 2019.
- Cook, G., 'The Economist Who Would Fix the American Dream', *The Atlantic*, 17 July 2019.
- Chetty, R. 'Visualizing the American Dream', *Talks at Google*, 12 December 2018.

Search Data against Coronavirus

The Infodemiology chapter of the *Coronavirus Tech Handbook* is at https://coronavirustechhandbook.com/infodemiology. It contains links to Bill Lampos's working paper, Patrick Berlinquette's interactive tools and Seth

Stephens-Davidowitz's *New York Times* op-ed, as well as the data sets Sophie and I uploaded.

Patrick's writing about using search data to understand heroin use, high school shootings and Covid-19 can be accessed via his profile page on OneZero: https://onezero.medium.com/@patrickberlinquette

The death of Tanzanian MPs was reported by Aljazeera (https://www. aljazeera.com/news/2020/05/tanzania-opposition-mps-boycott-parlia- ment-3-mps-die-200502055621809.html), night burials were reported by the BBC (https://www.bbc.com/news/world-africa-52505375) and John Magu- fuli's comments about the ineffectiveness of testing kits by the *Independent* (https://www.independent.co.uk/news/world/africa/coronavirus-tanzania- test-kits-suspicion-goat-pawpaw-positive-a9501291.html).

The academic paper which critiques Google Flu Trends is Lazer, D., Kennedy, R., King, G. and Vespignani, A., 'The Parable of Google Flu: Traps in Big Data Analysis.' *Science* 343 (6176), 2014, pp. 1203–5.

My paper with Roberto and Mark is: Foa, R. S., Gilbert, S. and Fabian, M., 'COVID-19 and Subjective Well-Being: Separating the Effects of Lockdowns from the Pandemic', Bennett Institute for Public Policy, Cambridge, 2020.

Chapter Five: It's Not All About 'Us'

This chapter greatly benefited from Dr Stephanie Diepeveen's seminar series 'Africa's Digital Communications Revolution: State, Publics, Power and Politics', and Dr Justin Pearce's lectures and seminars on the politics of Africa during the 2018–19 academic year at Cambridge. I am also grateful to David Garcia for drawing attention to the ways in which the Philippines bears the externalities of social media use in the West at the LSE & Oxford Internet Institute 'Connected Life' conference in 2019.

Statistics about Henry Olonga's cricketing career are from his player page on ESPN Cricinfo: https://www.espncricinfo.com/zimbabwe/content/ player/55675.html. The account of the armband protest draws on his memoir (Olonga, H., *Blood, Sweat and Treason: My Story*, Vision Sports Publishing, Kingston, 2010), an interview he gave in 2015 (https://www. youtube.com/watch?v=7W68J6v8gw0) and a BBC Sport retrospective (https://www.bbc.com/sport/cricket/21359274). The text of Olonga and Flower's statement is in a *Guardian* archive of the 2003 Cricket World Cup: https://www.theguardian.com/sport/2003/feb/10/cricketworldcup2003. cricketworldcup11

Evan Mawarire's original #ThisFlag video can be viewed at https://www.youtube.com/watch?v=xPSw-hSBlrY. The 2016 *BBC News* story 'Zimbabwe Shutdown: What Is Behind the Protests?' describes the protests Mawarire inspired: https://www.bbc.com/news/world-africa-36776401.

For an analysis of social media-enabled protest in Zimbabwe, see Gukurume, S., '#ThisFlag and #ThisGown Cyber Protests in Zimbabwe: Reclaiming Political Space.' *African Journalism Studies* 38, no. 2, 2017, pp. 49–70. On Baba Jukwa, see Karekwaivanane, G., 'Tapanduka Zvamuchese': Facebook, 'Unruly Publics' and Zimbabwean Politics.' *Journal of Eastern African Studies* 13, 1, 2018. On Robert Mugabe's governing style, see Levitsky, S. and Way. L. A., *Competitive Authoritarianism: Hybrid Regimes After the Cold War*, Cambridge University Press, Cambridge, 2010, pp. 239–47.

There are many accounts of the role of social media in the Arab Spring. I have mainly relied on Aouragh, M. and Alexander, A., 'The Arab Spring: The Egyptian Experience: Sense and Nonsense of the Internet Revolution.' *International Journal of Communication* 5, 2011, pp. 1344–58, and Bellin, E., 'Reconsidering the Robustness of Authoritarianism: Lessons of the Arab Spring', *Comparative Politics*, 44, 2, 2012, pp. 127–49.

The unintended consequences of #BringBackOurGirls are highlighted in Maxfield, M., 'History Retweeting Itself: Imperial Feminist Appropriations of "Bring Back Our Girls"', *Feminist Media Studies* 16, no. 5, 2016, pp. 886–900.

The Henry Olonga quote is from a retrospective interview on the armband protest with Martin Williamson for ESPN CricInfo, 'Standing Up for Their Principles', https://www.espncricinfo.com/story/_/id/22830886/standing-their-principles.

Zeynep Tufekci's book is Tufekci, Z., *Twitter and Tear Gas: The Power and Fragility of Networked Protest*, Yale University Press, New Haven, 2017.

Statistics on Facebook users by country are from the data aggregators Statista ('Leading countries based on number of Facebook users', https://www.statista.com/statistics/268136/top-15-countries-based-on-number-of-facebook-users/) and Internet World Stats ('Internet User Statistics', https://www.internetworldstats.com/stats.htm).

The data source for my analysis of the transfer of value between Facebook users in different regions of the world is 'Facebook Q4 2018 Results', available at https://s21.q4cdn.com/399680738/files/doc_financials/2018/Q4/Q4-2018-Earnings-Presentation.pdf

The references to John Rawls are from Rawls, J., *A Theory of Justice*, Belknap Press, Cambridge, 2005, p. 83, and Rawls, J., *The Law of Peoples*, Harvard University Press, Cambridge, 1999, p. 37.

My comparative analysis of advertising- and subscription-based business models draws on various sources, including:

- Facebook Q4 2018 Results
- World Bank (2016), 'Adjusted net national income per capita in current US$', World Development Indicators, https://data.worldbank.org/indicator/NY.ADJ.NNTY.PC.CD
- Comparitech summary of Netflix pricing, referenced in Clark, T., 'How Much Netflix Costs in Different Countries Around the World, and Which Ones Get the Best Deal?', *Business Insider*, 12 September 2018.
- eMarketer (2016), 'Paid Netflix Subscribers in Select Countries/ Regions', https://www.emarketer.com/Chart/Paid-Netflix-Subscribers-Select-CountriesRegions-Dec-2011-Dec-2015-thousands/173523.
- 'Number of Amazon Prime Video subscribers worldwide from 2016 to 2020, by region', aggregated by Statista at https://www.statista.com/statistics/693936/global-number-of-amazon-prime-video-subscribers-region.
- Apple Inc. Investor Relations 'Q4 2018 Unaudited Summary Data', https://www.apple.com/newsroom/pdfs/Q4-18-Data-Summary.pdf.

On the 'fog' created by political moralising, see Runciman, D., 'Political Theory and Real Politics in the Age of the Internet', *The Journal of Political Philosophy*: Vol. 25, No. 1, 2017, pp. 3–21.

Apple's Supply Chain

The Apple supply chain is analysed in Clarke, T., Boersma, M., 'The Governance of Global Value Chains: Unresolved Human Rights, Environmental and Ethical Dilemmas in the Apple Supply Chain', *Journal of Business Ethics*, 143, 2017, pp. 111–31.

Foxconn's plant at Longhua and Pegatron's in Shanghai are described respectively in:

- Merchant, B., 'Life and Death in Apple's Forbidden City', *Guardian*, 18 June 2017.
- Oster, S., 'Inside One of the World's Most Secretive iPhone Factories', Bloomberg, 25 April 2016.

Two reports in Quartz provide data points on pay, overtime and working conditions at Foxconn facilities, and on Apple's response to child labour:

Bhattacharya, A., 'Apple Is Under Fire for "Excessive Overtime" and Illegal Working Conditions in Another Chinese Factory' *Quartz*, 26 August 2016; and Fernholz, T. (2014), 'What Happens When Apple Finds a Child Making Your iPhone', *Quartz*, 7 March 2014.

China Labor Watch's findings were reported in Fullerton, J., 'Suicide at Chinese iPhone Factory Reignites Concern Over Working Conditions', *Daily Telegraph*, 7 January 2018.

The BBC *Panorama* episode referenced is 'Apple's Broken Promises', aired on BBC One on 18 December 2016.

Apple's 'Supplier Responsibility Center' is here: https://www.apple.com/supplier-responsibility.

The world's major cobalt refineries are listed at https://www.thebalance.com/the-biggest-cobalt-producers-2339726. Conditions in cobalt mines in the Congo are described by the Harvard researcher Siddharth Kara in the *Guardian*: https://www.theguardian.com/global-development/2018/oct/12/phone-misery-children-congo-cobalt-mines-drc.

On coltan mining in the Congo, see Smith, J. H., 'Tantalus in the Digital Age: Coltan Ore, Temporal Dispossession and "Movement" in the Eastern Democratic Republic of the Congo', *American Ethnologist* 38, no. 1, 2011, pp. 17–35. An interactive map of coltan mines is available from the International Peace Information Service: https://www.ipis-research.be/mapping/webmapping/drcongo/v5/#-1.2214940237301164/28.6591796876304/6/2/1/.

For further data points on cobalt and coltan, see O'Brien, C., 'Your Smartphone Is a Mine of Precious Metals and Elements', *Irish Times*, 19 April 2018.

Shoshana Zuboff refers to 'rogue capitalism' on five occasions in *The Age of Surveillance Capitalism*, Kindle edition, Loc 27, 362, 2059, 8442, 9434.

Moderation in All Things

Accenture sizes the global content moderation labour force in its brochure 'Content Moderation: The Future is Bionic' available at https://www.accenture.com/cz-en/_acnmedia/PDF-47/Accenture-Webscale-New-Content-Moderation-POV.pdf. TaskUs's global office locations are listed at https://jobs.jobvite.com/taskus-inc/.

Recruitment and pay for content moderators in Manila is discussed in Season Four, Episode Four of the IRL podcast, 'The Human Costs of

Content Moderation'. The *Washington Post* article 'Content Moderators at YouTube, Facebook and Twitter See the Worst of the Web – and Suffer Silently' (24 July 2019) describes the emotional and psychological costs.

Data points on Rodrigo Duterte's war on drugs are from:

- Etter, L., 'What Happens When the Government Uses Facebook as a Weapon?', *Bloomberg Businessweek*, 7 December 2017.
- 'Profile: Duterte the controversial "strongman" of the Philippines', *BBC News*, 22 May 2019.
- Johnson, H. and Giles, C., 'Philippines Drug War: Do We Know How Many Have Died?', *BBC News*, 12 November 2019.
- Alba, D., 'How Duterte Used Facebook To Fuel The Philippine Drug War', *Buzzfeed News*, 4 September 2018.

On the Rohingya ethnic cleansing in Myanmar, see:

- Habib, M., Jubb, C., Ahmad, S., Rahman, M. and Pallard, H., 'Forced Migration of Rohingya: An Untold Experience', Ontario International Development Agency, 2018.
- Human Rights Watch, 'Myanmar: Crimes Against Rohingya Go Unpunished', https://www.hrw.org/news/2019/08/22/myanmar-crimes-against-rohingya-go-unpunished.
- Amnesty International (2018), 'Military top brass must face justice for crimes against humanity targeting Rohingya', https://www.amnesty.org/en/latest/news/2018/06/myanmar-military-top-brass-must-face-justice-for-crimes-against-humanity-targeting-rohingya/

The deprecation of Facebook Graph Search and its implications for Open-Source Intelligence are discussed in Silverman, C., 'Facebook Turned Off Search Features Used to Catch War Criminals, Child Predators and Other Bad Actors', *Buzzfeed News*, 10 June 2019.

Sam Dubberley's quote is from his op-ed 'How Facebook's sudden change hinders human rights investigations', Amnesty International, https://www.amnesty.org/en/latest/news/2019/06/how-facebooks-sudden-change-hinders-human-rights-investigations.

The BBC Africa Eye episode 'Anatomy of a Killing' can be viewed at https://www.youtube.com/watch?v=XbnLkc6r3yc. Amnesty International's account of the investigation is at https://www.amnesty.org/en/latest/news/2018/09/digitally-dissecting-atrocities-amnesty-internationals-open-source-investigations/.

Chapter Six: Taking Over the Panopticon

This chapter greatly benefited from conversations with Dr Amanda Greene at University College London about the nature of digital power.

The stories of Bentham's life are from the lecture by Dr Christopher Meckstroth in Cambridge on 7 November 2018, which is described later in the chapter.

On self-driving car regulation in Germany, see Gershgorn, D., 'Germany's Self-driving Car Ethicists: All Lives Matter', *Quartz*, 24 August 2017. For more on self-driving cars and utilitarianism, see Chapter Nine.

Jeremy Bentham's description of the Panopticon is available via the Online Library of Liberty: https://oll.libertyfund.org/titles/bentham-the-works-of-jeremy-bentham-vol-4/simple#lf0872-04_head_010.

Long-reads on social media as a Panopticon include:

- Chu, A., 'The Social Web and the Digital Panopticon', *TechCrunch*, 18 October 2015.
- McMullan, T., 'What Does the Panopticon Mean in the Age of Digital Surveillance?', *Guardian*, 23 July 2015.

Is Facebook a Panopticon?

The *Newsweek* headline is from Baker, K., 'Facebook's Online Panopticon', *Newsweek*, 1 October 2012.

The Orwell quotes are from Orwell, G. *Nineteen Eighty-Four*, Signet Classics, New York, 1949.

The Foucault references are from:

- Foucault, M. and Sheridan, A., *Discipline and Punish: The Birth of the Prison*, Vintage Books, New York, 1995.
- 'Two Lectures' in Foucault, M., *Power/Knowledge: Selected Interviews and Other Writings, 1972–7*, Harvester, Brighton, 1980.
- Patton, P., 'Taylor and Foucault on Power and Freedom', *Political Studies*, XXXVII, 1989, pp. 260–76.
- Fornet-Betancourt, R., Becker, H., Gomez-Müller, A. and Gauthier, J. D., 'The Ethic of Care for the Self as a Practice of Freedom: An Interview with Michel Foucault on 20 January 1984', *Philosophy & Social Criticism*, 12(2–3), 1987, pp. 112–31.

On surveillance in early modern Europe, see Gorski, P. S., 'The Protestant Ethic Revisited: Disciplinary Revolution and State Formation in Holland and Prussia', *American Journal of Sociology*, Vol. 99, No. 2, 1993, pp. 265–316.

On the Beacon controversy, see:

- Taplin, J. T., *Move Fast and Break Things: How Facebook, Google and Amazon Have Cornered Culture and What It Means for All of Us*, Macmillan, London, 2017.
- Doyle, W. and Fraser, M., 'Facebook, Surveillance and Power' in Wittkower, D. (ed.) *Facebook and Philosophy: What's On Your Mind?*, Open Court Publishing Company, Chicago, 2010, pp. 222–3.
- Scharding, T., *This Is Business Ethics: An Introduction*, Wiley, London, 2018, p. 167.

Is Google a Panopticon?

Statistics on the numbers of users of Google Analytics, Google Ads and YouTube channels are from marketingland.com (https://marketingland.com/as-google-analytics-turns-10-we-ask-how-many-websites-use-it-151892) and Tubics (https://www.tubics.com/blog/number-of-youtube-channels). Newspaper circulation numbers are aggregated by Statista at https://www.statista.com/statistics/184682/us-daily-newspapers-by-circulation. Smartphone usage statistics are from Ofcom (2018), 'A Decade of Digital Dependency', https://www.ofcom.org.uk/about-ofcom/latest/media/media-releases/2018/decade-of-digital-dependency and Bank of America (2018), 'Trends in Community Mobility'.

Cambridge Power

The review of Cambridge's Seeley Historical Library that dissed the mechanical competence of humanities students is Banham, R., 'Reyner Banham Reviews James Stirling's Cambridge History Faculty', *The Architectural Review*, 14 November 1968.

Selfie deaths are analysed in Bansal, A., Garg, C., Pakhare, A. and Gupta, S., 'Selfies: A Boon or Bane?', *Journal of Family Medicine and Primary Care*, 7(4), 2018, pp. 828–31. The points of comparison with other causes of deaths is informed by the Florida Museum's 'International Shark Attack File': https://www.floridamuseum.ufl.edu/shark-attacks/odds/compare-risk/death.

Market Power

Statistics on lobbying spend by tech companies are from Kang, C. and Vogel, K. P., 'Tech Giants Amass a Lobbying Army for an Epic Washington Battle', *New York Times*, 5 June 2019.

Mike Moloney describes the ways Google featured snippets are detrimental to FilterGrade in this Twitter thread: https://twitter.com/moloneymike/status/1249865960338661377.

Google's vertical integration-enabling acquisitions are summarised in *Search Engine Watch* (https://www.searchenginewatch.com/2016/02/23/google-to-close-its-financial-comparison-service/) and *Wired* (https://www.wired.com/2011/04/google-ita/).

The European Commission's investigation into anti-competitive conduct by Apple was announced at https://ec.europa.eu/commission/presscorner/detail/en/IP_19_4291, and summarised by *TechCrunch* (https://techcrunch.com/2019/05/06/eu-will-reportedly-investigate-apple/).

Reach Power
Freedom House's website lists countries that are 'Not Free': https://freedomhouse.org/countries/freedom-world/scores?sort=asc&order=Total%20Score%20and%20Status.

Chapter Seven: Tech CEO Hubris

On Elizabeth Holmes, see Friedell, D., 'A Chemistry Is Performed', *London Review of Books*, Vol. 41, No. 3, 2019, and Carreyou, J., *Bad Blood: Secrets and Lies in a Silicon Valley Start-up*, Picador, London, 2018. Theranos funding and valuation statistics are from Marketwatch (https://www.marketwatch.com/story/the-investors-duped-by-the-theranos-fraud-never-asked-for-one-important-thing-2018-03-19) and Investopedia (https://www.investopedia.com/articles/investing/020116/theranos-fallen-unicorn.asp).

Adam Neumann's eccentricities are documented in Brown, E., 'How Adam Neumann's Over-the-Top Style Built WeWork: "This Is Not the Way Everybody Behaves"', *Wall Street Journal*, 18 September 2019, and Platt, E. and Edgecliffe-Johnson, A., 'WeWork: How the Ultimate Unicorn Lost Its Billions', *Financial Times*, 19 February 2020.

WeWork's mission statement is available on the company's corporate website: https://www.wework.com/newsroom/posts/wecompany.

WeWork's valuation at the time of its rescue by Softbank is per CNBC (https://www.cnbc.com/2020/05/18/softbank-ceo-calls-wework-investment-foolish-valuation-falls-to-2point9-billion.html). Comparative valuations of Tesco and Barclays are from https://lsemarketcap.com/ as at 29 May 2020.

Statistics on room dividers and oak flooring are from the cover story in the July 2018 issue of *Wired*, 'How WeWork Became the Most Hyped Start-up in the World'.

Neumann's leaked comments about his plans for his descendants to control WeWork were reported by Connie Loizos in *TechCrunch* (https://techcrunch.com/2019/10/18/adam-neumann-planned-for-his-children-and-grandchildren-to-control-wework/?guccounter=1).

SpaceX's mission statement can be viewed at the company's website: https://www.spacex.com/human-spaceflight/mars/. Elon Musk's quote on humanity as a 'multiplanet species' is from an interview with Chris Anderson at the TED conference, 'The Future We're Building – and Boring', the transcript of which is available at https://www.ted.com/talks/elon_musk_the_future_we_re_building_and_boring/transcript. On his interest in brain-computer interfaces, see footage of the Neuralink launch event at https://www.youtube.com/watch?v=r-vbh3t7WVI&feature=youtu.be; and on flamethrowers see https://www.boringcompany.com/not-a-flamethrower.

Anti-ageing investee companies of Bezos, Thiel, and Page and Brin include:
- Unity Biotechnology: https://unitybiotechnology.com/the-science/.
- Calico Labs: https://www.calicolabs.com/.
- Alcor Life Extension Foundation: https://alcor.org/FAQs/faq01.html#friends.

Billionaire milestone data is from Elkins, K., 'The Age When 17 Self-Made Billionaires Earned Their First Million', *Business Insider*, 11 February 2016 and Levy, L., 'How Steve Jobs Became a Billionaire', *Fortune*, 19 October 2016.

A summary of DARPA's role in building the foundations for the internet is available at https://www.darpa.mil/about-us/timeline/modern-internet.

On government subsidies to big tech companies, see Rushe, D., 'US Cities and States Give Big Tech \$9.3bn in Subsidies in Five Years', *Guardian*, 2 July 2018.

Thomas Piketty's book is *Capital in the Twenty-First Century*, Harvard University Press, Cambridge, 2014.

Linsey McGoey's book is *No Such Thing as a Free Gift: The Gates Foundation and the Price of Philanthropy*, Verso, London, 2015. For an overview of her critique of philanthrocapitalism, see McGoey, L., 'The Philanthropy Hustle', *Jacobin Magazine*, 10 November 2015.

Data on the Gates Foundation's trustees and endowment is from its website: https://www.gatesfoundation.org/who-we-are/general-information/foundation-factsheet.

Zuckian Liberalism

On the history, genealogy and definition of liberalism, see Freeden, M., *Liberalism: A Very Short Introduction*, Oxford University Press, Oxford, 2015; Fawcett, E., *Liberalism: The Life of an Idea*, Princeton University Press, Princeton, 2014; and Bell, D., 'What Is Liberalism?' *Political Theory*, 42(6), 2014, pp. 682–715.

The Zuckerberg Files digital archive is at https://www.zuckerbergfiles. org/. The transcripts cited are as follows:

- Zuckerberg, M. (2017a), 'Building Global Community', *Zuckerberg Transcripts*, 989.
- Dubner, S. and Zuckerberg, M. (2018), 'MZ Interview with Stephen Dubner on Freakonomics', *Zuckerberg Transcripts*, 859.
- Zuckerberg, M. (2015d), 'A Letter to Our Daughter', *Zuckerberg Transcripts*, 498.
- Zuckerberg, M. (2018a), 'MZ shares focus of FB goals in 2018', *Zuckerberg Transcripts*, 792.
- Facebook Investor Relations (2018), 'Facebook Q2 2018 Earnings', *Zuckerberg Transcripts*, 863.
- Klein, E., Zuckerberg, M. and *Vox* (2018). 'Mark Zuckerberg on Facebook's Hardest Year, and What Comes Next', *Zuckerberg Transcripts*, 950.
- Zuckerberg, M. (2016c), 'Facebook & Conservatives', *Zuckerberg Transcripts*, 865.
- Zuckerberg, M. (2016d), 'Voting in the 2016 Elections', *Zuckerberg Transcripts*, 621.
- Zuckerberg, M. (2016e), 'Zuckerberg Facebook Post about Social Feeds – 2016-09-06', *Zuckerberg Transcripts*, 217.
- Facebook, (2018b), 'Hard Questions: Q&A With MZ on Protecting People's Information', *Zuckerberg Transcripts*, 1002.
- Zuckerberg, M. (2019a), '2019 – Live at F8!', *Zuckerberg Transcripts*, 1010.
- Zuckerberg, M. (2018b), 'MZ Interview with Kara Swisher', *Zuckerberg Transcripts*, 949.
- Zuckerberg, M. (2017a), 'Live with Dreamers at My Home', *Zuckerberg Transcripts*, 992.
- Zuckerberg, M. (2017c), 'Announcing Facebook Communities Summit', *Zuckerberg Transcripts*, 713.
- Zuckerberg, M. (2017d), 'MZ w/ Muslim Students in Dearborn, MI', *Zuckerberg Transcripts*.

- Zuckerberg, M. (2016f), '#ProfilesForPeace', *Zuckerberg Transcripts*, 553.
- Zuckerberg, M. (2016d), 'Responding to Marc Andreessen's Comments About Facebook & India', *Zuckerberg Transcripts*, 535.
- Zuckerberg, M. (2015b), 'A Year of Books: *The Better Angels of our Nature*', *Zuckerberg Transcripts*, 371.
- Zuckerberg, M. (2018c), 'MZ shares article by Steven Pinker "The Enlightenment Is Working"', *Zuckerberg Transcripts*, 796.
- Zuckerberg, M. (2015c), 'A Year of Books: *Sapiens*', *Zuckerberg Transcripts*, 423.
- Zuckerberg, M. and Harari, Y. N. (2019), 'A Conversation with Mark Zuckerberg and Yuval Noah Harari', *Zuckerberg Transcripts*, 1011.
- Zuckerberg, M. (2019b), 'MZ discussion with Jonathan Zittrain', *Zuckerberg Transcripts*, 1007.
- Facebook (2014), 'Discussion on Acquisition of WhatsApp Conference Call', *Zuckerberg Transcripts*, 242. This is the earliest record of the phrase 'global community' in Zuckerberg's discourse.
- Facebook, 'Facebook Q1 2016 Earnings Call' (2016a), *Zuckerberg Transcripts*, 227.
- Zuckerberg, M. (2017b), 'MZ Post – Funding Philanthropy', *Zuckerberg Transcripts*, 756.
- Zuckerberg, M. (2016b), 'Note from Mark Zuckerberg', *Zuckerberg Transcripts*, 245.
- Zuckerberg, M. (2017b) 'Protecting the Security and Integrity of Our Services', *Zuckerberg Transcripts*, 645.
- Zuckerberg, M. (2018a), 'MZ shares a note – A Blueprint for Content Governance and Enforcement', *Zuckerberg Transcripts*, 857.

The Naughton quote is from Naughton, J., 'Mark Zuckerberg Should Try Living in the Real World', *Guardian*, 7 May 2017.

Zuboff's comments on 'Building Global Community' are at Zuboff (2019), Kindle edition, Loc 7313–57.

On Hegel's view of history, see Singer, P., *Hegel*, Oxford University Press, Oxford, 1983, Kindle Edition, Chapter 2.

On pluralism, see Berlin, I., Hardy, H. and Margalit, A., *The Power of Ideas*, Princeton University Press, Princeton, 2016, pp. 14–7; Nussbaum, M.C., *Creating Capabilities*, 2011, Kindle edition, Loc 224, 839, 1153.

On 'overlapping consensus', see Rawls (2005), pp. 388ff.

References to John Stuart Mill's 'On Liberty' are from Mill et al., *On*

Liberty, Utilitarianism and Other Essays, new edition, Oxford University Press, Oxford, 2015, pp. 8, 13, 15, 19, 50–2, 53ff.

The internal memo in which Andrew Bosworth refers to Rawls's original position was republished in the *New York Times*, 7 January 2020.

Zuboff's quote on WhatsApp data flows is from Zuboff (2019), Kindle edition, Loc 1878.

Karpian Realism

For an account of Edward Snowden's revelations see Greenwald, G. and MacAskill, E., 'NSA Prism Program Taps in to User Data of Apple, Google and Others', *Guardian*, 6 June 2013.

Eric Schmidt's comments on competition with China on 5G are from *The New Tech Cold War*, BBC Radio 4, 19 June 2020.

On Project Maven, see 'What is Project Maven? The Pentagon AI Project Google Employees Want Out Of', Global News, 5 April 2018.

The features and uses of Palantir's Gotham and Foundry products are outlined on the company's website at https://www.palantir.com/products/. For a product comparison with Palantir's competitors in the Business Intelligence software category, see Gartner's summary of customer reviews: https://www.gartner.com/reviews/market/analytics-business-intelligence-platforms.

For commentary on Palantir's more controversial contracts, see:

- US Immigration and Customs Enforcement (ICE): Woodman, S., 'Palantir Provides the Engine for Donald Trump's Deportation Machine', *The Intercept*, 2 March 2017.
- Relationship with the Trump administration: Sorkin, A. R., 'Why Tech's Split with Trump Could Set the Country Back', *New York Times*, 3 September 2018.
- Predictive policing: Winston, A., 'Palantir Has Secretly Been Using New Orleans to Test Its Predictive Policing Technology', *The Verge*, 27 February 2018.
- NHS: No Tech For Tyrants (2020), 'The Corona Contracts: Public-Private Partnerships and the Need for Transparency', https://privacy international.org/long-read/3977/corona-contracts-public-private-partnerships-and-need-transparency.

The sources for quotes and claims by Alex Karp are:

- 'Alex Karp, CEO of the Data-Mining Company Palantir, Reflects on His Career and What Led Him to Create software that is Used by the CIA, FBI and Others', https://charlierose.com/videos/12809, 11 August 2009.

- 'Interview: Alex Karp, Founder and CEO of Palantir', *TechCrunch*, 2012: https://www.youtube.com/watch?v=VJFk8oGTEs4&t=1s.
- 'Palantir CEO Alex Karp: Investors Will Be "Positively Surprised" At The Company's Margins', CNBC, 2018: https://www.youtube.com/watch?v=QwoCgLvoUvs.
- 'Palantir CEO Karp on Silicon Valley, ICE, 2020 Election', Bloomberg Politics, 2019: https://www.youtube.com/watch?v=1zHUXGd4gJU&t=97.
- 'Palantir Technologies CEO Alex Karp Joins CNBC's Andrew Ross Sorkin to Discuss the Company's Contract with ICE, How he Thinks About the Apple Privacy Debate, and its Plan to IPO', CNBC, 2020: https://www.youtube.com/watch?v=MeL4BWVk5-k.

Chapter Eight: Digital Legitimacy

For an extended definition of legitimacy, see Peter, F., 'Political Legitimacy', *The Stanford Encyclopedia of Philosophy*, Edward N. Zalta (ed.), 2017.

The distinction between input legitimacy and output legitimacy originates in the work of Fritz Scharpf. See Steffek, J., 'The Output Legitimacy of International Organizations and the Global Public Interest', *International Theory*, 7:2, 2015, pp. 263–93, 266–7.

On legitimacy versus justice, see Rawls, J., *Political Liberalism*, Columbia University Press, New York, 2005, pp. 225–6.

To compare countries' GDP to tech companies market capitalisation, see International Monetary Fund, 'World Economic Outlook Database', https://www.imf.org/external/pubs/ft/weo/2019/01/weodata/index.aspx. As at 31 December 2018, Facebook's market cap was $541 billion, comparable to the nominal GDP of Sweden ($551 billion) and Belgium ($533 billion).

The Zuckerberg quote about Facebook being 'like a government' is from Klein, E., Zuckerberg, M. and *Vox* (2018).

For a summary of David Ciepley's argument, see Ciepley, D., 'Beyond Public and Private: Toward a Political Theory of the Corporation', *The American Political Science Review*, Vol. 107, No. 1, 2013, pp. 139–58.

On Facebook's experiment with allowing users to vote on policy changes see Facebook (2009), 'Facebook Opens Governance of Service and Policy Process to Users', https://newsroom.fb.com/news/2009/02/facebook-opens-governance-of-service-and-policy-process-to-users/. For the critique, see Farrell, H., Levy, M., O'Reilly, T., 'Mark Zuckerberg Runs a Nation-state, and He's the King', *Vox*, 10 April 2018.

On the 'exercise fallacy', see Lukes (2005), p. 70, 109.

For a detailed account of Facebook's Oversight Board, see Klonick, K., 'The Facebook Oversight Board: Creating an Independent Institution to Adjudicate Online Free Expression', *Yale Law Journal*, Vol. 129, No. 2418, 2020.

On Facebook's moves to mitigate the harmful effects of reach power, see:

- 'What is the Page Transparency section on Pages?', https://www.facebook.com/help/323314944866264?helpref=popular_topics.
- Facebook Ad Library, https://www.facebook.com/ads/library/.
- 'WhatsApp Restricts Message-sharing to Fight Fake News', *BBC News*, 21 January 2019.
- Parloff, R., 'Facebook's Chris Cox Was More Than Just the World's Most Powerful Chief Product Officer', *Yahoo!*, 26 April 2019.
- Zuckerberg, M. (2019c), 'The Internet Needs New Rules. Let's Start in These Four Areas', *Zuckerberg Transcripts*, 1008.

On the 'liberalism of fear', see Shklar, J., 'The Liberalism of Fear' in *Liberalism and the Moral Life*, ed. Nancy L. Rosenblum, Harvard University Press, Cambridge, 1989; and Runciman (2017).

Tufekci's epithet is from Tufekci, Z., 'Why Zuckerberg's 14-Year Apology Tour Hasn't Fixed Facebook', *Wired*, 6 April 2018.

On humanity's unreasonableness, see Williams, B., 'A Fair State: Review of Political Liberalism by Rawls, J.' *London Review of Books*, Vol. 15, No. 9, 1993, pp. 7–8.

For a discussion of 'permissionless innovation', see Rosner, G. and Thierer, A., 'The Precautionary Principle vs Permissionless Innovation', *Governing the Internet of Things*, American University Internet Governance Lab, 14 March 2018.

The mantra 'Move fast and break things' was amended in 2014 to 'Move fast with stable infrastructure': Zuckerberg, M. (2014), '2014 F8 Developer Conference', *Zuckerberg Transcripts*, 149.

The Shklar quote about 'freedom from the abuse of power' is from Shklar (1989) p. 27; Zuckerberg's on 'doubt' is from Zuckerberg (2017a).

Should Digital Advertising-based Business Models be Outlawed?
For an example of Cook claiming Apple is more legitimate than Facebook, see Kafka, P., 'Tim Cook Says Facebook Should Have Regulated Itself, But it's Too Late for That Now', *Vox*, 28 March 2018.

Is More Privacy the Answer?

Facebook's 'pivot to privacy' is outlined in Zuckerberg, M. (2019b), 'A Privacy-Focused Vision for Social Networking', *Zuckerberg Transcripts*, 1006.

On the role of encrypted messaging in Brazil and India's elections see Magenta, M., Gragnani, J., Souza, F., 'How WhatsApp is Being Abused in Brazil's Elections', *BBC News*, 24 October 2018, and Ponniah, K., 'WhatsApp: The "Black Hole" of Fake News in India's Election', *BBC News*, 5 April 2019.

Should Social Media Companies be Regulated as Publishers Rather than Platforms?

On Facebook's enforcement of its rules, see Facebook (2019), 'An Update on How We Are Doing At Enforcing Our Community Standards', https://newsroom.fb.com/news/2019/05/enforcing-our-community-standards-3/.

The end of the Snopes fact-checking partnership is described in Green, V. and Mikkelson, D., 'A Message to Our Community Regarding the Facebook Fact-Checking Partnership', 1 February 2019.

On automated keyword-based censorship by WeChat, see Huang Yuan, 'National Trolls', *London Review of Books*, Vol. 39, No. 19, 2017, pp. 15–6.

Should We Break Up Big Tech?

Peter Thiel's advice to would-be monopolists is in Thiel, P. A. and Masters, B., *Zero to One: Notes on Start-ups, or How to Build the Future*, Virgin, London, 2014, p. 34.

The Zuckerberg quotes on Facebook's competitive position are from Facebook (2018), 'MZ Testifies before the EU Parliament', *Zuckerberg Transcripts*, 1000.

Mill writes about 'natural monopoly' in Mill, J. S., *The Principles of Political Economy: With Some of their Applications to Social Philosophy*. Project Gutenberg EBook, 1849, 241ff.

On historic infrastructure costs, see Ferguson (2017), pp. 160–2, pp. 256–7; on regulation of natural monopolies see Taplin (2017), pp. 258–9. Lanier's remarks on natural monopoly are in Lanier, J. and Simon, H., 'Delete Your Account Now: A Conversation with Jaron Lanier', *Los Angeles Review of Books*, 8 October 2018.

On the regulation of broadcasting in Germany after World War Two, see Wu, T., *The Attention Merchants: The Epic Struggle to Get Inside Our Heads*, Atlantic Books, London, 2017, p. 121.

Should Dual-class Stock Structures be Reformed?

The statistic on the gap between Zuckerberg's equity holding and the proportion of the company he controls is from Securities and Exchange Commission (2016), 'Proxy Statement Pursuant to Section 14(a) of the Securities Exchange Act of 1934: Facebook, Inc.', https://www.sec.gov/Archives/edgar/data/1326801/000132680116000053/facebook2016prelimproxysta.htm#s3D4B8526AA3DA88881A6CC93FD965687: 37–8.

On proposals for reforming dual-class stock structures, see Kupor, S., 'Limit Dual-Class Share Structures Rather than Shun Them', *Financial Times*, 20 November 2018; and Govindarajan, V., Rajgopal, S., Srivastava, A., Enache, L., 'Should Dual-Class Shares Be Banned?', *Harvard Business Review*, 3 December 2018.

For Facebook's purpose and mission statements, see The State of Delaware (2012), 'Facebook Inc. Restated Certificate of Incorporation', https://s21.q4cdn.com/399680738/files/doc_downloads/governance_documents/FB_CertificateOfIncorporation.pdf: ARTICLE III and Facebook Investor Relations, 'What is Facebook's Mission Statement?', https://investor.fb.com/resources/default.aspx.

Should We Allow Big Tech Companies to Control Internet Infrastructure?

On big tech companies' investments in internet infrastructure, see:

- Zuckerberg (2017f).
- Burgess, M., 'Google and Facebook are gobbling up the internet's subsea cables', *Wired*, 18 November 2018.
- Cooper, T., 'Google and other tech giants are quietly buying up the most important part of the internet', *Venture Beat*, 6 April 2019.

On the connection between control of infrastructure and imperial power, see:

- Ferguson (2017), p. 160.
- Lafrance, A., 'Facebook and the new colonialism.' *The Atlantic*, 11 February 2016.
- Friederici, N., Ojanperä, S. and Graham, M., 'The Impact of Connectivity in Africa: Grand Visions and the Mirage of Inclusive Digital Development.' *The Electronic Journal of Information Systems in Developing Countries* 79, no. 2, 2017, pp. 1–20.

On Google's roll-out of Loon in Kenya, see Adegoke, Y., 'How Google's balloons are bringing internet to new parts of Kenya', *Quartz Africa*, 14 July 2020.

Andreessen is quoted in Bowles, N., 'Why is Silicon Valley So "Tone Deaf" to India?', *Guardian*, 12 February 2016. Zuckerberg said 'I found the comments deeply upsetting, and they do not represent the way Facebook or I think at all' – see Zuckerberg (2016d).

Chapter Nine: Data Ethics for Big Tech

This chapter draws on a research report I wrote for the UK-China Global Issues Dialogue Centre at Jesus College, Cambridge, in collaboration with Professor Peter Williamson and Professor Stelios Zyglidopoulos. The original report can be downloaded at https://bit.ly/data_ethics.

Data on the share price impact of disasters is from Knight, R. F. and Pretty, D. J., 'The Impact of Catastrophes on Shareholder Value', Oxford Executive Research Briefings, Templeton College, Oxford, 1997.

For a definition and short history of data ethics, see Floridi, L. and Taddeo, M., 'What Is Data Ethics?' *Philosophical Transactions: Series A, Mathematical, Physical and Engineering Sciences*, 374(2083), 28 December 2016, Vol. 374 (2083).

Bias, Discrimination and Injustice in Algorithmic Decision-making

Cathy O'Neil's book is *Weapons of Math Destruction: How Big Data Increases Inequality and Threatens Democracy*, Penguin, London, 2017. For more on the use of algorithmic decisioning in criminal justice, see Fry, H., *Hello World: How to Be Human in the Age of the Machine*, Transworld, London, 2018.

On tech companies' tools to mitigate algorithmic injustice, see:

- Facebook (2018), 'AI at F8 2018: Open frameworks and responsible development', https://engineering.fb.com/ml-applications/ai-at-f8-2018-open-frameworks-and-responsible-development/.
- Google (2018), 'Introducing the What-If Tool for Cloud AI Platform models', https://cloud.google.com/blog/products/ai-machine-learning/introducing-the-what-if-tool-for-cloud-ai-platform-models.
- IBM (2018), 'Introducing AI Fairness 360', https://www.ibm.com/blogs/research/2018/09/ai-fairness-360/.

On the case for algorithmic transparency, see Gillis, T. B. and Simons, J., 'Explanation < Justification: GDPR and the Perils of Privacy', *Pennsylvania Journal of Law and Innovation*, 19 April 2019.

Artificial General Intelligence as an Existential Risk to Humanity

Results from the survey of AI experts are available in Grace, K. et al., 'When Will AI Exceed Human Performance? Evidence from AI Experts', https://arxiv.org/abs/1705.08807.

Nick Bostrom's book is Bostrom, N., *Superintelligence: Paths, Dangers, Strategies*, Oxford University Press, Oxford, 2014.

The Pi thought experiment is from Susskind, J., *Future Politics: Living Together in a World Transformed by Tech*, Oxford University Press, Oxford, 2018.

Meredith Whittaker's comments are from Crawford, K. and Whittaker, M. (2018) 'How Will AI Change Your Life?', *Recode Decode* podcast, 8 April 2019.

On Salesforce, see 'Ethical and Humane Use', https://www.salesforce.com/company/ethical-and-humane-use/; and 'US Customs and Border Protection Agency Selects Salesforce as Digital Modernization Platform', Cision, 6 March 2018.

On Google's ethics board, see 'Google's AI Ethics Board Might Save Humanity', *Huffpost*, 28 January 2014, and Piper, K., 'Google Cancels AI Ethics Board in Response to Outcry', *Vox*, 4 April 2019.

Elon Musk's tweet about superintelligence is available at: https://twitter.com/elonmusk/status/495759307346952192.

Job Displacement from Machine Learning and Robotics

The assessment of the risk of job displacement from AI and robotics is Frey, C. and Osborne, M., 'The Future of Employment: How Susceptible are Jobs to Computerisation?' *Technological Forecasting and Social Change* 114, 2013, pp. 254–80.

On the existential questions raised by joblessness, see Cohen, J., *Not Working: Why We Have to Stop*, Granta, London, 2018.

On tech CEO's concerns about machine-driven job displacement and calls for UBI, see Clifford, C., 'Y Combinator President and eBay Founder join Elon Musk in Addressing Crisis of Robots Taking Jobs', CNBC, 13 February 2017, and Kharpal, A., 'Tech CEOs Back Call for Basic Income as AI Job Losses Threaten Industry Backlash', CNBC, 21 February 2017.

Reconciling Differences in the World's Ethical Traditions

On ethical traditions in business context, see Hendry, J., 'Ethical Cultures and Traditions', Second Edition, 2013, available at http://johnhendry.co.uk/wp/wp-content/uploads/2013/05/Ethical-cultures-and-traditions.pdf.

The summary of ethical norms in business draws on Donaldson, T., 'Values in Tension: Ethics Away from Home', *Harvard Business Review*, Sep–Oct 1996.

Sources for the case study of Roadway are:

- Dun & Bradstreet company website, https://www.dnb.com/about-us. html.
- Chu, K., 'Dun & Bradstreet Fined, Four Sentenced in China', *Wall Street Journal*, 9 January 2013.
- 'Dun & Bradstreet Reportedly Fined RMB $1 Million for Illegally Obtaining Personal Information in China; Four Employees Imprisoned', Inside Privacy, 10 January 2013.
- Volkov, M., 'Dun and Bradstreet Pays $9 Million for FCPA Violations in China', 9 May 2018.

The lead generation market size is as aggregated by Statista in 'Digital lead generation ad spend in the US, 2019–2023'.

Beyond The Trolley Problem

Road traffic deaths are listed in World Health Organization, 'The Top 10 Causes of Death', 2018, https://www.who.int/news-room/fact-sheets/detail/the-top-10-causes-of-death, and self-driving car fatalities in Wikipedia, https://en.wikipedia.org/wiki/List_of_self-driving_car_fatalities.

The fatal accident involving an Uber self-driving was reported in Levin, S. and Wong, J. C., 'Self-driving Uber kills Arizona Woman in First Fatal Crash Involving Pedestrian', *Guardian*, 19 March 2018.

The trolley problem is posed in Foot, P., 'The Problem of Abortion and the Doctrine of the Double Effect' in *Virtues and Vices*, Basil Blackwell, Oxford, 1978. The image is from Image from Wikimedia Commons: https://commons.wikimedia.org/wiki/File:Trolley_Problem.svg. For a discussion in relation to self-driving cars, see Fry (2018).

On variations in ethical preferences, see Awad, E., Dsouza, S., Kim, R. et al., 'The Moral Machine Experiment', *Nature*, 563, 2018, pp. 59–64.

On the Cloudflare case study, see Roose, K., 'Why Banning 8chan Was So Hard for Cloudflare: "No One Should Have That Power"', *New York Times*, 6 August 2019.

Facts about Cloudflare are from the company website, https://www. cloudflare.com/. Prince's quote is from Prince, M. (2019), 'Terminating Service for 8chan', https://blog.cloudflare.com/terminating-service-for-8chan/.

Examples of 'value added services' being misused include:

- Stalking: Valentino-DeVries, J., 'Hundreds of Apps Can Empower Stalkers to Track Their Victims', *New York Times*, 19 May 2018.
- Livestreaming killings:
  - Tanakasempipat, P. and Thepgumpanat, P., 'Thai Man Broadcasts Baby Daughter's Murder Live on Facebook', Reuters, 25 April 2017.
  - Roose, K., 'A Mass Murder of, and for, the Internet', *New York Times*, 15 March 2019.
- Child abuse: Newton, C., 'The Big Disturbing Problem that Could Help End Encryption', *The Interface*, 30 September 2019.

The Virtuous Big Tech Company
Google's Privacy Controls are at https://safety.google/privacy/privacy-controls/.

'Co-creating' the Jobs of the Future
On co-creating the jobs of the future, see Leadbeater, C., 'The RSA Future Work Awards – Meeting Anxiety with Innovation', *RSA*, 6 February 2019.

For an example of AI and human doctors working in concert to fight cancer, see McKinney, S. M., Sieniek, M., Godbole, V. et al., 'International Evaluation of an AI System for Breast Cancer Screening', *Nature*, 577, 2020, pp. 89–94.

The account of food delivery platform dynamics is from Perrig, L., 'Matching Users' and Developers' Beliefs: The Algorithmic Management of Uncertainty', Presentation at *Connected Life: Data & Disorder*, London School of Economics, 2019.

On Mondragón, see Agirre Lehendakaria Center for Social and Political Studies, 'Mondragon Will Count on Mariana Mazzucato in its Commitment to Social Innovation', 2019.

Putting More Data into the Public Domain
On the philosophical barriers to treating data as private property, see Prainsack, B., 'Logged Out: Ownership, Exclusion and Public Value in the Digital Data and Information Commons', *Big Data & Society*, 6(1), 2019, 2053951719829773.

On the hampering of Open-Source Intelligence, see Chapter Five and Dubberley (2019).

Conclusion

Jamie Bartlett's book is Bartlett, J., *The People Vs Tech: How the Internet Is Killing Democracy (And How to Save It)*, Ebury, London, 2018.

John Naughton calls Zuckerberg 'a sociopath' in the presentation referenced in Chapter One, and in an article 'Has Zuckerberg, Like Frankenstein, Lost Control of the Monster He Created?', *Guardian*, 29 July 2018. Shoshana Zuboff characterises Sandberg as 'Typhoid Mary' in Zuboff (2019), Kindle edition, Loc 1682.

The publishers would like to thank the following sources for their kind permission to reproduce the pictures in this book.

The Economist Group Limited: 34
Copyright Guardian News & Media Ltd 2021: 8
Properati: 55
Retromash.com: 119

All other photographs courtesy of the author

Every effort has been made to acknowledge correctly and contact the source and/or copyright holder of each picture and Welbeck Publishing apologises for any unintentional errors or omissions, which will be corrected in future editions of this book.

INDEX

Ad Preferences Center 29–31
Ads Manager 35, 172, 173, 241
*Age of Surveillance Capitalism,
   The* 5, 154–5
Aleric 215, 216
Algorithms 40, 45, 53, 54, 112,
   130, 134, 155, 160, 168, 170,
   190, 207. 214, 247–9, 251,
   259, 265, 266, 271
Allan of Hallam. Lord 208
Allworth, James 105
Alternative für Deutschland 60,
   61
Altman, Sam 252
Amazon 10, 34, 105, 121, 150,
   151, 185, 188, 196, 197, 221,
   240, 242, 244, 252
Amnesty International 158, 160
Analects, The 253
Andreessen, Marc 243
AnswerThePublic 99,122–5
Apple 10, 41, 150–54, 185, 188,
   197, 221, 234, 242
Aristotle 259
authoritarians 9, 142, 146, 157,
   190, 202, 216, 222, 225, 240
automation 252, 264, 266

Baidu 92, 267
Bartlett, Jamie 271

behavioural data 5–8, 27, 28, 29,
   31, 46, 50, 53, 58, 59, 104, 106,
   122, 231, 267
Benioff, Marc 252–3
Bentham, Jeremy 163–7, 169, 170,
   172, 179, 180, 182, 201, 233,
   257
Berlin, Isaiah 205
Berlinquette, Patrick 127–31
Better Angels of Our Nature, The
   204
Bing 124, 125, 132, 233, 238,
   267
Bolsonaro, Jair 235
Bostrom, Nick 250
Bosworth, Andrew 'Boz' 205
Bought By Many 2, 3, 19–26, 34,
   35, 36, 39–43, 80, 81, 82, 84, 85,
   87–92, 95, 103, 105, 186, 190,
   199, 278
Bouglé, Célestin 207
Bowling Alone 205
Bragazzi, Nicola 100–02, 107
broad targeting 31

Cadwalladr, Carole 2–3, 272
Cambridge Analytica 2–3, 9, 15,
   25, 35, 47–50, 52, 64, 65, 67,
   226, 227, 268
Cambridge power 177–84, 269

Capital in the Twenty-First Century 198
Chahali, Evarist 128–9
Chetty, Raj 119–21
Chopra, Rohit 66
Cieplay, David 223–4, 229
Citymapper 118, 137, 287
Clegg, Sir Nick 208
Clinton, Hillary 59
Cloudflare 259–61, 263
Coley, Sophie 99, 122–5, 127
concentrated control 200, 201, 226, 230
Confucius 253
Congress, US 15, 105, 189
Cook, Tim 151, 152, 154, 234
Coronasearch 126, 127
coronavirus *also* Covid-19 107–8, 122–34, 216, 267, 271, 274
Coronavirus Tech Handbook 122, 125
Cox, Chris 236
Coyle, Diane 98, 99, 103
Crisis of Liberalism, A 206–7
Cummings Dominic 50–1, 190
Custom Audiences 45, 47, 51, 53
Customs and Border Protection Agency 251, 263

Daedalus 193, 197, 215, 216
data ethics 246–7
data openness 11, 109, 112, 122, 137
demand taxonomy 73, 74, 82, 84, 88, 93, 103
Democracy in America 205
deontology 257, 258

digital advertising 3, 10, 16, 48, 52, 221, 232, 233, 235, 273
Digital Culture, Media and Sport, Department of 29, 227
digital legitimacy 229, 232, 237, 274
digital marketing 3, 4, 10, 59, 75, 77, 92, 104, 124, 127, 143, 147, 148, 149, 278
digital revolution 98
digital technology 11, 143, 145–7, 154, 208, 217, 254, 261, 273
Digital Verification Corps 158, 159
Discipline and Punish 177
Dubberley, Sam 160
Dun & Bradstreet 254, 255, 256, 259
Duterte, Rodrigo 8, 156, 157, 190, 224

Economist, The 33–4
8chan 259, 260, 263
Einiö, Elina 102
entitledto 115–6
Everybody Lies 100
Experian 2, 24, 39, 42, 53, 54, 56, 57, 58, 65, 66, 72, 73, 77, 78, 82, 112, 255, 271, 272, 278

Fabian, Mark 133, 134
Facebook 2–10, 15–20, 22–33, 35–6, 39–53, 58–67, 87, 88, 92, 113, 145, 146, 148–51, 152, 154, 155, 156, 157, 158, 159, 167, 168, 170, 171–5, 176, 177, 185, 190, 191, 197, 200–9, 211, 215, 221, 223, 224–8, 231, 232–9, 241, 242, 243, 249, 252, 264, 268,

Facebook Messenger 157
Facebook workshop 39–46, 53
Ferguson, Niall 28
FilterGrade 186, 187, 189
Flower, Andy 140–43, 145, 147
Foa, Roberto 133
Foot, Philippa 257
Forward Internet Group 74–6, 78,
    83
Foucault, Michel 169–70, 173, 177,
    182, 184
Foundry 214–6
Free Basics 243
Frey, Carl Benedikt 252
Future Politics 250

Gates Foundation 198
Gates, Bill 125, 197, 198, 201, 271
*GDP: A Brief but Affectionate
    History* 98
GDPR (General Data Protection
    Regulations) 31, 32, 104, 116,
    167
geodemographics 55–6, 59, 233
global community 200, 202, 204,
    205, 206, 208, 213
Global South 150, 153, 226, 232,
    233, 234, 243
Goldman, Paula 251
Google 10, 16, 33, 71, 72, 73, 74,
    76, 83, 89, 90, 92, 93, 97, 98,
    100, 101, 102, 105, 123, 124,
    125, 127, 128, 129, 130, 131,
    134, 148, 152, 154, 165, 167,
    176–7, 185, 186, 187, 188, 189,
    190, 196, 197, 200, 211, 221,
    224, 234, 238, 241, 242, 243,
    249, 250, 251, 252, 256, 267

Google Ads 22, 73, 127, 130, 176,
    233, 238
Google Chrome 89,
Google Earth 158, 267, 268
Google Flu Trends 130, 131,
    132
Google Maps 158, 272
Google Trends 99, 103, 107, 123,
    125, 127, 128, 130–35, 136
Graph API 64–66, 208, 227
Great Hack, The 35
Guardian, the 2, 8, 65, 124, 165,
    272

Harari, Yuval Noah 204
Hatch, Orrin 15
Hegel 204
Hitwise 72–4, 78, 82, 90, 93,
    103–5, 107, 108, 109, 122, 123,
    124, 125
Hobbes, Thomas 223
Hobson, J.A. 204, 207
Holmes, Elizabeth 194–5
Hopkins, Claire 126
Huawei 210, 271, 273
hubris 193, 196, 197, 198, 201,
    210, 217
Hutchinson, Neil 75

Icarus 193, 197, 215
illegitimacy 6, 7, 9, 50, 221, 224,
    225, 279
infodemiology 100, 125, 130
informed consent 6, 261

Johnston, Steve 23, 73, 74, 83, 94,
    103
Jolie, Angelina 101–2

Jumpshot 104, 105, 107, 109, 121, 189

Just Cages 76, 77

Kaiasm 73, 82, 83

Kant, Immanuel 258

Karp, Alex 211–7

Karpian realism 210–7

Kogan, Aleksandr 49, 64

Koutaniemi, Eeva 102, 127

Lampos, Bill 125–6, 131, 132

Larsen, Kristian 45–7, 50, 52

legitimacy 60, 62, 66, 190, 221, 222–44, 274, 277

Leviathan 223

liberalism 201, 202, 203, 204, 205, 206, 207, 208, 209, 210, 211, 217

Lookalike Audiences 4, 53–4, 58–61, 63–4, 190, 209, 232, 273

Maloney, Sean 39

market power 184–9

Martínez, Antonio García 9

MATLAB 98, 99

Maven, Project 211, 212, 214

Mawarire, Evan 145–6, 174, 190

McGee, Liam 23, 73, 74, 83

McGoey, Linsey 198

micro-targeting 25, 31

Microsoft 10, 124, 132, 196, 197, 214, 221, 233, 238, 240, 242, 244, 252

Mill, John Stuart 179, 201, 206, 239

Minos of Crete, King 193

Minotaur 193

Moloney, Matt 186

Moloney, Mike 186

MoveOn 174, 190

Mugabe, Robert 142, 144, 145, 146, 190

Murray, Joe 76

Musk, Elon 196, 197, 250, 251

Myanmar 8, 157, 209, 235

Nadella, Satya 252

Naughton, John 5, 28, 226

Neumann, Adam 194, 195–6, 198, 213

Neumann, Rebekah Paltrow 198

Nineteen Eighty-Four 168–9, 173

95 Theses about Technology 28

Nix, Alexander 48, 49

Nussbaum, Martha 205

O'Neil, Cathy 248

Obama, President Barack 51

Observer, the 2

OCEAN segmentation 47–50

Olonga, Henry 139–43, 144, 145, 147, 160

Omidyar, Pierre 252

On Liberty 206

open banking, 110–14

open data 116–21

open-source intelligence 158, 159

Opportunity Insights 119–21, 137, 215

optimisation 46, 47, 50, 51, 52, 171, 270

Orwell, George 168–9, 170

Osborne, Michael 252

Palantir 211-7
Panopticon 165-72, 174-7, 186, 188, 190, 233
People vs Tech, The 271
Pichai, Sundar 211
Piketty, Thomas 198
Ping An 90-5
Pinker, Steven 204
PL & Partners 45, 48
Prince, Matthew 260-1
probabilistic inference 17, 18, 113
profile data 57, 18-9, 26, 27, 29, 47, 48, 50, 59, 65, 159
Project Maven 211, 212, 214
Properati 118, 119
psychological manipulation 47-50
pug insurance 86-7, 93, 95, 105, 190, 270
Putnam, Robert 205

Rawls, John 149, 201, 205
reach power 189-91
realism 210, 212
Rohingya Muslims 8, 157, 159, 190, 209, 226, 235, 238
Runciman, David 151, 163

Salesforce 251
Salvini, Matteo 8
Sandberg, Sheryl 271
Sapiens 204
Schmidt, Eric 210, 211, 213, 215
Science 131
Shanghai Roadway 254-5, 256, 258, 259, 263
Shklar, Judith 228, 229
Snowden, Edward 210

Space X 196
Square and the Tower, The 28
Stephens-Davidowitz, Seth 72, 99, 127
Sun, Mr 90-1
surveillance capitalism 4-8, 11, 16, 18, 19, 28, 32, 47, 48, 50-2, /59, 66, 105, 140, 147, 186, 202, 221, 224, 225, 233, 235, 271
Susskind, Jamie 250

Tanzania 128-9
Techlightenment 3, 24
Theory of Justice, A 205
Theranos 194-5
#ThisFlag 145, 174
Thompson, Ben 105
Tocqueville, Alexis de 201, 205
trolley problem 257-8, 259
Trump, Donald 8, 9, 59, 100, 217
Tucker, Richard 76, 77
Tufekci, Zeynep 5, 28, 148, 226, 228, 233
Turnbull, Mark 48, 49
Twitter and Tear Gas: The Power and Fragility of Networked Protest 148

Vaidhyanathan, Siva 5, 226
vertical integration 188, 189, 240, 241
Vestager, Margrethe 240
Vote Leave 9, 50-1

Walgreens 194
Walker, Abigail 126
Weapons of Math Destruction 248
WeChat 92, 238

weWork 195–6, 198–9
Whittaker, Meredith 250–1
will.i.am 32–3, 37
Wilson, Nigel 66–7
WorldStores 76, 77, 78
Wylie, Christopher 2–4, 272

Yelp 65
YouGov 133–5

Zuboff, Shoshana 5, 154–5, 202,
   207
Zuckerberg Files, The 202, 208
Zuckerberg, Mark 15, 35, 61, 64,
   170, 171 172, 173, 174, 190,
   197, 200–10, 213, 223, 226, 227,
   231, 235, 241, 242, 271
Zuckian liberalism 202–3, 205–9,
   217, 226, 228, 235